T5-AGM-051

EDUCATION AND TRAINING FOR WORK

HOW TO ORDER THIS BOOK

BY PHONE: 800-233-9936 or 717-291-5609, 8AM–5PM Eastern Time

BY FAX: 717-295-4538

BY MAIL: Order Department
Technomic Publishing Company, Inc.
851 New Holland Avenue, Box 3535
Lancaster, PA 17604, U.S.A.

BY CREDIT CARD: American Express, VISA, MasterCard

BY WWW SITE: http://www.techpub.com

PERMISSION TO PHOTOCOPY–POLICY STATEMENT

Authorization to photocopy items for internal or personal use, or the internal or personal use of specific clients, is granted by Technomic Publishing Co., Inc. provided that the base fee of US $3.00 per copy, plus US $ .25 per page is paid directly to Copyright Clearance Center, 222 Rosewood Drive, Danvers, MA 01923, USA. For those organizations that have been granted a photocopy license by CCC, a separate system of payment has been arranged. The fee code for users of the Transactional Reporting Service is 1-56676/96 $5.00 + $ .25.

VOLUME 1—PLANNING PROGRAMS

EDUCATION
and
TRAINING
for
WORK

Edited by Dr. Clifton P. Campbell
Professor, The University of Tennessee

TECHNOMIC
PUBLISHING CO., INC.
LANCASTER · BASEL

0156391

Education and Training for Work—Volume 1
aTECHNOMIC ᵖpublication

Published in the Western Hemisphere by
Technomic Publishing Company, Inc.
851 New Holland Avenue, Box 3535
Lancaster, Pennsylvania 17604 U.S.A.

Distributed in the Rest of the World by
Technomic Publishing AG
Missionsstrasse 44
CH-4055 Basel, Switzerland

Copyright ©1996 by Technomic Publishing Company, Inc.
All rights reserved

No part of this publication may be reproduced, stored in a
retrieval system, or transmitted, in any form or by any means,
electronic, mechanical, photocopying, recording, or otherwise,
without the prior written permission of the publisher.

Printed in the United States of America
10 9 8 7 6 5 4 3 2 1

Main entry under title:
   Education and Training for Work: Planning Programs—Volume 1

A Technomic Publishing Company book
Bibliography: p.
Includes index p. 275

Library of Congress Catalog Card No. 96-60623
ISBN No. 1-56676-417-3

To the Department of Human Resource Development,
The University of Tennessee
and its dedication to the improvement and advancement of
workforce education and training

Contents

0156391

3. The Content of Instruction   109

DENNIS R. HERSCHBACH—*University of Maryland*

4. Employability Skills   133

GREGORY C. PETTY—*The University of Tennessee*

5. How Young Adults Learn: Theory and Practice   153

PAUL A. BOTT—*California State University–Long Beach*

6. How to Foster High Expectation and Motivation   169

ROGER B. HILL—*University of Georgia*

7. Structured On-the-Job Training: Pitfalls and Payoffs   195

DAVID C. BJORKQUIST—*University of Minnesota*
BRIAN P. MURPHY—*HRD Resource Group, Inc.*

8. An Approach to Program Evaluation   223

DAVID D. L'ANGELLE—*California State University–Long Beach*

Acknowledgements

THE editor wishes to express sincere thanks and appreciation to his colleagues in the Department of Human Resource Development at The University of Tennessee for their patience and support while this work was being prepared. I particularly want to thank my esteemed friends Dr. Gerald D. Cheek and Dr. Roger W. Haskell for shouldering an excessive load of academic advising and committee functions. As always, the department provided the stimulating and encouraging atmosphere necessary for research and writing.

An expression of profound gratitude is extended to the authors, who committed their extensive knowledge and experience, as well as valuable time, to writing these chapters. The editor is also deeply indebted to the perceptive editorial panel, whose impartial chapter reviews and collective advice resulted in valuable improvements to this work.

Special appreciation is extended to my wife Linda for her skillful word processing, in-depth editing, and patient proofreading of the many chapter revisions. Her insightful suggestions for both substance and style are woven into the fabric of this work. I shall be ever grateful for her help and support.

A note of thanks is due Mrs. Elaine Whitehead for her expert word processing and valuable assistance with all the correspondence and express mailings to the geographically dispersed authors and editorial panel members.

I am also grateful to Dr. Joseph Eckenrode, Mr. Steve Spangler, and the production staff of Technomic Publishing Company for contributing their many professional talents to the production of this work. Their careful attention to detail and diligent efforts made this two-book project a reality.

Finally, as chairman of the board for the National Association for Trade and Industrial Education (NATIE), I wish to acknowledge that the authors, editors, and others generously donated their time and talent to this publication project. NATIE receives the royalties from the sale of these books and the proceeds will be used for the advancement of workforce education and training.

Introduction

THE future of the U.S. economy, productivity, and global competitiveness depends on the nation's ability to prepare and maintain a highly qualified workforce. Employers are increasingly recognizing this pragmatic need as essential to their own organizational success. As job competencies constantly interface with technological advances and organizational changes, they become increasingly more complex. Nevertheless, employers expect that vocational and technical education and training will effectively and efficiently provide the skilled workforce so desperately needed.

This work seeks to be of assistance in dealing with such an expectation. It presents current and comprehensive information on the development of knowledge, skills, abilities, understandings, attitudes, work habits, and appreciations needed by students, trainees, apprentices, and so forth, to enter the workforce and progress in a career. For some time, there has been a need for a book that presents the best practices (methods, approaches, and strategies) for planning and delivering vocational and technical education and training. The authors accepted the challenge of identifying and describing the best practices and, in doing so, they addressed the full range of needs, from basic entry-level skills to technical skills requiring a high degree of specialization and competence.

This work is intended to be a reference or text for practicing and aspiring instructors, curriculum developers, counselors, administrators, consultants, and others engaged in workforce development in public and private schools, post-secondary technical and community colleges, and teacher training programs in colleges and universities. It is also appropriate for training in business, industry, government, and the armed services.

One of the problems faced in preparing this work was semantics. First, there was the dilemma of what is meant by vocational and technical education. In its broadest sense, this term could mean formal and non-formal preparation for entering all occupations and, thus, encompass the entire education process. In a narrower sense, it could assume the meaning given in much of the literature and refer only to those formal education courses and programs that prepare students for direct entry into skilled trades, crafts, industries, and businesses. Since the intent was not to enter a debate on semantics, use of the term *vocational and technical education and training* (VET) was decided upon. This term provides a generic description for a full range of education and training delivery methods—formal (school-based) and non-formal (workplace-based). Other semantic problems are resolved in the Glossary, which provides definitions of the key words and terms used.

In terms of structure, this work consists of seventeen chapters organized into two books. The first book provides detailed guidelines for planning, while the second book presents the latest proven methods and techniques for delivering instruction. Together, the two books offer, for consideration and hopefully application, practical information on the best practices for planning, developing, delivering, and evaluating VET courses and programs.

The content is based on the chapter authors' extensive knowledge and experience, the generally available professional literature, and the less available but valuable documentation resulting from research and application by the armed services. Tables, figures (diagrams, illustrations, etc.), and examples supplement the text in explaining the content.

An important characteristic of this work is that each chapter focuses on a specialized topic, which is addressed within the contextual framework. The outcome is chapters that stand on their own and can, therefore, be read in various sequences. This organizational approach makes it possible for readers to focus on their personal interests and sequence their reading accordingly.

For the keen reader who wishes to know more about a subject or topic, further readings are, of course, essential. In order to facilitate this, the sources used by the authors are appropriately cited in the text, with complete reference information located at the end of each chapter.

The authors brought a wide variety of educational and occupational backgrounds to bear on their chapters. The editor hopes that readers find their distinct interpretations and writing styles refreshing, and that their individual viewpoints add interest to the important content of these two books.

CLIFTON P. CAMPBELL

Editorial Panel

THE five members of this editorial panel provided impartial peer reviews of all manuscripts submitted. This book greatly benefitted from their expertise and the quality of their efforts.

- Dr. Lowell D. Anderson—Indiana State University, Terre Haute, Indiana
- Dr. Clifton P. Campbell—The University of Tennessee, Knoxville, Tennessee
- Mrs. Linda L. Campbell—Professional Associates, Knoxville, Tennessee
- Dr. Dennis R. Herschbach—University of Maryland, College Park, Maryland
- Dr. Walter S. Mietus—University of Maryland, College Park, Maryland

CHAPTER 1

Determining the Market Demand for Skilled Workers

CLIFTON P. CAMPBELL—*The University of Tennessee*

RELEVANT and effective vocational and technical education and training (VET)[1] is an important means of improving working and living conditions, enhancing the dignity of individuals, and increasing their ability to participate fully in the economic life of their communities. Accordingly, the training/skill/employment triad must focus on the realities of current and future skilled worker needs as a prerequisite for the efficient functioning of the labor market.

There are many organizations, both public and private (proprietary), involved in providing VET. The main providers include (a) secondary schools; (b) post-secondary institutions, such as trade and technical institutes and 2-year colleges; (c) job training programs operating under various government agencies; (d) the military; (e) apprenticeships; and (f) employer (workplace-based) programs. For ease of presentation and brevity, all these public and private schools, institutions, programs, employers, and so forth, are referred to, in this chapter, as VET providers.

VET providers offer courses and programs in a variety of disciplines (service areas), including trade and industrial, health, business and office, agriculture, home economics, marketing and distribution, cooperative, and technical education and training. Each of these disciplines prepares participants for particular occupations within an economic sector (industry, e.g., construction).

GUIDING TRAINING DECISIONS

The utopian dream is total freedom to choose our work, to be the master of our own destiny. Toward this end, it is generally accepted that a person's interest in and aptitude for a particular type of work as well as the satisfaction they obtain from performing it should guide their occupational choice. This sentiment is held, in part, because satisfaction at

1

work is so important. Nevertheless, the low pay, unfavorable working conditions, and a negative image result in recruitment problems for some occupations, while the potential for high earnings, favorable working conditions, and social prestige attract large numbers to other occupations. In any case, employment possibilities for different occupations have a profound influence on rational career decisions.

More often than not, young adults choose an occupation for which there is a realistic opportunity for fulfilling and secure employment within their personal geographic mobility potential. When young adults choose to remain in their local area, the job opportunities in the geographic proximity should guide their VET options. However, those who prefer to leave the local area need training for jobs to be found in the region or nation.

Differences of view with respect to geographic mobility exist, however, among national, state, and local governments. The federal government is interested in nationwide matching of supply to demand and sufficient geographic mobility to achieve that purpose. Nevertheless, a local community may have little interest in providing VET courses or programs deliberately aimed at outmigration.

Another consideration reflects a somewhat controversial point of view that has two focal points: (a) public (taxpayer-financed) education and training should be relevant to the needs of the economy; and (b) public resources devoted to education and training should be used effectively, thus avoiding the wastage of inappropriate education and training and initial over-education simply because of societal demand. This view is supported by evidence that the return on investments in education and training is not fixed or automatic, but depends on opportunities to use the knowledge and skills acquired (relevant job opportunities).

In this respect, policy statements and planning documents express a growing concern about the social pressure for young adults to pursue a 4-year college education, given (a) projections that, by the year 2000, more than 70% of jobs will not require a college degree; (b) estimates that more than 50% of college students never graduate; and (c) the rising number of over-educated and under- or unemployed graduates (projected to be nearly 30% by 2005). Shelley (1994) reported that, "Because the number of college-graduate job seekers will grow more quickly than the number of college-level jobs, nearly 25% of new entrants [graduates] are expected to settle for jobs that do not require a college degree" (p. 9). Clearly, college is not advisable for all, nor does a 4-year degree guarantee a professional job or a high income. Furthermore, graduates, depending on their program of study, cannot rely on college to provide them with the knowledge and skills necessary for gainful employment. What counts is having marketable skills. Moreover, in the opinion of many, financing the overproduction of 4-year college graduates is not justified when it is at the expense of the many who need VET in order to be qualified for existing jobs.

It is, therefore, increasingly believed that public investments in education and training should reflect the needs of the economy for a relevant and qualified workforce. This supports the notion that VET should be targeted at occupations with favorable employment prospects. If this is not done, there is a serious risk of ineffectively using limited resources and preparing trainees for non-existent jobs. The "acid test" for success is employment in the occupation trained for and favorable prospects for a productive and satisfying career.

Consequently, responsible planning calls for VET courses and programs to be offered based on individual preferences tempered by a clear understanding of the trainees' ability to benefit from such training in terms of current and future employment possibilities. Apart from these considerations, it is implicit in the idea of economic development that the size and scope of VET programs should meet the quantitative and qualitative requirements for skilled workers, in a time of rapid technological and organizational change as well as international challenge.

DEMAND AND SUPPLY

Problems of labor market demand and supply plague the nation. There are too many assemblers, yet too few practical nurses; waiting lines for apprenticeship programs, yet empty shops in some formal training programs. Furthermore, there are jobs for carpenters in Atlanta, while carpenters in Pittsburgh are being laid off. In a very real sense, all of these problems are related, and they are best treated by VET planning.

Essentially, VET planning is a balancing problem. It can be thought of as an attempt to balance an equation. On one side of the equation is the labor market demand for skilled workers. On the other side are the interests, aptitudes, preferences, and mobility of potential trainees.

Labor market information includes data on demand (the number of workers needed with particular skills) and supply (the number of individuals available with particular skills). The comparison of demand and supply data answers the question, "What VET courses and programs are needed?"

Public VET Providers

Historically, taxpayer-financed VET has not been sufficiently responsive to demand and supply factors. The match between VET offerings and regional as well as local labor markets has been less than satisfactory, with too great a lag between labor market demand changes and course/program modifications. As a result, public VET providers often create a surplus of graduates for declining-demand occupations and inadequate numbers for growing-demand occupations or those where skilled workers are in short supply. Notwithstanding this problem—or perhaps on that very account—graduates find it difficult to keep up their personal dignity and favorable attitudes about work when the jobs for which they were prepared are not readily available. Furthermore, skills can atrophy if not practiced and, hence, much of the proficiency attained through VET is wasted. Conversely, preparing trainees in occupations with present and future employment opportunities helps assure them of a promising future, while maintaining a high level of employment for all who can work. Keeping the labor market supplied with well-prepared workers also contributes to the competitiveness of business in both domestic and international markets.

Proprietary VET Providers

Private schools offer a cost-effective alternative to public sector VET that fails to respond to labor market demand. Because of their profit motive, and because decision making is in the hands of the owner, private schools are more sensitive to market forces and are both willing and able to respond in a timely fashion to meet employers' needs for skilled workers. Since tuition is their primary source of income, proprietary schools must attract trainees to survive. And those trainees, who are paying for their VET, will exercise quality and relevance control on the school. In order to attract and hold trainees, private schools need to present a convincing case that their courses and programs facilitate quick qualification for jobs in demand in the regional/local labor market.

Consequently, a school's reputation for providing quality instruction, marketable skills, and good placement is essential if it is to thrive.

Thus, proprietary schools evaluate workforce projections and forecasts and undertake selected labor market signalling approaches. They work closely with potential employers and heed their advice. As a result, many proprietary schools quickly alter program content and change their offerings to assure that their graduates are realistically prepared to meet the needs of the marketplace.

When placement opportunities for graduates of a particular program dry up, the program is dropped (supply is ended). In some cases, the school may close. From a business point of view, it makes no sense to offer VET that employers do not want or need. Consequently, proprietary schools consider themselves employment brokers, providing only the VET that enables graduates to get jobs.

By contrast, this openness and flexibility are not part of the traditional mentality of public VET providers who appear to suffer from inertia. This may be attributable to the bureaucracy at the national, state, district, and local levels. But even where there is substantial autonomy, site-based decision makers may lack the resources or incentives to respond to imbalances between the demand for and supply of skilled workers. And as for dropping programs that have outlasted their need, the size of the original capital investment in plant and equipment, as well as the problem of reassigning tenured instructors, may make it nearly impossible (Castro & de Andrade, 1989).

Summing Up

Although VET providers cannot be held accountable for eliminating all skilled worker surpluses and shortages or providing a perfect fit between training and jobs, imbalances in supply and demand can and should be anticipated. Improvements in the speed with which VET offerings adjust in response to changes in labor market demand and reductions in the level of structural unemployment are two measurable aspects of progress toward achieving this goal.

VET can and should play a fundamentally important role in a strong, efficient, and productive economy. That role is to provide skilled workers in the myriad of occupations the nation requires, thereby eliminating inflationary bottlenecks in production and services that may otherwise constrain economic growth. Retraining in higher-demand jobs, for re-dundant workers, can also reduce problems of structural unemployment and the waste of human resources.

The need for skilled workers is far too often identified only after serious bottlenecks emerge. When the profitability of a technological innovation for the production of goods or services depends on the availability of skilled workers, investment projects may be cut back or falter, unless VET providers respond to labor market needs. By assuring an adequate supply of appropriately skilled workers, VET makes a positive impact on economic development (Vermeulen, 1981).

METHODOLOGICAL CONSIDERATIONS

Given the influential use of workforce projection and forecasting as well as labor market signalling approaches to chart labor market de-mands, it is crucial that VET planners be informed about them.[2] How-ever, many planners, as well as other decision makers, are only remotely aware of these approaches, their various purposes, advantages, disadvan-tages, and how they can be used for planning purposes. Nevertheless, it is supremely important that VET planners know what can be legitimately concluded from them and understand the data's imperfections and limi-tations.

Once gathered and analyzed, employment estimates can be compared with data on the numbers of trainees being prepared for each occupation. This is essential in arriving at informed judgments about (a) expanding, curtailing, dropping, or modifying existing courses and programs; or (b) offering different courses and programs to supply the skilled workforce needed. The main objective is to ensure that the VET offered coincides with the skilled worker needs of the economy.

There are a variety of approaches to gathering labor market data, such as sophisticated long-term (more than 5 years) manpower requirements, econometric, and input-output studies. Other approaches, which gather current and short-term data (up to 5 years), include reporting by employ-ment services, employer surveys, and key informants; plus the analysis of job advertisements and follow-up study information. All these ap-proaches provide information on labor market needs, thereby enabling VET providers to offer appropriate courses and programs.

This chapter does not attempt to predict the specific jobs that will be available over the long-term planning horizon. To do so would be foolhardy. Changes in technology, the organization of work, consumer patterns, international competition, and so forth, will result in very different needs. In addition, this chapter does not fully discuss the supply of skilled workers or the particular reasons why various VET providers fail to adjust supply (their output) to demand. It does, however, address the need for VET planners to be informed about the approaches used to gather labor market demand information. In addressing this issue, it provides an overview of the main methods and techniques relied upon to determine present and future demands for skilled workers in the various economic sectors (industries) and occupations. These include the traditional workforce projection and forecasting approaches, as well as the labor market signalling approaches which place more responsibility on VET planners themselves to collect and utilize the necessary information. The chapter concludes by discussing how partnerships among formal (school-based) VET providers and employers lead to a better fit between VET offerings and employer needs.

Not all of the approaches for gathering labor market demand information that are presented in this chapter are appropriate in every situation. VET planners must consider the advantages and disadvantages of each and determine those that should be consulted and those that ought to be conducted locally. In an effort to enhance understanding, the specialized vocabulary and technical jargon often used by economists and workforce planners/analysts is minimized.

Terminology

It is important at this point to provide clarification between three often-confused concepts: projection, forecast, and planning. Each of these words has a specific meaning—they are not substitutes for one another. Nevertheless, the words projection and forecast are used interchangeably in much of the literature.

Projection is a generic word encompassing several approaches (methodologies). It is a protraction in the future of a past trend, in accordance with assumptions of extrapolation or deviation. The procedures used are mechanical and are not based on any explicit formulation of how labor markets function. Projections are not forecasts unless they involve a probability.

A *forecast* is an assessment of what will happen between the present (base year) and a future date (target year). The time period is a major consideration. Assessments are usually quantified, made with a certain degree of confidence in their probability, and subject to assumptions concerning the nature and direction of future trends. Assumptions are the backbone of a forecast. A variety of approaches can be used to forecast demand. Each approach has its own special properties of detail, conditional restraints, and applicability to reality.

Planning is the application of foresight, approaching the future with the aid of systematic analysis, so as to minimize uncertainty and mistakes. As used in this chapter, planning means anticipating and taking corrective action to avoid workforce imbalances (shortages and surpluses), based on the best possible information about labor market demand. Thus, VET planning aids in the intelligent and effective preparation of human resources.

Planning and Labor Market Demand

The planning of VET should correspond more closely to regional and local needs than the planning of other educational experiences. Furthermore, there is a broad consensus that VET opportunities ought to closely match the needs of the economy. This is especially true when unemployment among qualified workers co-exists with a skilled workforce shortage. However, the needs of the economy are not easily and precisely determined. Profiles of job and skill requirements are a consequence of the changes taking place in technology, work organization, consumer patterns, and the restructuring of the world-wide economic system.

Experience has shown that the data from long-term national workforce projection and forecasting studies are not always accurate and, therefore, are not dependable. Even though some point out well-known difficulties and question the utility and validity of projecting or forecasting skilled workforce demands in a free market economy, public agencies and research institutions as well as private consulting firms continue the practice in one form or another. This is largely for two reasons. First, decisions need to be made about the full utilization of existing and the availability of new VET facilities and instructors, the number of trainees to be admitted to different courses/programs, and so forth, in advance of labor market entry by those who are to be trained. The longer the duration of training, the greater is the need to plan ahead of labor market demand (Lauglo, 1993, p. 8).

The second reason is that national growth or decline in industries and occupations can have a variety of effects on regional/local planning. For example, if an industry is growing locally but not nationally, the national decline could imply that the local industry may soon experience the same decline. Industries experiencing growth at both the national and local levels provide the most promise for employment. National growth is also important because it supports the regional/local market situation.

In response to criticism, workforce projection and forecasting is now often confined to a sectoral or regional level, where it is more apt to provide useful information. The trend is toward collecting more valid and reliable information for short-term forecasts (5 years or less), which tend to be more accurate than long-range forecasts, and making adjustments based on routine monitoring through employment service data, employer surveys, key informants, job advertisements, follow-up studies, and other generally accepted techniques. Even the best of planning needs adjustments which are, in fact, part of good planning. And the faster the economy changes, the more vigorous the adjustments need to be.

Appendix A provides a checklist to help determine what approaches are being applied in assessing demand for skilled workers and by what agency or institution. Questions are included to determine the way in which existing methods and practices need improvement.

WORKFORCE PROJECTION AND FORECASTING APPROACHES

When the planning horizon is long term, predicting skilled worker demands is a hazardous undertaking. The future is filled with uncertainties and, the longer the planning horizon, the greater the problem. Workforce demand is affected by many factors, some of which, even after great effort, can be foreseen only imperfectly and imprecisely.

In any case, much has been learned from long-term studies in the U.S. and abroad, since the U.S. Department of Labor's Bureau of Labor Statistics (BLS) began the process in 1940. By 1994, the *Occupational Outlook Handbook*, produced biannually by the BLS, described future employment estimates for about 500 occupations, and the projection and forecasting approaches have become more sophisticated.

The literature has recorded many models dealing with workforce projection and forecasting, albeit in a limited way and often from a strict disciplinary framework. These models are all somewhat different; consequently, the three dominant approaches were selected for discussion here. They are the (a) manpower (workforce) requirements approach, (b) econometric models, and (c) input-output models. All three aim at quantifying the long-term workforce demands of the economy.

Manpower (Workforce) Requirements Approach

The workforce requirements approach relates forecast or planned economic growth to the output of VET providers based on a number of plausible assumptions. A general assumption is that certain sectoral economic growth rates are reachable targets (Lauglo, 1993, p. 7). The output of VET providers is then planned to meet requirements derived from these targets.

The workforce requirements approach, as usually practiced, has five main steps:

(1) Forecast employment levels in the target year (some future point in time) for each economic sector/subsector.

(2) Estimate the distribution of various occupations (staffing patterns) in each sector/subsector.

(3) Convert the employment projections into a set of projections by occupation.

(4) Project occupational replacement needs—those arising from job turnover (retirements, disabilities, deaths, promotions, and occupational mobility).

(5) Combine steps three and four for each occupation to estimate job (employment) possibilities.

Advantages

The methodology is straightforward, transparent, and appeals to common sense. It is readily comprehensible and has remained popular with economists and policy-makers (Middleton, Zinderman, & Van Adams, 1993, chap. 5). Data requirements vary according to variations of the model with regard to different levels of aggregation and detail. On the whole, however, data requirements are relatively modest. This approach provides long-term quantitative skilled worker requirements.

Disadvantages

A set of evaluations of workforce requirements studies concluded that while employment forecasts at the sectoral level (step 1 in the previous list) have been reasonably accurate, their conversion to occupations (step 3) is problematic (Hinchliffe, 1993). Furthermore, the reliability of this approach depends essentially on the accuracy of the central assumptions. Unfortunately, experience has shown that reliability remains an elusive goal; the discrepancy between actual and forecast workforce requirements is usually substantial (Mingat & Tan, 1988, p. 107). The reasons include weaknesses caused by overly-optimistic estimates of employment growth as well as increasingly rapid economic change. Other weaknesses are the frequent lack of allowance for technological advances, changing business practices, occupational mobility (e.g., resignations, lay-offs, and discharges), and the movement of individuals out of and back into employment (e.g., quit to raise a child, then return). Additionally, jobs are often filled by those who lack the skills theoretically required but who will work for less.

As a rule, accuracy and reliability diminish with longer-term projections and with a low level of aggregation, particularly greater occupational and geographic detail (Bertrand, 1992, chap. 1; Lauglo, 1993, p. 7). This dilemma is at the root of a general dissatisfaction by VET planners who insist that accurate training needs assessment requires detailed—rather than macro-type—projections.

Finally, the actions taken on the basis of workforce requirements forecasts cause obsolescence in the forecasts themselves. As public and private steps are taken to overcome prospective imbalances in demands and supplies, some of the assumptions on which the projections were based are no longer valid. Therefore, new forecasts must be made.

Econometric Models

These models, which have undergone considerable refinements, represent a set of equations describing the complex inter-relationships of the different economic sectors. Econometric studies are a sophisticated long-term forecasting approach customarily conducted by economists. Their output is a set of estimates of levels of employment in various sectors for the target year (Bertrand, 1992, chap. 1). Users of this information must avoid reading into this long-term forecast any commitment to a straight-line trend at intermediate points between the base year (year of the study) and the target year.

Advantages

This approach is sensitive to a variety of factors affecting the level and structure of employment, taking into account indirect and local inter-sectoral effects. Methodological improvements allow for replacement needs to compensate for retirements, deaths, occupational mobility, and so forth. According to the U.S. Department of Labor (1992), "In most occupations, replacement needs provide more job openings than does growth" (p. 440).

Disadvantages

Data requirements, as well as model and data base maintenance costs, are considerable. In addition, due to the technical complexity of the model's documentation, the techniques applied pose problems of accessibility and comprehensibility to VET planners and policy-makers. Also, the data are national and are not entirely useful for regional or local planning.

Accuracy is also a problem with models which are based on projections of population, workforce productivity, consumption, and overall output. This is because of the difficulty in forecasting economic activity, technological change related to productivity, and specific needs, which change due to labor and capital mobility in given market areas (American Institutes for Research, 1976, p. 45).

Input-Output Models

Each industry within an economy relies on other industries to supply inputs—intermediate products or services—for further processing. For example, a truck manufacturer must purchase steel, glass, and so forth to produce trucks. The input-output model shows these purchases by the manufacturer. Analysis of such interrelationships results in a more precise projection of each industry's production than is possible from final demand alone.

These models have been used in centrally planned, socialist, free market, developed, and developing economies. They are capable of producing highly detailed employment projections. Input-output models consist of matrices or tables that show the flow of goods and services among producing and purchasing industries over a stated period of time. Industrial output is translated into employment demands within industries. Total employment within an industry is related to its total output and expressed in terms of a workforce input coefficient. These coefficients show the workforce requirements of an industry per unit of output (Bezdek, 1974, p. 3-13).

Advantages

Input-output tables can be easily understood and interpreted. By tying industry output forecasts to detailed industry employment, workforce, and skill requirements, this approach can illuminate likely bottlenecks or workforce imbalances. It is equally appropriate for impact analysis (e.g., the effects of government programs on a regional economy) and for short-term employment projections.

Disadvantages

The construction of a national input-output table is a complex, laborious, and expensive undertaking. First, an immense volume of quantitative information must be gathered from many and varied sources and then ordered. Next, an enormous amount of statistical compilation, estimation, correction, balancing, and reconciliation must be completed. Consequently, only organizations with skilled specialists and sophisticated computer availability can construct input-output tables.

The fundamental problem of input-output model analysis is to calculate the necessary output levels of each industry required to achieve a final output. Apart from this, the approach does not provide a substitute for insight and informed judgment on the part of a VET planner (Hewings, 1985).

A comparison of some advantages and disadvantages of the three workforce projection and forecasting approaches is presented in Table 1.

Table 1. Advantages and disadvantages of workforce projection and forecasting approaches.

Advantages	Disadvantages
Manpower (Workforce) Requirements Approach	
• Straightforward, transparent, and appeals to common sense • Readily comprehensible • Popular with economists and policy-makers • Relatively modest data requirements	• Reliability affected by uncontrollable factors, such as overly optimistic estimates of employment growth, rapid economic change, lack of allowance for technological advances, changing business practices, occupational mobility, and withdrawal from and return to the workforce • Accuracy and reliability diminish with longer-term projections and with greater disaggregation • General dissatisfaction by vocational training planners
Econometric Models	
• Sensitive to a variety of factors which affect the level and structure of employment • Methodological improvements allow for replacement needs to compensate for retirements, deaths, occupational mobility, etc.	• Extensive data requirements • High data base maintenance costs • Highly technical and, therefore, difficult for vocational training planners and policy-makers to access and/or comprehend • National data not entirely useful for regional or local planning • Accuracy problem with models based on population, workforce, productivity, consumption, and overall output projections
Input-Output Models	
• Capable of producing highly detailed employment projections • Tables easy to understand and interpret • Can illuminate likely bottlenecks and workforce imbalances • Equally appropriate for short-term forecasting and impact analysis	• Extensive data requirements • High data base maintenance costs • Requires skilled specialists and sophisticated computers to construct tables

LABOR MARKET SIGNALLING APPROACHES

Rather than rely exclusively on sophisticated long-term projections and forecasts, VET planners need to consider the merits of various labor market signalling approaches. These approaches involve the frequent collection and careful monitoring of data on workforce demand and supply in regional/local labor markets where the process of matching jobs and people takes place.

For example, a rising number of unfilled job vacancies for plumbers, or the inability of sheet-metal program graduates to find employment, are labor market signals. They reflect, respectively, a shortage of plumbers and a possible surplus of sheet-metal workers (Middleton et al., 1993, chap. 5).

Labor market signalling approaches include reporting of the transactions of employment services (unemployment registration, notification of job vacancies, and placements). Quantitative and qualitative information is also available from other labor market "stakeholders" such as individual employers, economic development authorities, employers' and workers' organizations, VET providers, and so forth. The collective data provides a basis for determining demand/supply imbalances and trends.

Labor market signalling approaches supplement existing long-term workforce projections and forecasts which are too aggregate, contradictory, or out of date. In addition, they direct VET planners toward current and short-term (future) job opportunities rather than highly speculative long-term possibilities. These approaches are a response to the realization that labor market action, by and large, is at the regional/local levels.

Reporting by Employment Services

Labor market signals can be captured by monitoring overall workforce activity and movements in the employment and unemployment (layoffs and resignations) of workers with particular skills. Most state employment services keep records on unemployment, job openings, and placements. However, in many cases, presentation of the data takes the form of a mere compilation of statistics. Such administrative data is devoid of detailed and informative analyses of workforce supply and demand situations and trends.

For example, calculating the number of job openings is not only useful in itself, but makes it possible to monitor trends in the shifting demand for and supply of skilled workers. Thus, when job opening rates fall, unemployment rates rise, or employment growth declines for workers with particular skills, this signals a downturn in the need for these skills and, hence, in the benefits of providing VET to produce them. There is a great and growing need for the sorts of information only a public employment service could supply. However, such information must be reliable and available in a usable form.

Advantages

Public employment services act as an intermediary between people looking for jobs and employers looking for workers. Consequently, they are in touch with labor market happenings at the state and local levels. As a result, they are in a position to collect, analyze, and report information on job openings and unemployment rates by occupation and job title. This information is valuable to VET planners, who can use it in determining the need for VET in a particular occupation or job. The generation and dissemination of this information does not require investment of considerable new resources, but mainly requires broadening the focus to include labor market information analysis.

Disadvantages

Since the registration of people looking for jobs and the notification of vacancies by employers do not cover the whole of these phenomena, the data available from public employment services is more or less incomplete. Furthermore, the data may not be representative of the overall labor market situation. For example, little is known on the extent to which employers are willing to report vacant jobs to the local employment service, and whether or not the reporting rate varies over time and between employers. Thus, the information available may be inadequate and could be misleading.

Furthermore, public employment services are more highly concentrated in urban areas catering to the formal (wage-earning) sector. They appear to function largely as a job exchange for the unemployed, with unemployment registration taking up much of their staff time. Any collection, generation, analysis, and dissemination of labor market information is usually considered a side-line. In other words, the full potential of their recordkeeping and ability to capture and report labor market signals is far from being adequately developed.

Employer Surveys

Ultimately, employers are the ones who decide on hiring. Theirs is the last word on what the market wants; they are the market. It makes sense, therefore, to seek their input. The idea is neither new nor original. The problem is how to do it. The most straightforward way is to survey private and public sector employers directly. Mailed questionnaires and personal interviews are widely used methods of collecting information. Questionnaires and interview schedules can vary from open-ended to closed-ended instruments. The closed-form instrument is recommended when categorized data is needed; whereas, the open-ended is best-suited for preliminary exploration of untried situations. Telephone interviews are limited in use and not usually appropriate for a comprehensive survey.

Large, medium, and small businesses within a geographic area (including all places that workers are willing to travel without changing their residence) are identified and asked to estimate their present and future workforce requirements. They are also asked to provide information on associated training needs, as well as any constraints in hiring VET graduates. This information helps to identify which industries and occupations are growing and which are declining. It augments the data gathered from other approaches, such as reporting by employment services.

Advantages

Employer surveys are relatively easy to conduct, go right to the source of labor market demand, and can provide good information in a reasonably short time. By directly involving employers in needs determination and by considering their views regarding occupational projections and forecasts derived from other approaches, employers' willingness to cooperate in providing information is increased (American Institutes, 1976, p. 44).

The personal interview method of data collection provides a high response rate and a host of other opportunities. For example, VET planners can use the occasion to inquire about anticipated changes in technology and to inform employers about the advantages of hiring VET graduates. This is also an opportunity to discuss the feasibility of partnership arrangements between VET providers and employers which lead to more relevant, effective, and efficient VET. Appendix B provides guidance on preparing for and conducting in-person interviews.

Disadvantages

Not all employers are able (or willing) to provide detailed predictions of target-year occupational demand and training needs, especially those needs beyond the immediate future (not much more than one year). This is because many employers don't gather the data necessary for reliable estimates. In addition, when estimates are provided, they are apt to be biased toward overestimation if the employers feel that their replies will positively affect the availability of skilled workers. For example, if the skills concerned are scarce, employers will tend to overestimate their needs (Bertrand, 1992, chap. 2).

Furthermore, different ways of classifying jobs by various employers (often incompatible with national standard classifications) have detrimental effects on the comparability of the information collected. Comparability also suffers as changes in the workplace alter job requirements, especially when the jobs are not reclassified. Moreover, surveys that ask employers to provide relatively long-range estimates by industry and occupation may not provide valid or reliable data. This is especially true during periods affected by extreme structural change and/or severe economic fluctuations. Unfortunately, when a questionnaire is used, response rates are often low and the information provided is not always complete or adequate for planning purposes. As a result, confidence in the accuracy of survey information is usually low.

While surveying employers may not provide valid or reliable quantitative information on labor market demand, it is, nevertheless, an essential component of the qualitative analysis of the content and evolution of jobs and an assessment of labor market functioning (Bertrand, 1992, p. 34).

A further drawback of this approach is that costs vary from reasonable to high levels depending on the (a) data collection method used (mailed questionnaire or personal interview), and (b) number of employers surveyed. In any case, the main problem is that employer surveys typically do not cover skilled worker demand in the informal (self-employed) sector, particularly in rural areas.

Key Informant Interviews

Interviews of individuals who are knowledgeable on workforce demand and the supply of skilled workers in a geographic area or economic sector offer another way to obtain relevant labor market information. In some cases, no useful information would have been available if no interviews had been undertaken.

An essential precondition for the satisfactory outcome of key informant interviews is the careful selection of knowledgeable, competent, and unbiased individuals from (a) regional/local businesses; (b) public agencies; (c) economic development authorities; and (d) employer, worker, and professional organizations. Other important factors include the use of a structured interview schedule limited to well-constructed core questions, the timely analysis of the information obtained, and regular and frequent follow-up of the signals captured. Core questions focus on current and expected workforce demand and supply imbalances. They also seek to determine factors underlying such imbalances, and the most critical workforce issues for the next 5 years. Other questions ask about employer screening, hiring, and training practices. Appendix B provides guidance on preparing for and conducting in-person interviews.

It is important to add that active contact with key informants, to inquire about workforce demand and supply problems, is a prudent practice. Experience has shown that carefully selected individuals are willing to participate and are pleased to provide input.

Advantages

Key informant interviews are straightforward and modest in cost. They yield current indicators of workforce demand and supply imbalances in regional/local labor markets, give early warning signals about forthcoming changes, and/or confirm trends previously documented. In addition, information can be gathered on the various screening, hiring, and training practices in use. For example, are skilled jobs filled by promoting and training semi-skilled employees, or are apprenticeship programs used to prepare skilled workers? If these or other screening practices are used, there may be little opportunity for applicants who have already received school-based VET and, therefore, expect skilled-worker jobs and wages.

Key informant interviews can be held with individuals and groups, conducted in both the public and private sectors, and used in formal as well as informal labor markets. Selection of key informants may be based on brief interviews, cross-checked by the question: Whom do you consider most knowledgeable on workforce demand and supply in this area? Conduct of interviews and analysis of information collected can be entrusted to employment services, local labor and other government departments, research institutes, universities, and, last but not least, VET providers.

Disadvantages

Key informants provide mainly qualitative information which reflects personal views and perceptions. Consequently, it must be weighed with other information. Since the primary selection criterion for a key informant is "knowledge" (and not "randomness"), informants will not be representative in terms of research rigor. Whether or not these disadvantages are significant depends largely on the kind and scope of workforce information which VET providers have agreed as being essential for the effective and efficient planning of VET courses and programs.

Job Advertisements

Little systematic use has been made of collecting and analyzing job advertisements in newspapers, trade publications, professional journals/magazines, and other print media. Yet, help-wanted ads constitute the only public listing of job opportunities, with the exception of notices displayed by some employment service and civil service offices. Monitoring these publicized listings over a specified period of time can produce a valuable picture of the present labor market demand.

Job advertisements provide a great body of current, convenient, and usable information. More often than not, they even provide a point of contact, an address and/or telephone number which can be used to obtain further information. What is more, the information can be collected at a time when employers are most interested in that particular job and when they have given explicit thought to their requirements and expectations.

The main reason for reluctance to use this approach seems to be that the advertisements alone do not reveal all the information necessary for a labor market analysis. As a result, contact must be made with the advertising establishments/employers to collect further details, such as (a) whether the job was newly created or a replacement, (b) the number of applicants and their qualifications in relation to the skills required, and (c) the occupational profile of those hired. Skill gaps on the part of applicants point to the need for more training or the upgrading of qualifications.

Advantages

Major newspapers, especially the Sunday editions, often contain voluminous sections of job advertisements which literally go begging for analysis with regard to identifying demand. Such analysis would at least complement the (incomplete) signals received from employment service records. It could be easily undertaken by VET planners who, in discussing ads with the employers who floated them, could benefit directly from the views and attitudes of those employers regarding the skills required. The analysis of job advertisements is an inexpensive approach which provides information on the latest trends in the employment market.

Disadvantages

Job advertisements vastly underrepresent the volume of actual job openings. Among the reasons are that they cover only a small segment of the labor market and focus primarily on large metropolitan areas. Another problem is that many employers do not even use want ads, and those that do tend to be the bigger employers, who list the same jobs with the employment service. Furthermore, the number of advertisements in regional or local newspapers may be insufficient to construct a sample large enough for analysis to yield useful conclusions.

Moreover, this approach deals with present needs and not with future needs of the region/locality. It is also static—it does not predict the future growth of present or new industries (American Institutes, 1976, p. 46). In any event, the assumption that job advertisements provide an accurate picture of labor market demand has not been tested adequately. No known research has attempted to analyze systematically the content of help-wanted ads and, in turn, their utility to VET planners as labor market indicators.

Follow-up (Tracer) Studies

Follow-up studies, usually conducted as part of the process for evaluating VET courses and programs, are increasingly recognized as important sources of information for VET planners. They are used to monitor labor market trends affecting graduates. Like employer surveys, follow-up studies use a questionnaire or personal interview to collect information. For a variety of good reasons, the mailed questionnaire is generally used.

A follow-up questionnaire is developed, pilot-tested, and then mailed to course/program graduates. Appendix C presents a process for conducting follow-up studies. Among other things, graduates are asked whether they (a) are available for employment, (b) are working full- or part-time, and (c) found a job for which they were trained. In addition, the studies seek to find out how useful they consider their training to have been for their actual job. The questionnaire also asks graduates (a) how much they earn, (b) how they found their job, (c) how long they looked before finding it, and (d) if different training would have made finding employment easier. (See Appendix D for a prototype follow-up questionnaire.) An analysis of responses to these and other questions helps to determine the demand relevance of particular VET courses or programs and sheds some light on the circumstances of entry into and experiences in the labor market.

For best results, follow-up study questionnaires must be short and simple to complete. It is recommended that follow-up studies be conducted from 4 to 6 months after graduation, at the end of the first year, and again at the end of the second and third years. Important information revealed by a three-year follow-up includes answers to the following questions:

(1) Is it getting harder or easier to find a particular job?
(2) Are there shifts in the economic sector (industry) in which graduates are employed?
(3) Do the self-employed earn more or less than salaried graduates?

(4) What are the trends in earnings by job title and sector of employment?

(5) Is a match between VET and a graduate's job an early career phenomenon?

(6) Is VET important as a source of skills for entry into the labor market, while work experience and on-the-job training become more important than VET in later career stages?

It is not necessary at the outset to conduct large-scale studies in order to gain an idea of graduates' labor market experiences. To begin with, a study can be made of small populations, giving priority to courses or programs of questionable efficacy and which create the most urgent problems (Bertrand, 1992, chap. 7). Experience shows 10 respondents to be the minimum number for reliable reporting. Appendix E presents a tally sheet format which is helpful in tabulating responses from small population studies.

A significant problem is that rates and periods of unemployment, and wages/salaries earned, do not indicate on their own the success or failure of a particular VET course or program. This information needs to be put in perspective by comparisons with (a) the labor market experiences of a control group, (b) feedback from employer interviews, (c) different VET courses and programs, (d) other training institutions, and (e) current market conditions (regional/local employment opportunities). The number of vacant jobs and the available pool of graduates with the training to fill them are clearly key parameters affecting the probability that any graduate will be able to obtain a job that fits (matches) his or her training.

Advantages

Follow-up studies supplement other sources of labor market information by revealing what has actually happened to VET course/program graduates. They are not an instrument for projections or forecasts, but they are a feedback mechanism for collecting information so that courses and programs can be adjusted, when necessary, to meet labor market requirements. Information on the employment and wages of graduates provides effective signals on the balance of supply and demand, by job title, in local markets.

Since the population surveyed is a group of graduates who completed training at the same time and who were looking for employment at the same time and under similar conditions, VET planners can make good use of this tool for both labor supply and, to a lesser extent, demand and trend analysis. Follow-up studies using questionnaires are relatively inexpensive.

Disadvantages

Problems arise when too many objectives are set for follow-up studies other than those related to assessing how graduates fared in the labor market. In addition, when questionnaires get unduly long or complicated, requiring considerable time to complete, response rates and the quality of the answers tend to diminish. Low response rates may result from out-dated or incomplete addresses, as well. There is also a problem with the data—information provided by graduates has questionable validity.

In general, follow-up studies are time-consuming and contribute little to identifying the need for different VET offerings. However, this in no way diminishes their importance as a mechanism for monitoring the relationship between courses and programs completed and the consequent labor market experiences of graduates.

A comparison of some advantages and disadvantages of the five labor market signalling approaches is presented in Table 2.

Table 2. Advantages and disadvantages of labor market signalling approaches.

Advantages	Disadvantages
Reporting by Employment Services	
• Employment services stay in touch with state and local labor market happenings and can collect, analyze, and report data on unemployment and job openings by occupation and job title	• Data available is more or less incomplete
	• Data may not be representative of overall labor market situation
• No sizable investment of new resources is required for generating and disseminating the data	• Employment services are more highly concentrated in urban areas catering to the formal sector

Table 2. (continued).

Advantages	Disadvantages
Employer Surveys	
• Relatively easy to conduct • Go right to the source of labor market demand • Provide good data in a relatively short time • Employers' willingness to cooperate is increased, because their views and suggestions are considered	• Not all employers are able (or willing) to provide reliable and detailed predictions of target-year occupational demand and training needs • Estimates provided by employers may be biased, if they feel that their replies will positively affect the availability of skilled workers • Different employers may classify jobs in different ways, thus affecting the comparability of the information collected • Comparability suffers as changes in the workplace alter job requirements, especially when the jobs are not reclassified • Employers may not provide valid or reliable long-range information during periods of structural change or economic fluctuation • Employer surveys do not cover skilled worker demand in the informal sector, particularly in rural areas
Key Informant Interviews	
• Straightforward and cost-effective • Information yields current indicators of workforce demand and supply imbalances in regional/local labor markets • Information gives early warning signals about changes in workforce demand and supply, and/or confirms trends previously documented • Information can be gathered on employers' screening, hiring, and training practices • Can be conducted in both formal and informal labor market sectors	• Information is mainly qualitative, reflecting personal views, opinions, and perceptions • Information is not representative in terms of research rigor

(continued)

Table 2. (continued).

Advantages	Disadvantages
Job Advertisements	
• Provide a great body of current, convenient, and usable information • Analysis of advertisements could complement signals received from employment services records • Analysis could be easily undertaken by VET planners who could, at the same time, benefit directly from views of the employers who floated the advertisements • An inexpensive approach which provides an up-to-date record of trends	• Cover a small segment of the labor market and focus on large metropolitan areas • Many employers do not advertise, and those that do tend to be bigger • The number of advertisements in regional or local newspapers may be insufficient to construct a sample for analysis • Deal with present needs, not future needs • Analysis does not predict future growth of present or new industries
Follow-up (Tracer) Studies	
• Reveal what actually happened to graduates in the labor market • Monitor training courses/programs, thereby facilitating adjustments to meet labor market requirements • Information collected on employment and wages of graduates provides signals on the balance of supply and demand by job title in local markets • Relatively inexpensive	• Problems arise when including objectives that are not related to how graduates fared in the labor market • Response rates and the quality of answers may diminish if questionnaires are too long or complicated • Poor response rates result from out-dated or incomplete addresses • Information provided by graduates has questionable validity • Time consuming • Contribute little toward identifying the need for new training courses/programs

SOME CLOSING THOUGHTS

The underlying hypothesis of this chapter is that VET offerings must adjust to labor market demand. In principle, VET providers cannot force increases in demand. Therefore, they must use information collected from workforce projection and forecasting as well as labor market signalling approaches in making informed decisions about (a) expanding, curtailing, dropping, or modifying existing courses and programs; or (b) offering different training. The consequences of a mismatch between VET offerings and employment possibilities include the demoralization of graduates who cannot find a job for which they were prepared, as well as a severe waste of material and human resources. Neither individuals nor society can afford to invest in VET that the labor market does not want or need.

The overview of the major workforce projection and forecasting approaches presented in this chapter is by no means exhaustive. But it does point out that, despite the care that goes into their preparation, there are no perfect projections or forecasts; there are only best estimates based on the most comprehensive approaches and the most complete information. Since these approaches will continue to be primarily the responsibility of economists or workforce planners/analysts, in view of their relevance to wider issues of employment and labor market policies, in addition to VET planning, those concerned with the latter might be satisfied with gaining overview knowledge in this respect. However, such knowledge must include an understanding of the various advantages and disadvantages of each approach and its potential for assessing labor market demand. It is worth noting here that the BLS's long-term forecasts are the soundest available. Accordingly, their publications— the *Occupational Outlook Handbook,* which projects for roughly a decade ahead, and the *Occupational Outlook Quarterly*—have gained wide acceptance for VET planning.

The five labor market signalling approaches described provide information on current and short-term (future) job demand trends at the regional/local level. These approaches can be undertaken by VET planners, thereby eliminating the need to wait for economists or workforce planners/analysts to fill labor market information gaps which, in many instances, are considerable.

Reporting by employment services, employer surveys, key informant interviews, analyses of job advertisements, and follow-up (tracer) studies are strong candidates in this respect. They have proven successful in a number of trials and are now beginning to be applied more broadly. It is for this reason that a checklist is presented in Appendix A, to determine which of the methods described is applied and what use is made of their results for VET planning. The checklist is followed by guidelines for preparing and conducting interviews and follow-up studies.

The last, and perhaps the most important point to be made is that none of the approaches described can claim predominant significance or provide complete insight. Consequently, the use of any single approach should be avoided. In fact, there is merit in the use of a combination of several approaches to collect the requisite information. Reliance on a host of selected labor market demand approaches enables VET planners to form judgments based on a composite of information.

Given the past emphasis placed on long-term mechanistic workforce projection and forecasting approaches—with controversial results— there is room to conduct a variety of labor market signalling approaches. The process nature of workforce demand and supply interactions, as reflected in [ever-changing] labor supply and demand imbalances, and the special importance of capturing these changes in a timely fashion, also suggest the importance of labor market signalling approaches. These approaches involve routine data collection and analysis—rather than the workforce projections and forecasts which are made at a single point in time.

Determining the demand for skilled workers has been discussed, within this chapter, in the context of:

(1) Reducing lag time in adjusting to labor market demand and supply imbalances
(2) Avoiding skilled worker surpluses
(3) Avoiding bottlenecks due to skilled worker shortages
(4) Tracing VET graduates to determine if they are working at jobs where their talents and training are fully utilized

The overall purpose is to match VET offerings more closely with the realities of current and future skilled worker needs. Some VET courses/programs create a surplus of graduates in declining-demand occupations and too few in emerging-demand occupations and those where skilled workers are in short supply. Effective planning at the regional and local levels and accountability by VET providers is necessary if VET is to utilize limited resources more effectively to avoid these imbalances and serve as an effective instrument of economic growth and social development.

A Movement toward the Reform of Formal VET

VET providers, trainees, employers, government, and society all have something to gain when VET is responsive to labor market demand. Nevertheless, there may be reasons why some VET providers do not respond at the speed required or on a scale sufficient to adequately address imbalances between supply and demand, for example, the lack of physical, financial, and staff resources, or the lack of accountability. In most cases, however, there are at least some adjustments that can be made. There is a fair amount of consensus that *the main deterrent to responsiveness is a lack of up-to-date information on present and anticipated job vacancies.* As this chapter shows, labor market demand information can be collected and should be used to reduce the gap between the supply of and demand for skilled workers.

If the approaches presented thus far do not provide acceptable choices for action, then expanded partnership arrangements among formal (school-based) VET providers and employers or craft unions will, among other things, lead to a better fit between VET offerings and marketplace needs. By bringing together those who are on the supply side (VET providers) and those on the demand side (employers), there is every reason to expect more relevant, effective, and efficient VET. Through such partnerships, businesses and craft unions can better communicate their concerns and skill needs to VET providers, and VET planning can better respond to the realities of the labor market. For example, workplace requirements will determine the form, content, scope, and duration of training, ensuring relevance and timeliness.

Partnership benefits such as these are the reason for the growing number of school-to-work transition schemes in the U.S. and abroad. Austria, Germany, and Switzerland present examples of schemes at their highest level of development. In these countries, the outcome of work-based VET is employment as a skilled worker, not education and training for its own sake (Campbell & Armstrong, 1993, chap. 4).

Linking Schooling and Work

Transition schemes are aimed at satisfying both the VET needs of young adults and the needs of the economy for a relevant and qualified workforce. They facilitate alternating periods of learning in school and structured training on the job. Variations include (a) youth apprentice-

0156391

ships, (b) cooperative vocational training, work-study contracts, (c) internships, and (d) a host of other collaborative approaches.

Under the *ideal* transition scheme, initial VET takes place in schools, institutions, and so forth, as well as in the workplace, namely, businesses, industries, enterprises, firms, plants, factories, hospitals, and construction sites. While the workplace is the focal point for the development of skills and positive work socialization behaviors, it shares with the school the responsibility for providing young adults with the best possible job and personal qualifications.

The workplace takes the lead and provides practical experiential training and productive work experience, while the school provides integrated occupation-related and applied general education. This coordinated combination of on-the-job training/practice and schooling breaks down the artificial barriers between work and schooling by creating the preconditions for all-around meaningful, relevant, and effective learning.

Trainees are highly motivated because they feel secure, in knowing that their training provides marketable skills and that it is clearly relevant to employment. Furthermore, they may be offered a job, based on their performance and achievement.

Apart from providing a genuine incentive to learn, this form of VET channels the youths' time and energies to economically and socially useful purposes. Because it is conducted in an adult environment, it can also counteract the influence of negative teenage peer pressure by constructively promoting the maturation process, on a one-to-one basis, under the guidance of a workplace mentor.

While businesses naturally provide training to meet their anticipated requirements, they also train a pool of skilled workers to meet labor market demand. Graduates not hired by the sponsoring business are sought after by other employers because of their quality training, experience, and credential.

In carrying out their training responsibilities, businesses and craft unions

(1) Impart the occupational knowledge and skills necessary for the attainment of learning objectives, through structured workplace training by qualified on-the-job instructors
(2) Provide the necessary supervised work experience, where knowledge and skills are applied, using state-of-the-art equipment and production methods

(3) Cultivate positive work socialization behaviors, namely, dependability, a willingness to accept supervision and follow work rules, getting along and cooperating with others, a sense of responsibility beyond their own job, pride in work, etc., through workplace mentoring and coaching

(4) Care for trainees' health, safety, and well-being, while promoting their maturation in the workplace alongside supportive adults

Monitors (coordinators/overseers) periodically visit trainees at their workplace to determine progress through the various phases of the occupation and to help resolve problems. They also provide assurance that trainees receive the requisite training from a qualified person, are closely supervised by a designated mentor, and are not exploited as "cheap labor." Apart from looking after trainee progress and potential abuse, monitors act to forestall situations where incumbent workers are at risk of being displaced by trainees.

In making career choices and searching for a workplace or craft union in which to train, young adults are guided by an extensive vocational counseling network. In addition to services provided by the state department of labor (e.g., one-stop career information centers), school-based efforts include

(1) Counseling and guidance toward career opportunities relevant to labor market demand

(2) Day visits (field trips) to workplaces and craft union training sites

(3) Fundamental pre-vocational training in related occupational groups (clusters)

(4) Short-term unpaid experiences (e.g., job shadowing, work observation, etc.) in a variety of workplaces

(5) Information and advice on transition scheme opportunities (includes parental involvement)

(6) Work placement assistance

Workplace training is provided in stages, beginning with an orientation and familiarization, then broad-based transferable VET, which is followed by a gradual integration into the operational process and increasing specialization. It ends with a criterion-referenced examination (competency demonstration) based on nationally accepted occupational standards. The examination is organized and administered by an impartial body of equally represented employers, incumbent skilled workers, and VET instructors. Those who pass the final examination are awarded a widely recognized, respected, and portable credential (certificate, diploma, etc.) that has value in the workplace because it ratifies the knowledge and skills acquired.

Role of Tripartite Bodies

The *ideal* transition scheme is organized, implemented, and administered in accordance with policies developed by autonomous tripartite bodies (boards, councils, etc.). These bodies have equal representation and balanced participation by knowledgeable and influential persons from business (private sector), organized workers (unions), and government. VET instructors also serve, but only in an advisory capacity. The policies developed by tripartite bodies provide a course of action to

(1) Influence employers to participate in a transition scheme and provide training in occupations consistent with present and anticipated workforce demand.

(2) Develop and deliver curricula using performance-(doing-) based methodology and evaluate using criterion-referenced examinations.

(3) Identify changes in job knowledge and skills within occupations and continually update the curricula.

(4) Establish official occupational qualifications (credentials) which certify competence, based on industry-driven, nationally-accepted skill standards, and oversee the examinations which grant the qualifications.

(5) Ensure that trainee progress is based on individual achievement (attainment of learning objectives).

(6) Set regulations that ensure uniform high quality workplace training and cost-effective decentralized program oversight.

(7) Facilitate a seamless passage for trainees between and among various levels of VET.

(8) Conduct research and experimentation efforts, then disseminate information on how to solve the problems studied. Also, improve the quality and accessibility of labor market demand information, as well as provide technical assistance and guidance to employers and VET providers on training and related matters.

Successful policies depend on a mechanism for sharing the costs of training. In this regard, tripartite bodies must address the need to pool resources from a host of private, public, and philanthropic organizations. One approach is to have employers, government, and trainees contribute. In such a case, the higher income deferred by a trainee while in the scheme should be recognized as a contribution. The principle of joint funding may be expensive at the front end to a party who would prefer to be exempt, but this approach broadens the base of support, creates a healthy partnership, and produces genuine incentives for all parties to help the scheme succeed. Moreover, joint funding has a multiplier effect with other sources, such as foundations.

The Business Decision to Participate

Businesses and craft unions train and nurture young adults because they are convinced that, given the projected slowing of labor force growth, it is the best way to ensure a reliable supply of skilled and productive workers who practice positive work socialization behaviors. Toward this end, businesses are increasingly realizing that they must deal with VET providers as suppliers of human capital. That means dealing with them similar to the way they deal with other suppliers—getting involved and collaborating on quantity and quality requirements. Economists and employers advocate transition schemes because ". . . mismatches of [skilled] workers to jobs are less likely than when we rely on occupational projections . . ." (Lerman, 1994, p. 45). More specifically, businesses of all sizes are willing to take on the quasi-public responsibility of training young adults, despite the costs, when they are faced with, or anticipate, skilled worker shortages. Moreover, the decision to participate often includes the following motives (what's in it for them) that make economic sense:

(1) Employers are free to decide how many and which trainees they will take on and for what occupations, and don't have to pay them as much as they pay skilled workers. Admittedly, the trainees are not as productive as experienced skilled workers, but the employer still gets a bargain. Nevertheless, an employer that wants to attract good applicants and hold on to skilled workers after their training offers reasonable wages and other incentives during the training period as well.

(2) A fully trained skilled worker is more productive and flexible, can more readily solve work-related problems, produce better products and deliver better service, and assimilate new knowledge and skills, thereby contributing to the overall economic vitality of the business. Over time, a training investment in young workers returns more than its cost by preparing highly capable and motivated employees that contribute to the business's increased competitiveness and profitability.

(3) The chance to observe and evaluate trainees over a lengthy period, under actual work conditions and standards, before making hiring decisions eliminates the expensive, time-consuming, and risk-laden process of recruiting and screening skilled workers. By training their own potential workers, employers are assured of the skills and on-the-job social behaviors of those they choose to hire. Because these new hires have been part of the business for a while, it doesn't take them long to "get up to speed"—essentially, they can "hit the ground running" and be productive, high performance workers right from the start. Moreover, employers gain from their investment through reduced time, effort, and costs associated with hiring, orienting new employees to their jobs, and terminating those who do not meet expectations.

(4) Workplace training promotes high morale and leads to an understanding of and identification with the business or craft. Furthermore, businesses and craft unions provide training out of a sense of social responsibility and are proud of the skilled workers they prepare. Offering workplace training means enhanced community relations.

For these and other reasons, workplace training for anticipated job vacancies is viewed as a good investment with high long-term economic and social returns.

Concluding Remarks

In the final analysis, the employment prospects of those who participate in a transition scheme, such as the one described, are better than those of graduates from an exclusively school-based VET program. The salient employability advantages are (a) a respected credential that is portable to other employers across the country (making it easier to move to where the jobs are), (b) meaningful and productive work experience, and (c) positive work socialization behaviors. Even if graduates could not find a job for which they were trained, the above-listed advantages, for which there is a common need across occupations, make them excellent candidates for numerous related jobs. Furthermore, the acquisition of positive work behaviors and maturity, which are molded in the workplace by caring and influential instructors, mentors, and co-workers, along with an understanding of employer expectations, are benefits that enable graduates to enter full-time jobs and successfully adjust to the situation. These benefits also help graduates compete more effectively in the labor market and will serve them well over a lifetime of employment and career progression.

APPENDIX A

A Checklist on the Actual Use of Various Workforce Projection and Forecasting Approaches and Labor Market Signalling Approaches

This checklist was prepared to help VET planners obtain as complete a picture as possible on what approaches are being applied in assessing demand for skilled workers. The checklist is intended as an illustration of major considerations; it does not include all questions which the VET planner might wish to raise.

1. Which approaches are being applied and by what agency/institution?
   1.1 Workforce projection and forecasting approaches
       ☐ Manpower (workforce) requirements approach
       Agency: _____
       ☐ Econometric models
       Agency: _____
       ☐ Input-output models
       Agency: _____
       ☐ Other approaches/models used _____
       Agency: _____
   1.2 Labor market signalling approaches
       ☐ Reporting by employment services
       Agency: _____

  ☐ Employer surveys
   Agency: _____
  ☐ Key informants
   Agency: _____
  ☐ Job advertisements
   Agency: _____
  ☐ Follow-up (tracer) studies
   Agency: _____

2. Do the results of these approaches discuss VET implications?
  ☐ Yes ☐ No

3. Do the results call attention to possible constraints, pitfalls, or reservations to be considered in their use for VET needs assessment and planning?
  ☐ Yes ☐ No

4. Assess the approaches identified in items 1.1 and 1.2. Then list those that are most appropriate for your situation.
  4.1 Workforce projection and forecasting approaches

   _____
   _____
   _____

  4.2 Labor market signalling approaches

   _____
   _____
   _____

APPENDIX B

Guidance on In-Person Interviews

Introduction

Interviews may be conducted with one individual or a group, in person or by telephone. The interviews may be formal, highly structured interchanges with prepared questions, or they may be informal, with considerable flexibility. Guidance on in-person interviews is briefly presented here.

Prepare for the Interview

Activities that help in preparing for the interview are:

- Know the purpose for the interview, what labor market information you expect to gain.
- Select a skillful, understandable interviewer with a pleasant personality and the ability to listen attentively.
- Develop a plan or guide to help keep the interview on track. This will ensure that the purpose is achieved and that the needed information is collected. Carefully planned interviews take less time to conduct.
- Know the subject to be addressed and how you are going to compare the responses. This will ensure the cost-effectiveness of the time and effort invested.
- Contact those to be interviewed (interviewees) to request their cooperation (letter of request, followed by a telephone call for an appointment).
- Choose the time and place of the interview wisely. This choice will have an impact on the information collected. For best results, make sure that the time and place are acceptable to the interviewee(s), and that the location is quiet, comfortable, and free from distractions.
- Find out personal information about the interviewee(s). This will help in setting a realistic time frame and pace for the interview.

Begin the Interview

Points to be observed when beginning the interview are:

- Be on time and start the interview with "small-talk" to "break the ice" and build rapport. This will create a favorable impression and enhance the interviewee's willingness to provide needed information.
- Explain the purpose for the interview, and discuss how the information will be used. Emphasize that their input is important and their participation is valued.
- Ask for permission to take notes. Write so that the interviewee(s) can see what you have recorded. This reduces anxiety. A tape recorder may also be used. Note-taking may be disturbing and audiotaping threatening to some individuals.

Conduct the Interview

Points to be observed when conducting the interview are:

- Use prepared questions to ensure that you get all the information needed. Ask simple questions first.
- Practice active listening skills and observe non-verbal messages (body language) in order to understand what is said and meant.
- Use probing techniques, as necessary, to elicit complete, specific information.
- Clarify misunderstood questions and reconcile conflicting information.

Conclude the Interview

Items to consider when concluding an interview are:

- Give the interviewee(s) an opportunity to ask questions.
- Summarize what was recorded during the interview.
- Tell the interviewee(s) that additional information may be needed at a later date.
- Thank the interviewee(s) for their important help.

Follow-up

Send a thank-you note that emphasizes how valuable their input was.

APPENDIX C

Guidance on Follow-up (Tracer) Studies

Introduction

The practical side of conducting a follow-up study using a mailed questionnaire to collect data is briefly presented here as an 11-step process. Mailed questionnaires are normally a cost-effective method of collecting quantifiable information from large numbers of geographically dispersed graduates.

Prepare for the Study

- Prepare a budget based on estimated costs associated with developing, pilot-testing, duplicating, and mailing a questionnaire, as well as tallying, interpreting, and reporting the data collected.

- Inform trainees who are about to complete their course or program about the purpose and importance of the follow-up study. Show them the type of questionnaire they will receive and encourage them to participate in the study. Make it clear that the purpose is to determine what happens to them after they graduate, so that future training can be more relevant to the labor market. These measures will help to allay possible mistrust later on.

- Have trainees complete a baseline information form which includes their name, address, phone number, gender, age, work experience, etc. Add individual training performance data (attendance, grades, etc.) and statements about the trainee's behavior to the form. This information is useful when interpreting data collected from the study.

- Set up a control group of individuals who will enter the labor market at about the same time as the trainees, but who did not follow a training course or program. *This is an optional, but highly desirable step.* The characteristics of these individuals should be similar to those of the trainees. A control group makes it possible to compare the labor market experiences of those who received training with the experiences of those who did not receive training.

- Develop the questionnaire. It is important to *ask only those questions that will yield essential information.* Demographic and other information available in existing records is omitted and all nice- or interesting-to-know, but non-essential, items are left out in order to keep the questionnaire as short as possible. Experience has shown that graduates tend to prefer 3 to 5 pages. Appendix D provides a prototype follow-up questionnaire which was developed to gather labor market information. It includes an appropriate combination of closed-ended questions (e.g., Part 3, items 8 and 9), partially closed-ended questions (e.g., Part 3, item 7), and open-ended questions (e.g., Part 3, items 10 and 11). After deciding on the type of item to use, it must be carefully worded so that all respondents interpret the question as intended. Finally, a neat, well-organized, and attractive questionnaire, with sufficient space to answer each question, should increase the critically important response rate.

- Select a sample of trainees to pilot-test the questionnaire. During the pilot test, the trainees are asked to indicate if any items are unclear, confusing, or difficult to answer. The questionnaire is revised based on pilot-test results.

- Prepare a cover letter. The cover letter to course/program graduates should be clear and to the point, providing all the necessary explanatory information. An effective cover letter (a) states why the graduate has received the questionnaire, (b) identifies the purpose of the follow-up study, (c) explains why the questionnaire should be completed and returned, (d) assures confidentiality of the responses, (e) provides directions on how and when to respond, and (f) expresses appreciation for participating in the study. This information may also appear on the questionnaire. The cover letter ought to be on letterhead stationery and signed by someone known by the graduates.

Conduct the Study

- Mail the cover letter and questionnaire, along with a self-addressed, stamped envelope, to all course/program graduates, or to a random sample if the population is large. Find correct addresses for mail returned because of incorrect address. Send a second mailing to non-respondents after a 2-week waiting period. It may be necessary to telephone or interview the remaining non-respondents after an additional 2-week waiting period. The potential for high response rates is enhanced when mailings avoid holiday and vacation periods.
- Tally the data collected. Appendix E provides manual tally sheets, which follow the prototype questionnaire. Sheets like this can be used for compiling the information collected from small populations or when automated (computer) data summaries are not available. When tally sheets are prepared at the same time as the questionnaire, they show how the collected information will appear. As a result, open-ended items are often converted into closed-ended questions so that the data will be easier to tabulate, analyze, and report.

Prepare a Report

- Write a report which documents the results of the follow-up study. The data should be presented in a clear, concise, and easy-to-understand manner. For example, it can be outlined in narrative text and graphically displayed in tables and charts. Based upon your conclusions, make recommendations about the course/program studied.
- Collect information about the costs incurred in developing and delivering the training course or program. This information is neces-

sary to calculate the resources expended on the training of each participant, in terms of facilities, equipment, materials, personnel, and so forth. Such information is essential to calculate the cost effectiveness of training. This is an optional, but highly desirable, step. The last action is to distribute the follow-up study report.

APPENDIX D

A Prototype Follow-up Questionnaire

Name _____ Date _____
Current address _____
Home phone number (   ) _____

The purpose of this follow-up survey is to find out about your employment since graduation. Your responses will be confidential. Please take a few moments today to complete this survey and return it in the enclosed, self-addressed, stamped envelope. Your responses are valuable and your assistance is greatly appreciated. Thank you.

Part 1 (for EVERYONE)
  1. Course/program completed: _____
  2. What is your present status? (Check all that apply.)
    ____ Employed by a private enterprise (company)
    ____ Employed by a government agency
    ____ Self-employed
    ____ Working in a family business
    ____ In the military service
    ____ Pursuing further education/training (please specify)

    _____
    ____ Other (please specify) _____
    ____ Unemployed
       (If currently unemployed, proceed to Part 4)

Part 2 (ONLY for those who are currently employed)
  3. Are you working: (Check all that apply.)
    ____ Full-time
    ____ Part-time
    ____ In a job that you were trained for
    ____ In a job related to your training
    ____ In a job that does *not* use your training

4. What is your job title? _____

5. How did you find this job? (Check one.)
   ___ Direct application to employer (walk-in)
   ___ Training institute job placement service
   ___ Public employment service
   ___ Private employment agency
   ___ Friend or acquaintance
   ___ Parent(s) or other relative
   ___ Help-wanted ads (flyer, newspaper, journal, or magazine)
   ___ Other (please specify) _____

6. How long did you look (wait) before finding this job? (Check one.)
   ___ Less than 1 month   ___ 3 to 4 months
   ___ 1 to 2 months   ___ More than 4 months

Part 3 (ONLY for those who are currently employed)

7. In which economic sector (industry) are you employed? (Check one.)
   ___ Business & repair   ___ Manufacturing
   ___ Wholesale & retail trade ___ Mining
   ___ Construction   ___ Public utilities
   ___ Insurance & real estate ___ Service
   ___ Agriculture, forestry,   ___ Transportation
       & fishing
   ___ Other (please specify) _____

8. What was your starting hourly wage rate? (Check one.)
   ___ Less than $6.00   ___ $10.00 to $11.99
   ___ $6.00 to $7.99   ___ $12.00 to $13.99
   ___ $8.00 to $9.99   ___ $14.00 or more

9. What is your present hourly wage rate? (Check one)
   ___ Less than $6.00   ___ $10.00 to $11.99
   ___ $6.00 to $7.99   ___ $12.00 to $13.99
   ___ $8.00 to $9.99   ___ $14.00 or more

10. What subjects/topics in the training received did you find to be *most useful* in your job?
    _____
    _____
    _____

11. Which subjects/topics did you find to be *least useful*?
    _____
    _____
    _____

12. Would you have been employed without job training?
    ___ Yes   ___ No
13. Did your training qualify you for a higher-level job than your present employment?
    ___ Yes   ___ No
14. Does your employer value the training you received?
    ___ Yes   ___ No
15. Have you received any job training from your employer?
    ___ Yes   ___ No

Part 4 (ONLY for those who are currently unemployed)
16. Are you actively seeking employment?
    ___ Yes   ___ No
17. How long have you been looking for employment?
    ___ Less than 4 months   ___ 4 months or more
18. Would a different training course or program have improved your chances for employment?
    ___ Yes   ___ No
    If Yes, what would have made the difference? _____

Part 5 (for EVERYONE)
19. Please add any particular observations, comments, and/or suggestions about the training you received and about possible ways to improve it. (For example: Needed more practice in performing job skills.)

_____

_____

_____

You are now finished with the survey. Please return it in the addressed and stamped envelope provided. Thank you for taking the time to help us. *(Add name and address of the person to whom the questionnaire should be returned since questionnaires can be separated from the envelope and cover letter.)*

Note. For particulars on questionnaire development, see *Follow-Up and Follow-Through in Employment and Training Programs: An Action Planning Guidebook* (Research and Development Series No. 219), by S. Pritz, 1983, Columbus, OH: The National Center for Research in Vocational Education.

APPENDIX E

Tally Sheets for Follow-up Study Responses*

Part 1 (for EVERYONE)

Present Status

	Total Number of Responses	Course/Program Completed		
		Plumbing	Electrical	Carpentry
Status: Employed by a private enter-prise Employed by a government agency Self-employed Working in a fam-ily business In the military service Pursuing further education/ training (specify) —————— —————— Others —————— —————— —————— Unemployed				

*Manual tally sheets such as these are cost-efficient for small (less than 100 individuals) populations. If information is collected from a large number of individuals or the data requires a quick and extensive analysis, then the use of automation (a computer) will eliminate much of the labor-in-tensive activities of entering and analyzing the data.

Part 2 (ONLY for those who are currently employed)

Job/Training Relatedness and Job Title

	Total Number of Responses	Course/Program Completed		
		Plumbing	Electrical	Carpentry

Job/training related-ness:
    Full-time
    Part-time
    Job trained for
    Job related to
        training
    Non-related job
Job titles:
 	
_____
_____
_____				

Part 2 *(continued)*

How Job Found and Length of Job Search

	Total Number of Responses	Course/Program Completed		
		Plumbing	Electrical	Carpentry
How did you find this job?				
Direct application to employer				
Training institute job placement service				
Public employment service				
Private employment agency				
Friend or acquaintance				
Parent(s) or other relative				
Help-wanted ads				
Others				
_____				
_____				
_____				
How long did you look (wait) before finding this job?				
Less than 1 month				
1 to 2 months				
3 to 4 months				
More than 4 months				

Part 3 (ONLY for those who are currently employed)

Sector in Which Employed

	Total Number of Responses	Course/Program Completed		
		Plumbing	Electrical	Carpentry
Sector (industry) in which employed: Business & repair Wholesale & retail trade Construction Insurance & real estate Agriculture, forestry, & fishing Manufacturing Mining Public utilities Service Transportation Others _____ _____ _____				

Part 3 *(continued)*

Starting and Present Hourly Wage Rates

	Total Number of Responses	Course/Program Completed		
		Plumbing	Electrical	Carpentry
Starting hourly wage rate:				
Less than $6.00				
$6.00 to $7.99				
$8.00 to $9.99				
$10.00 to $11.99				
$12.00 to $13.99				
$14.00 or more				
Present hourly wage rate:				
Less than $6.00				
$6.00 to $7.99				
$8.00 to $9.99				
$10.00 to $11.99				
$12.00 to $13.99				
$14.00 or more				

Part 3 *(continued)*

Usefulness of Training Received

	Total Number of Responses	Course/Program Completed		
		Plumbing	Electrical	Carpentry
Subjects/topics that were: Most useful				
_____ _____				
Least useful				
_____ _____				
Would you have been employed without job training? Yes No				
Did your training qualify you for a higher-level job than your present employment? Yes No				
Does your employer value the training you received? Yes No				
Have you received any job training from your employer? Yes No				

Part 4 (ONLY for those who are currently unemployed)

	Total Number of Responses	Course/Program Completed		
		Plumbing	Electrical	Carpentry
Are you actively seeking employment? Yes No How long have you been looking for employment? Less than 4 months 4 months or more Would a different training course or program have improved your chances for employment? Yes No If Yes, what would have made the difference? _____ _____ _____				

Overall response to questionnaire

Number of Questionnaires Sent	Total Number of Responses (*n*) and Rate of Return (%)	Number of Responses by Course/Program Completed		
		Plumbing	Electrical	Carpentry
	n = ___ % = ___			

AUTHOR NOTE

The work of Lochtar Richter, a manpower consultant with extensive international experience, served to guide the author in organizing parts of this chapter.

Needless to say, the chapter content does not present a single perfect approach that can be used by all VET providers to determine the demand for skilled workers. Nevertheless, it does represent a step in the right direction and provides a basis for further study. Current problems that contribute to the shortcomings include:

(1) Much of the available literature was written by economists using highly specialized and somewhat complex language. In addition, the literature base on workforce projection and forecasting approaches includes numerous contradictions.

(2) Most workforce projection and forecasting approaches are not able to reflect, accurately and in a timely manner, the direct and indirect effects of changes in government priorities and policies on the labor market. In addition, none of the methods are widely accepted or dependable for long-term projections and forecasts.

ENDNOTES

1 In the context of this chapter, the phrase *Vocational and Technical Education and Training* is used as the generic description for a full range of training delivery methods—formal (school-based) and non-formal (workplace-based). The abbreviated form of the phrase, "VET," is often used. Initial and continuing VET use practical work experiences and theoretical insights to prepare trainees (students/apprentices)

for (a) gainful employment as skilled workers or as technicians or middle-level professionals in recognized vocations, or (b) enrollment in advanced technical education programs.

VET is concerned with the development of skills, abilities, understandings, attitudes, work habits, and appreciations needed by trainees to enter and progress in employment on a useful and productive basis. It provides a range of skill levels, from basic entry-level skills to technical skills requiring a high degree of specialization and competence.

VET courses and programs are offered at the secondary, post-secondary, and adult levels, but by definition exclude occupations which require a baccalaureate or higher degree.

2 Vocational and technical education and training (VET) planners work in a variety of capacities, including but not limited to: department chairperson, dean of vocational-technical education, vocational supervisor, principal, state or local director of vocational education, and superintendent of a vocational-technical school district. Planners are, perhaps, more identifiable by their responsibilities, which include:

(1) Determining the present (actual) and future (anticipated) training needs of businesses, industry, and the trainees

(2) Deciding what VET courses and programs to establish, expand/curtail, restructure, or drop based on information about current and emerging employment opportunities

REFERENCES

American Association for Vocational Instructional Materials. (1978). *Conduct a student follow-up study* (Module A-10). Athens, GA: Author.

American Institutes for Research. (1976). *Assessing manpower needs and supply in vocational education* (VECS Module 4). Washington, DC: U.S. Government Printing Office.

Bertrand, O. (1992). *Planning human resources: Methods experiences and practices* (Fundamentals of Educational Planning series, No. 41). Paris: UNESCO, International Institute for Educational Planning.

Bezdek, R. H. (1974). *Long-range forecasting of manpower requirements.* New York: Institute of Electrical & Electronics Engineers.

Campbell, C. P., & Armstrong, R. B., Jr. (Eds.) (1993). *Workforce development in the Federal Republic of Germany.* Pittsburg, KA: Press International.

Castro, C. M., & de Andrade, A. C. (1989). Who should be blamed when training does not respond to demand? (Discussion Paper No. 45). Geneva, Switzerland: International Labour Office.

Hewings, G. J. D. (1985). *Regional input-output analysis.* Beverly Hills, CA: Sage Publications.

Hinchliffe, K. (1993). Manpower forecasting and rapid labor market analysis: The demand for technical school graduates in Egypt. *The Vocational Aspect of Education, 45*(3), 239–250.

Lauglo, J. (1993). *Vocational training: Analysis of policy and modes.* Paris: UNESCO, International Institute for Educational Planning.

Lerman, R. I. (1994). Reinventing education: Why we need the school-to-work initiative. *Vocational Education Journal, 2*(11), 20–21 & 45.

Middleton, J., Zinderman, A., & Van Adams, A. (1993). *Skills for productivity: Vocational education and training in developing countries.* New York: Oxford University Press.

Mingat, A., & Tan, J. P. (1988). *Analytical tools for sector work in education.* Baltimore, MD: The Johns Hopkins University Press.

Richter, L. (1986). *Training needs assessment and monitoring.* Geneva, Switzerland: International Labour Office.

Shelley, K. J. (1994). More job openings—even more new entrants: The outlook for college graduates, 1992–2005. *Occupational Outlook Quarterly, 38*(2), 5–9.

U.S. Department of Labor, Bureau of Labor Statistics. (1992). *Occupational outlook handbook* (Bulletin No. 2400). Washington, DC: U.S. Government Printing Office.

Vermeulen, B. (1981). Accelerating the transition from schools to careers. In P. B. Doeringer & B. Vermeulen (Eds.), *Jobs and training in the 1980s* (pp. 158–179). Boston: Martinus Nijhoff.

CHAPTER 2

Instructional Systems Development

CLIFTON P. CAMPBELL—*The University of Tennessee*

TECHNOLOGICAL developments and various other needs for preparing a quality workforce are changing the priorities for vocational and technical education and training (VET). While the fundamental goals for VET remain, emphasis is shifting from a focus on subject matter orientation to a recognition of the importance of a systems approach. As a consequence, professionals involved with VET are increasingly aware of the need for more rigor in the process by which courses and programs are developed, implemented, and evaluated.

The purpose of this chapter is to present Instructional Systems Development (ISD) in a condensed, yet complete, form. Collected here is essential information on ISD for the development of relevant, effective, and cost-efficient performance-based VET. For those preparing a new course or program, this logical, organized, and applied approach provides a road map. Additionally, the procedural steps presented are useful when modifying and revising existing courses and programs.

Notwithstanding years of research and debate, there is still some controversy over what practices are best for achieving course/program accountability. Nevertheless, most experts in the field agree on the appropriateness of ISD methodology for planning, developing, implementing, and evaluating performance-based VET. This comprehensive systems approach ensures that trainees are taught the knowledge and skills essential for successful job performance.[1]

Accountability, the driving force behind performance-based VET, is substantially increased when the principles and processes of this carefully conceived systems approach are used. This is because the derivative and iterative character of the methodology ensures, when its procedures are resolutely carried out, that instruction will meet job requirements.

Certain components of ISD, such as job analysis, job performance measures, learning objectives, criterion-referenced testing, instructional materials, validation, and course/program evaluation, are not new or

55

unique to ISD. They are well known and used by many professionals. In spite of that, the application is often haphazard and fragmentary. Instructional Systems Development ties these and other components, which may have been previously omitted, together in a coherent whole. The critical distinctions with ISD are (a) a performance-based philosophy, (b) emphasis on an integrated instructional system, and (c) the use of feedback to keep training relevant, effective, and cost-efficient.

The application of ISD is preceded by the identification of a need to develop or revise instruction. Chapter 1, "Determining the Market Demand for Skilled Workers," focuses on this need as it applies to initial VET.

The ISD approach was developed for and refined by the U.S. Department of Defense. Concepts used in designing the approach were drawn from the disciplines of systems engineering, behavioral and cognitive psychology, and instructional technology. The result is a methodology for gathering and analyzing job information, preparing job performance measures, writing learning objectives and criterion-referenced tests, preparing and validating instructional materials in a variety of media, conducting instruction, and evaluating as well as improving the effectiveness of training. This approach is based upon evidence that the tasks performed on a job can be identified and analyzed, and that learning objectives and instructional strategies to attain these objectives can be developed and structured so that instruction, which qualifies graduates in job requirements, will be effectively and efficiently conducted (*CNTT-A10*, 1976, p. 2-i).

Over the years, the ISD approach has been depicted in a variety of ways. Nevertheless, the most useful models organized ISD procedures in five phases: (I) Analyze, (II) Design, (III) Develop, (IV) Implement, and (V) Control. Figure 1 presents these phases, each of which is made up of a series of steps. Symbolically, this structure illustrates the relationship of the five phases and 19 procedural steps. It also shows that the entire procedure, each ISD activity and product, is subjected to quality improvement through a feedback and revision cycle. This comprehensive model is based upon years of research and successful application by a host of users. Components of the model are necessarily depicted in a linear sequence and some steps, especially in Phases I and II, must be performed sequentially. However, many of the steps can be performed simultaneously, by a team using a parallel development plan.

Practical information on the essentials of each phase of the ISD model is furnished in subsequent pages. These concise descriptions were care-

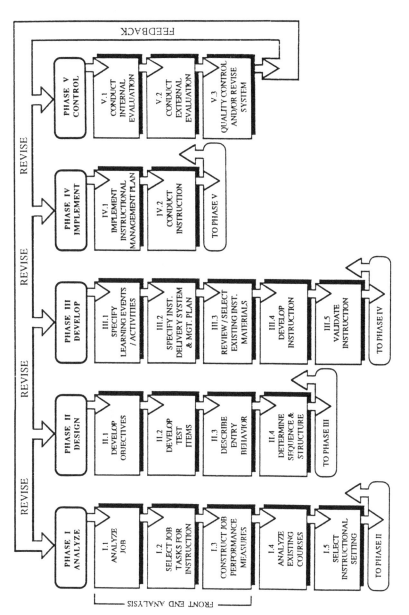

FIGURE 1 Instructional systems development model.

57

fully prepared based on an analysis and synthesis of the documents cited in the reference list. Figures and tables are included to help structure the presentation, and supplementary materials are arranged in the appendices. It is hoped that this chapter will help both the expert and novice to develop, conduct, and evaluate effective and cost-efficient VET courses and programs.

PHASE I, ANALYZE

Analyze Job (Step I.1)

The analysis phase begins when the requirement for a new or revised VET course/program has been established. The first procedural step is to analyze the job under consideration. This is done to identify and describe the knowledge and skills required of a successful job incumbent. Job analysis answers the questions of what tasks, performed in what manner, under what conditions, to what standards, make up the job. It is a means for basing training on job performance requirements instead of arbitrarily derived subject matter. Job analysis is the foundation for sound VET and the basis for determining the job-relevant behaviors that trainees must be capable of performing when they complete instruction.[2] Therefore, this fundamental procedural step must be initiated before any others.

A document study (review of literature) should be conducted at the outset. This is done to find out as much as possible about the job and to collect any available job analysis information. Once the literature has been reviewed, one or more of the various job analysis techniques are selected for use. The technique(s) selected will depend on its relative utility and whether the purpose is to identify and describe the tasks and elements of tasks that make up the job or to verify existing job analysis information.

The more common job analysis techniques are (a) observation of job incumbents doing the job, (b) in-person or telephone interviews of job incumbents and their supervisors, (c) questionnaire surveys of job incumbents and their supervisors, and (d) a jury or panel of job incumbents and supervisors (consensus group). While the observation and interview techniques are recommended for gathering detailed job information, this recommendation does not imply that other techniques are unacceptable.

In any case, no one method of job analysis is best for all situations. In fact, there is merit in the use of a combination of techniques, such as observation and interviews, to counteract bias and generate more quality information.

When several individual or combinations of techniques offer reasonable alternatives, the advantages and disadvantages of each, as listed in Appendix A, should be considered. Which technique(s) to use is decided based on constraints such as (a) time, (b) budget, (c) qualified help, (d) the number of job incumbents, (e) the type of job, and (f) the availability of existing task lists.

Regardless of how well the remaining 18 procedural steps are carried out, if the job analysis information gathered in this pivotal step is not valid and reliable, the training course or program will fail to produce graduates who can perform in a competent manner on the job (*NAVEDTRA 106A: Phase I,* 1975, p. 1).

Select Job Tasks for Instruction (Step I.2)

Job analysis output includes a list of all tasks that make up the job under consideration. There is a strong likelihood that among those tasks, some (a) can be performed without instruction (trainees may already be proficient), (b) are noncritical and categorized as "nice to know," (c) can be performed effectively using job performance aids (JPAs), (d) are relatively easy to learn on the job, or (e) are best learned at the workplace. In addition, a few may seldom be required on the job and only minimum job degradation would result if they were performed inadequately by an entry-level worker. On the other hand, many tasks are fundamental to successful job performance, and their complex nature, difficulty (to learn or accomplish), or frequency of performance makes instruction essential.

The needs of the job and training constraints such as cost, equipment, facilities, time, personnel, and feasibility require "best judgment" decisions when determining which tasks to include in a VET course or program. The purpose here is to make sure that all requisite tasks are trained and that resources are not expended on tasks that are not essential to successful job entry performance (*AFP 50-58: Vol. II,* 1978, pp. 2-16 & 2-17).

Figure 2 illustrates the procedure to follow in selecting job tasks for instruction. As indicated, this procedure includes "best judgment" deci-

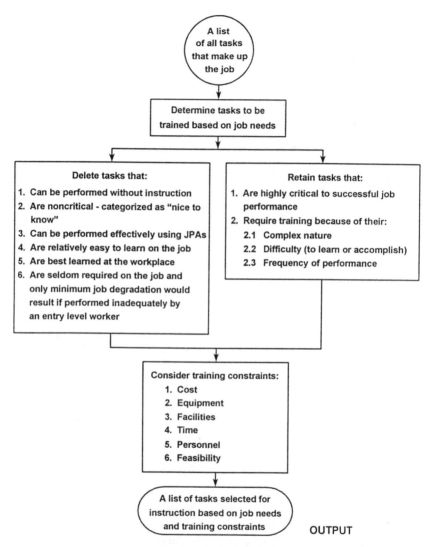

FIGURE 2 Selection of job tasks for instruction.

sions which are based on (a) an understanding of all the tasks that make up the job, and (b) consideration of expert advice provided by individuals who are familiar with the job and training constraints. The importance of task selection should not be underestimated since rejected tasks are not reconsidered until the external evaluation step. This step is performed after a training cycle is completed and graduates are on the job.

Construct Job Performance Measures (Step I.3)

The use of job performance measures (criterion-referenced performance tests) improves the effectiveness, control, and accountability of VET courses and programs. They are derived from tasks and provide the most direct, complete, and realistic method of testing a trainee's ability to perform those tasks. Therefore, they are constructed for those tasks considered *absolutely essential* to successful job performance.

Job performance measures test manipulative task proficiency against job requirements by using actual tools and equipment under real or closely simulated work conditions and workplace standards. They can be categorized as process and/or product tests. When the outcome is the completion of procedural steps which are observable but transient, a process test is used. However, when the final outcome is a tangible product which can be physically inspected, a product test is appropriate. Job performance measures often test processes which result in a product in order to provide feedback on process errors. Notwithstanding this advantage, not all job performance measures test both the process and product.

Carefully constructed job performance measures furnish the following benefits:

(1) They provide a valid, reliable, and objective measure of the trainees' ability to perform a task by distinguishing between those who are knowledgeable and skilled enough to meet attainment standards and those who are not. At the same time, they allow trainees an additional opportunity for practice.

(2) They facilitate uniform evaluation of all trainees, so that each individual is rated like all others.

(3) Bluffing is impossible and the advantages of being "test wise" or lucky at guessing are eliminated. They also reduce test phobia—a fear that some people experience with paper-and-pencil tests which evaluate recall. In addition, individuals generally prefer applying the knowledge and skills learned.

(4) They reveal specific difficulties and weaknesses in knowledge and skills which are promptly corrected through prescriptive remediation and/or additional practice.

(5) They reveal whether a trainee can deal with the stress and pressure of task performance.

(6) They provide the best way of determining whether a trainee can

transfer what was learned during instruction to task performance on the job.

(7) They provide authoritative information on the maintenance of quality instruction and course or program effectiveness.

These and other benefits justify the investment of resources required to construct, validate, and administer job performance measures.

Appendix B provides an example of a job performance measure. It includes (a) a task statement, (b) the performance conditions under which the test is administered, (c) an initiating cue (signal to perform an action), (d) the overall attainment standards which are a measure of the adequacy of performance, (e) examinee (trainee) directions, (f) administrative instructions, and other key information. The all-important process test checklist in Appendix B contains the task elements and/or steps that are the actions which make up the total performance. The checklist also contains the standards required for successful performance and a place to indicate whether or not the standards were attained. A product test appears at the end of Appendix B.

Job performance measures are a means of keeping training consistent with job requirements. They serve as a connecting link between the tasks and the terminal learning objectives. Therefore, the task statement (behavioral action), conditions, and standards of the job performance measure mirror, when practical, actual task performance (*Principles of Training*, 1985, p. 3-5). These tests are validated at the workplace if resources and time permit. If not, their accuracy must at least be verified by subject matter experts.

Job performance measures are useful in (a) formulating terminal learning objectives (Step II.1), (b) writing test items (Step II.2), and (c) evaluating the performance of graduates on the job (Step V.2). Because of their multiple uses, job performance measures are fundamental to the development and control of instruction. While worthwhile, it must be pointed out that considerable time and effort are involved in constructing and validating these tests, albeit a one-time expenditure (*NAVEDTRA 110*, 1978, p. 13).

Analyze Existing Courses (Step I.4)

In order to avoid unnecessary duplication of effort, existing course documentation and other available material should be reviewed. This endeavor may reveal that all or portions of the analysis and other phases have already been done by someone else and are suitable for use. It would not be cost-effective, however, to use materials from another source which have not been validated or are essentially extraneous.

Select Instructional Setting (Step I.5)

As a final step in Phase I, the tasks selected for instruction are examined in order to determine the most appropriate instructional setting(s); for example, classroom, shop, or on-the-job training (*MIL-STD-1379A,* 1976, p. 5). The optimal setting is the one that provides the necessary resources (facilities, equipment, personnel, and time) as well as the most effective and efficient instruction. One of the simplest ways to examine the tasks for resource requirements is to ask questions such as:

(1) What types of facilities are necessary?
(2) How much space is required?
(3) What equipment is needed (training, test, etc.)?
(4) What quantities of equipment are required?
(5) Is an instructor needed?
(6) What are the costs of the facilities, equipment, instructors, etc.?
(7) Are the facilities, equipment, and personnel available at the time and for the period(s) necessary?

Answers to these and other appropriate questions help to determine the optimal setting.

The list of tasks with their instructional setting nominations is customarily reviewed by administrators and others in authority. In order to arrive at the most cost-effective decision, trade-offs are made on the basis of requirements, available resources, and existing constraints.

PHASE II, DESIGN

Develop Objectives (Step II.1)

The first three steps in Phase I, referred to as front-end analysis, concentrated on job performance requirements and the selection of job tasks for instruction. Phase II represents a shift in focus, and development of learning objectives based on job analysis information is the beginning step in designing training to meet job performance requirements. Once the learning objectives are available, they become the focal point for all instructional design and development that follows.

A learning objective can be defined as a statement that specifies measurable behavior (performance) that trainees will be required to exhibit after instruction. Some of the benefits of behaviorally stated learning objectives are (a) a clear and precise description of the knowledge and skills that are to be attained by the trainee, (b) a sound basis for determining appropriate instructional content and for writing test items, (c) guidance for selecting and preparing instructional materials, (d) a framework for organizing training, and (e) determination of the most suitable instructional strategy.

When learning objectives are written down, they can be given to trainees and other interested parties. Disclosure of all the learning objectives provides the most complete understanding of what the course or program consists of and will deliver. In addition, research and experience have shown that when learning objectives are included on instructional materials, they help trainees learn (*AFM 50-2*, 1979, p. 4-3).

Objectives need to be action oriented and expressed in specific terms which ensure that the instructional intent is clear. Vague concept-related words and phrases which describe internal states or mental processes must be avoided. The following examples, unlike performance, are neither observable nor measurable (see Appendix C for a more complete list):

(1) Be aware of
(2) Become familiar with
(3) Develop an appreciation of
(4) Have knowledge of
(5) Understand

Problems arise when ambiguous language is used. A poorly written statement like "The trainee will *understand* the importance of maintaining accurate records of the patient's temperature" is vague and the intent obscure. How will an instructor observe or measure "understanding"? There is no overt activity. Behaviorally stated, the learning objective might read: "Measure a patient's temperature using an oral thermometer to within one-half of one degree and record the reading on the patient's

chart in accordance with clinical procedures and without assistance."
Now the trainees, instructor, and all who work with the learning objective
can determine the instructional intent and when the objective has been
attained.

There are two types or levels of learning objectives: (a) terminal and
(b) enabling. Both have the same three essential parts:

(1) Behavioral action statement

(2) Performance conditions

(3) Attainment standards

Inclusion of these three essential parts in all terminal and enabling
objectives is more important than the format used to write the objectives.
Nevertheless, format does affect the ease of preparation and revision as
well as the use of learning objectives.

Format

The three parts of a learning objective have traditionally been written
in a *single sentence or paragraph.* An example is included in the text
under the heading, Attainment Standards. Objectives can also be written
in *columns,* with their component parts separated. When columns are
used, the parts are layered, side by side, as shown in Table 1, or vertically,
as illustrated in the learning objective worksheet (Figure 4). The column
formats are recommended because they (a) help assure that all three parts
are completed; (b) make writing the objective easier, by avoiding gram-
mar, punctuation, and other problems; and (c) facilitate the use of each
component part for planning and developing instruction (*AFM 50-62,*
1984, chap. 5). Experience has shown a reluctance to revise learning
objectives written in a single expression, while the worksheet orientation
of the column formats facilitates improvements and "fine tuning."

Behavioral Action

The behavioral action statement specifies the activity to be performed
by trainees. It is derived from a task, element, knowledge, or skill
identified in the job analysis. The focus is on the behavior of the trainee,
not the instructor. Effective statements describe behavior that is both
observable (you can see the performance) and measurable (you can check
the performance). When writing a behavioral action statement, begin

Table 1. Writing the three parts of a learning objective.

Behavioral Action (What the trainee does)	Performance Conditions (What the trainee is given)	Attainment Standards (How well it is done)
Use action verbs that are: Observable Measurable Verifiable Reliable (not prone to varying interpretation) Appropriate to task performance	Inputs include: Environment (setting) Tools, equipment, furniture, materials, and supplies Safety considerations Job performance aids, references, and special instructions Special physical demands	Criteria include: Quality, degree of excellence Accuracy, within tolerance limits Number of allowable variations or permissible errors Quantity, rate of production Standard(s) and/or criteria in reference documents Time limit (speed) Amount of supervision or assistance provided
Examples of action verbs: assemble, bend, cut, dig, erect, fasten, haul, install, join, knurl, load, multiply, nail, oil, paint, repair, saw, and type	Example of conditions: (Type a 3-sentence memorandum)—using a self-correcting electric typewriter, given a dictionary and bond paper	Example of standards: (Type a 3-sentence memorandum)— without assistance, within 5 minutes, and with *no* uncorrected errors
Sample learning objective: Multiply eight decimal numbers, two to four digits long, by a one-digit number and record the results of each calculation	Using a hand-held calculator, given a sheet of problems and a pencil	Without error and without assistance, within 3 minutes

Note: Learning objectives have three essential parts. The parts can be easily remembered by the following formula: Learning objective = behavioral objective + performance conditions + attainment standards.

with a present-tense action verb like "type": Type a memorandum (the subject "you" is understood). Action verbs such as those listed in column one of Table 1 and in Appendix C are the key to performance—they tell what must be done.

Behavioral actions with more than one action verb are rewritten as separate statements. For example, "Take dictation and type a memorandum" becomes "Take dictation" and "Type a memorandum."

Since typing is a manipulative activity, it is easily expressed with an action verb. In the case of a knowledge requirement, where there is no overt activity to observe, trainees must perform some activity in order to demonstrate that they have the required knowledge. For example, if the lesson was on the safety rules to be followed when using a drill press, the behavioral action statement might be: List the safety rules that apply when using a drill press. Here the activity is listing. The cliché "you don't really know it until your behavior shows it" needs to be applied when writing behavioral action statements.

Performance Conditions

Circumstances that exist during performance of the behavioral action make up the conditions. They are dictated by the job itself and come from job analysis information whenever possible. This part of the learning objective specifies "where" and "with what" the behavioral action is to be performed. By stipulating, aiding, and limiting conditions in a learning objective, trainees know what resources they will have to work with (e.g., with the help of a checklist) and what limitations are placed on their performance (e.g., while lying down). If the behavioral action is to "type a memorandum," the trainee needs to know precisely what equipment will be provided.

EXAMPLE

Correct: Using a self-correcting electric typewriter

Incorrect: Using appropriate equipment

Performance conditions are necessary to simulate all the circumstances under which the behavioral action will be performed on the job. The overall training goal is to develop knowledge and skills that will be transferred from the training to the job setting.

Circumstances that need to be considered when specifying performance conditions are the (a) environment (setting); (b) tools, equipment, furniture, materials, and supplies; (c) safety considerations; (d) job performance aids, references, and special instructions; and (e) special physical demands. Appendix D provides examples of performance conditions for each of these five items.

When the performance conditions are *clearly* implied, they need not be stated. Listing all the conditions may become a bit pedantic when some are self-evident. For example, when most behavioral actions are performed in daylight, it is not necessary to state "in daylight." Thus, the decision on what conditions to include in the learning objective depends, to a large extent, on the situation and reasonable judgment. Nevertheless, it is better to err by being too specific than by omitting important conditions.

Attainment Standards

It is necessary to specify the criteria for how well a trainee must perform the behavioral action given performance conditions. Take the learning objective: "Type a three sentence memorandum using a self-correcting electric typewriter, given a dictionary and bond paper, without assistance, within 5 minutes, and with *no* uncorrected errors." This objective specifies the amount of assistance to be provided (without assistance), a time limit (within 5 minutes), and the number of permissible errors (with *no* uncorrected errors). In other situations, the attainment standards can be further defined by specifying the (a) amount of supervision to be provided; (b) number of allowable variations; (c) quality, degree of excellence; (d) accuracy, within tolerance limits; (e) quantity, rate of production or amount produced; and (f) standards and/or criteria in reference documents.

Like performance conditions, attainment standards are derived from job analysis information. However, attainment standards can be less than job standards when job entry requirements are less than those expected of fully qualified workers. Examples of criterion statements for each of seven different attainment standards categories are provided in Appendix E. Various combinations of these criteria are used to specify observable and measurable attainment standards.

Standards should not be implied in terminal objectives. However, they may be implied in enabling objectives where they are (a) the same as those expressed in the terminal objective to which the enabling objective is subordinate, and (b) self-evident to all who read the objective. Nevertheless, the inclusion of all attainment standard criteria enhances the capability of the learning objective to define trainee behaviors precisely (U.S. Department of Energy, 1992, p. 8).

A vaguely stated standard such as ". . . with at least 90% accuracy" must be avoided. Appendix F lists this and other obscure attainment standards which are troublesome and open to criticism because of their poorly specified criteria.

The job entry standards of the workplace and/or trade dictate how well a learning objective shall be performed. However, if the information is not available, the alternative is to begin with a trial set of criteria based on the opinion of expert workers who are performing the job. Later, by testing and verifying against on-the-job performance, the trial criteria can be revised and actual standards established.

Terminal and Enabling Objectives

As noted previously, there are two types or levels of learning objectives, terminal and enabling. *Terminal objectives* are derived from and formulated for critical tasks performed on the job. The source of behavioral action statements for each terminal objective is a critical job task selected for instruction in Step I.2. Figure 3 shows the relationship between the terminal objectives and the job tasks selected for instruction. Job performance measures constructed in Step I.3 include all three parts of a terminal objective.

Each terminal objective is subjected to a hierarchical analysis to derive subordinate or *enabling objectives.* These enabling objectives provide the level of detail necessary to specify the behavioral elements and the knowledge and skills that help the trainee attain a terminal objective. In many cases, the resultant enabling objectives specify the same behavioral actions as the elements of the job task itself. Other objectives pertain to supporting knowledge and skills which must be acquired.

Learning objectives bridge the gap between task performance in the actual workplace and learning how to perform that task in an instructional setting. They serve as a control over the content and output of instruction. The ability to develop learning objectives (and to teach and test those objectives) is fundamental to a successful performance-based VET course or program (*NAVEDTRA 106A: Phase II,* 1975, p. 1).

Figure 4 shows a worksheet which includes a box with a heading for each part of a learning objective. This format organizes the three component parts and guides the development of an objective. In addition, it

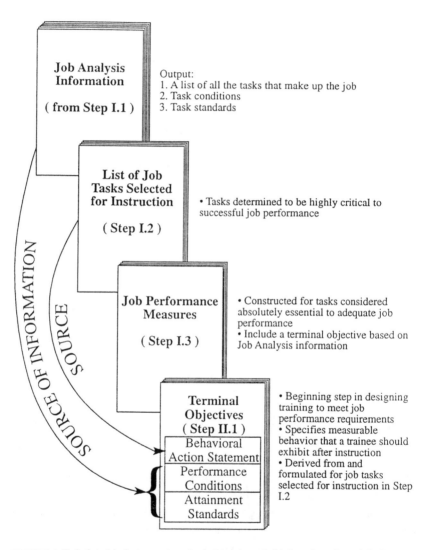

FIGURE 3 Relationship between terminal objectives and job tasks selected for instruction.

COURSE/PROGRAM TITLE:	TASK NO.:	UNIT/BLOCK OF INSTRUCTION:
Basic Skills Training	5.0	Mathematics (Calculator Orientation)

FILL OUT ONE ROW ONLY	☒ TERMINAL	Terminal objective no.: 5.3	Enabling objective numbers that are supportive: 5.3.1 & 5.3.2
	☐ ENABLING	Enabling objective no.: N/A	Terminal objective number supported: N/A

BEHAVIORAL ACTION STATEMENT:

    Multiply eight decimal numbers, two to four digits long, by a one-digit number, and record the results of each calculation.

PERFORMANCE CONDITIONS:

    Using a hand-held calculator, given a sheet of problems and a pencil.

ATTAINMENT STANDARDS:

    Without error and without assistance, within 3 minutes.

TEST ITEMS:

Form A	Form B
1. 107.2 x 5 = _____	1. 983.5 x 3 = _____
2. 961.0 x 3 = _____	2. 96.37 x 5 = _____
3. 2.773 x 8 = _____	3. 752.9 x 8 = _____
4. 91.50 x 6 = _____	4. 61.74 x 6 = _____
5. 7.16 x 7 = _____	5. 537.3 x 7 = _____
6. 540.2 x 9 = _____	6. 4.60 x 9 = _____
7. 87.29 x 4 = _____	7. 61.83 x 4 = _____
8. 4.165 x 7 = _____	8. 835.7 x 7 = _____

FIGURE 4 Learning objective worksheet. (Note: Performance is not limited to physical/manual manipulation, such as "building" or "splicing." There also is performance when multiplying numbers.)

makes missing information apparent. A separate worksheet is used in formulating each learning objective. This facilitates sequencing the objectives in a later step.

Develop Test Items (Step II.2)

After developing the learning objectives, test items called criterion-referenced measures are written to directly measure their attainment. These criterion-referenced measures are based solely on the requirements specified in the learning objectives.[3] As a result, the wording in the objectives and test items may be the same. For example, an appropriate test item for the learning objective "Parallel park a car with an automatic transmission between two other vehicles without hitting either vehicle and within 5 minutes" would be to require the trainee to actually parallel park a car under the conditions and to the standards specified in the objective. In this case, the objective itself is a good test item; in others, some re-wording or elaboration may be necessary.

For contrast, a norm-referenced test is one in which a trainee's performance is compared to the average (norm) performance on the test. This comparison is interesting and informative, but it does not tell whether a trainee can perform a task essential to successful job performance.

With a criterion-referenced measure, trainees are rated on their ability to attain the learning objective. This is a go, no-go type of test used to reliably measure what trainees can do and/or the product of their performance. How others score on the test has no bearing on an individual's grade (*AFP 50-58: Vol. III,* 1978, p. 1-2).

The nature of the learning objective determines the type of test item needed. By way of illustration, paper-and-pencil (written) items are most useful when assessing knowledge, while criterion-referenced performance items are especially suited to evaluating manipulative skills. The job performance measure in Appendix B shows under item 7 that a criterion-referenced performance measure can be used to test a process and/or a product. The behavioral action (task) statement "Replace a tire/wheel assembly" requires a criterion-referenced performance type process and product test.

Sufficient written items should be prepared for each learning objective so that alternate forms, not just scrambled versions, of a test can be administered. Using equivalent test items, like those shown in Figure 4, allows the scope and difficulty of the test to remain constant and trainee performance, as well as course or program effectiveness, to be evaluated over time. Trainees who do not meet acceptable performance standards on their first test are remediated and then retested using an alternate form of the test.

Where learning objectives are the same as job requirements, tests may be identical to the job performance measures constructed earlier. When this is the case, there is no need for an alternate form. The grouping of test items into pre-tests, progress tests, and post-tests is done in Step II.4.

Describe Entry Behavior (Step II.3)

After the test items have been written, those that were designed for lower level enabling objectives should be administered to a representative sample of the trainee population. This is done to determine what prospective trainees already know and can do before receiving instruction.

Estimates of trainee capabilities are verified or adjusted according to test results so that instruction meets trainees at the point of their need. When the test shows that some of the enabling objectives have already been acquired, they and their corresponding test items should be deleted from the training course or program unless overlearning is desirable. Whenever the test indicates that trainees lack prerequisite knowledge and skills, additional learning objectives and test items must be developed to close the gap between assumptions made about prior learning and the true entry-level behavior of trainees.[4]

Entry-level behavior also can be determined by testing training program participants just prior to the beginning of instruction. This approach is best reserved for use when a sample of the trainee population is unavailable earlier, because it leaves little or no time to make any modifications.

Determine Sequence and Structure (Step II.4)

This procedural step is to determine and specify how the terminal objectives and their respective enabling objectives are to be sequenced and structured (organized) to facilitate optimum learning. These decisions are based, to the extent possible, on learning factors rather than on how it was done in the past. Sequencing decisions attempt to identify and capitalize on prerequisite relationships (if any) among the learning objectives.

Before learning objectives are sequenced for instructional purposes, they must be analyzed and placed in one of the following three categories:

(1) *Dependent*—to attain one learning objective, it is first necessary to attain the other(s).

(2) *Supportive*—the learning involved in attaining one objective transfers to the other(s), making learning involved in attaining the other(s) easier.

(3) *Independent*—attaining one learning objective does not necessarily simplify the attainment of others.

Once identified, the dependent objectives are sequenced in accordance with the existing hierarchy of knowledge and skills so that prerequisite learning occurs first. This facilitates transfer of learning from one objective to another. Next, supportive objectives are placed as close to each other as possible without interfering with the dependent sequencing. The sequencing of learning objectives is likely to be more effective the greater the accuracy of categorizing and sequencing dependent objectives and facilitating supportive relationships.

Independent learning objectives are sequenced last. They can be arranged within a course or program in accordance with such principles as (a) simple to complex; (b) known to unknown; (c) general to specific; (d) the order performed on the job; (e) the frequency of performance or relative importance on the job; or (f) any other order that is practical, as long as they do not interfere with dependent and supportive learning objectives. If trainees would benefit from an early success, some interesting but easily attained objectives are presented first, before the more challenging ones. Finally, identical learning objectives are deleted and those objectives with the same behavioral actions are grouped together so that each is taught only once (*NAVEDTRA 110*, 1978, pp. 96–98).

To the extent that seems logical, the sequenced learning objectives are grouped (structured) into units, blocks, or modules of instruction, or other organized and manageable sets of objectives in the way that they will be presented to trainees.[5] Grouping is an arbitrary matter based on rational judgments regarding (a) commonality of subject matter, (b) anticipated transfer of learning, (c) meaningful relationships, and (d) a natural beginning and ending point (*AFP 50-58: Vol. IV*, 1978, p. 2-5).

Because test items measure specific learning objectives, they are structured at the same time as the learning objectives. This facilitates the grouping of test items into pre-tests, progress tests, and post-tests.

PHASE III, DEVELOP

Specify Learning Events/Activities (Step III.1)

Once the content of a course or program has been determined and described by learning objectives and these objectives are organized, appropriate learning events/activities can be specified. Learning principles are applied in planning and developing learning activities which will produce the desired learning outcomes. These principles can help make learning and retention easier, faster, more efficient, and more effective. Four principles which are broadly applicable in creating appropriate experiences are:

(1) Inform trainees of the learning objective(s).
(2) Provide active participation and purposeful practice.
(3) Provide guidance and prompts.
(4) Provide feedback.

These learning principles are described in the following paragraphs.

Inform Trainees of the Learning Objective(s)

Trainees are more successful in attaining learning objectives when they have a clear understanding of the instructional intent—what is expected of them. To create this understanding, the instructor should disclose and discuss, at the beginning of a lesson, the learning objective (a) behavioral action statement, (b) performance conditions, and (c) attainment standards. In addition, including learning objectives on instructional materials helps trainees learn (*NAVEDTRA 106A: Phase III*, 1975, p. 4).

Provide Active Participation and Purposeful Practice

Frequent opportunities to review knowledge and practice skills are critical to learning and the retention of what is learned. Trainees need physical activity to refine the coordination between visual and tactile senses. Furthermore, when the activity involves manipulating real objects, all the cues for later performance are available. While hands-on practice may be the only way to achieve coordination, continual practice of a learning experience which has already been correctly performed can be tiresome. Nevertheless, some degree of overlearning is desirable in order to enhance retention and assure the transfer of knowledge and skills to the job. The most practical way to achieve overlearning is by repeatedly performing a task correctly (skill comes from drill). Extensive practice on a single task should be interspersed with short rest periods.

Trainees learn by applying, in a meaningful, varied, and concrete way, what they are taught. Applied learning, done in the context of performing a task, enables trainees to use, rather than lose, new knowledge. In addition, applied learning experiences proceed most effectively and tend to be most permanent when they are personally meaningful. Finally, learning is an individual process in which trainees gain knowledge and skills and shape attitudes through their own activities, experiences, and motivation (*AFM 50-2,* 1975, p. 5-2).

Provide Guidance and Prompts

Trainees should be told and shown how to do something (perform). They need clear explanations of how to perform and step-by-step directions on what to do. Performance needs to be as error-free as possible the first time, since an error once made is likely to recur. First impressions are important. A trainee who performs an activity incorrectly the first time may have difficulty unlearning in order to learn the correct performance. Therefore, verbal and visual prompts should be provided before, during, and after practice to prevent guesswork and ensure correct performance (*NAVEDTRA 106A: Phase III,* 1975, pp. 6–8).

Provide Feedback

Honest, objective, and constructive feedback on how trainees are doing can improve performance and reinforce learning. Such feedback must be informative and received as soon as possible after performance. It should provide information on what is right or wrong as well as what corrective action to take. Effective feedback addresses both strengths and weaknesses. It reflects the instructor's consideration of the trainee's need for self-esteem, confidence, recognition, and the approval of others.

Knowledge and performance tests, as well as written work, ought to be used as teaching tools by fairly assessing the attainment of learning objectives. The evaluation process provides reinforcement for correct performance and includes corrective action for mistakes (*AFP 50-58: Vol. IV,* 1978, p. 2-6).

These four guidelines serve as an aid in establishing appropriate learning events/activities for each objective. The learning activities then specify what the instructor and/or the instructional materials must do to help the trainee attain the learning objective.

Specify Instructional Delivery System and Management Plan (Step III.2)

Choosing an optimum *instructional delivery system* is a complex decision, one that cannot be fully proceduralized. Since there are numerous teaching methods and a variety of media to choose from, the instructional delivery system includes a combination of appropriate methods, optimal instructional media, and a system of organizing trainees and instructors to accomplish all learning objectives. The types of teaching methods and media, along with representative examples of each, are listed in Table 2.

Methods and media are selected on the basis of careful analysis of the instructional situation from several standpoints: (a) learning objective, (b) learning activities, (c) learning stage, (d) characteristics of the trainee population, (e) instructional staff, (f) equipment and facility constraints, (g) time and cost advantages, and (h) whether group-paced or self-paced instruction is used[6] (Braby, Henry, Parrish, & Swope, 1978, pp. 7 & 8).

An *instructional management plan* consists of the policies and procedures used in organizing, controlling, and evaluating the delivery of instruction. This plan indicates (a) how the course or program is to be conducted, (b) how the trainees are to be managed, (c) when and where the trainees will be tested, (d) what the instructors and support personnel are to do, and (e) how each of the many elements within the plan work together. Documents that are a part of the management plan specify the procedures to be used in orienting incoming trainees, scheduling, instructing, remediating, monitoring, and evaluating both the trainees and instructors, and whatever else is needed to operate the course or program (*NAVEDTRA 110*, 1978, p. 189). Without a management plan, the faculty, staff, and administration are likely to lose track of trainees, resources, and even themselves.

Review/Select Existing Instructional Materials (Step III.3)

Developing instructional materials is a time-consuming and costly activity. In addition, special abilities, facilities, and equipment are required if the prepared materials are to be of good technical and pedagogical quality. Furthermore, experience has shown that by adopting existing materials or adapting them as necessary, the cost of instructional materials is reduced. For these reasons, it is essential to search out and

Table 2. Examples of teaching methods and media, by type.

Type	Representative Examples
Teaching Methods	
Presentation methods	1. Lecture 2. Demonstration 3. Indirect discourse (e.g., role playing, gaming, panel)
Verbal interaction methods	1. Questioning 2. Trainee query 3. Seminar 4. Discussion
Application methods	1. Performance (interaction with tools, equipment, etc.) 2. Coaching (performance taught/ supervised by a coach) 3. Case study
Media	
Printed materials	1. Books 2. Workbooks 3. Modules 4. Job performance aids 5. Instruction sheets 6. Manuals
Audiovisual media	1. Audio tape recordings 2. Microcomputer software 3. Overhead transparencies 4. 35 mm slides 5. Videotapes (cassettes) 6. Video disks
Manipulative aids	1. Actual objects 2. Models 3. Mock-ups 4. Cutaways 5. Trainers 6. Simulators

Note: The examples provided are representative and are not meant to be all-inclusive.

consider the suitability of existing items before committing resources to the development of new materials (*NAVEDTRA 106A: Phase III*, 1975, pp. 198 & 199).

Relevant existing materials from all possible sources ought to be identified, located, collected, and reviewed (examined) to determine their appropriateness. Requirements addressed by previous steps in the ISD model provide the criteria for examining and deciding which items are appropriate. The four criteria are

(1) Consistency with learning objectives

(2) Appropriateness to trainee characteristics

(3) Appropriateness to learning principles

(4) Compatibility with the delivery system and management plan (including available equipment)

Materials developed elsewhere that are not entirely adequate can be adapted (modified) as necessary to suit needs (*Handbook for Implementation*, 1979, p. 11). Modification of existing items may include deleting, updating, or resequencing materials. Another way to adapt existing instructional materials is to prepare adjunct or associated materials to supplement the existing items. This approach is particularly useful when remedial materials are needed for the less-advanced trainee (*NAVEDTRA 106A: Phase III*, 1975, p. 208). Even the use of some portions of existing materials may be economically advantageous.

A common error to avoid is the selection of instructional materials which present non-essential "nice-to-know" information. Providing a broad knowledge background can be costly if it increases the training time without increasing job task proficiency. Task-oriented training provides the trainee with greater reinforcement than hours spent gaining so-called related knowledge in a classroom.

The ISD approach asserts that training should be linked to performance rather than general knowledge or theory. Consequently, the training program ought to be task-oriented from beginning to end. The necessary supporting knowledge evolves in the context of task performance (*AFP 50-58: Vol. II*, 1978, pp. 3-8 & 3-9). The transmittal of knowledge is considered by some to be easier than training a learner to perform a task. This is no doubt one of the reasons why instructional materials are more readily available for supporting knowledge acquisition than for task performance.

At this point, appropriate existing instructional materials have been selected for use—some without alteration and others requiring modification. All that remains is to utilize the preceding analysis and planning to produce the necessary additional materials.[7]

Develop Instruction (Step III.4)

This is the point at which the preceding analysis and planning are used in developing new instructional materials that meet learning objectives. Among the different types of instructional materials are (a) job performance aids, (b) instruction sheets, (c) modules (instructional packages), (d) programmed texts, (e) overhead transparencies, (f) sound-slide sets, and (g) videotapes. Initially, these materials should include only the bare minimum of instruction. Instructional materials are then augmented as needed for trainees to attain the learning objectives. This "lean" strategy prevents the inclusion of extraneous information and instruction.

Draft instructional materials need to be reviewed, as they become available, by individuals who have the requisite expertise and who are constructive critics. There are essentially three types of reviews to be performed, all of which provide valuable information. First, there is a need for a technical review by someone with up-to-date knowledge and skills who will scrutinize the accuracy, currency, and completeness of the instructional content. The second review is for quality of content, clarity of presentation, and composition. This should be done by someone with training and experience in editing. The third review is an attempt to prejudge the relative effectiveness and value of the materials. As a result of these reviews, oversights, flaws, mechanical difficulties, and other problems are identified and resolved prior to the use of materials by trainees.

Once the materials are ready, they are tried out by a few capable trainees, with improvements and enrichment made as necessary. This assures the economies of minimal instruction and the correction of deficiencies. Quantitative information about the effectiveness of instruction is obtained through validation procedures which provide further opportunities for revision (*CNTT-A10,* 1976, p. 3-86).

Validate Instruction (Step III.5)

Validation assesses the effectiveness of small segments of instruction with the intention of making all necessary improvements. It is the process of repetitive cycles of tryouts and revisions until there is evidence that instructional materials are effective (*AFM 36-2234*, 1993, sect. F). *Validation procedures include both individual and group trials* by selected members of the training population or representative learners. First, instructional materials are individually tried out by two to five trainees, revised based on data and feedback, and tried again until the defects are corrected. Typical problems identified are (a) vague and incomplete directions, (b) lack of supporting instructional materials, (c) improper sequencing of the instruction, and (d) insufficient practice time.

After the individual trials are completed and all necessary revisions to the instruction have been made, the materials are tried out on a small group of ten to twenty trainees. These tryouts are continued until there is valid and reliable evidence that trainees can attain the learning objectives as measured by criterion-referenced tests.

Once the instructional materials are validated, they are ready for duplication and use in a teaching-learning setting. When materials are used without being validated, continual revision, based on actual experiences, must be anticipated.

PHASE IV, IMPLEMENT

Implement Instructional Management Plan (Step IV.1)

The implementation of the instructional management plan developed previously is the terminal step in planning and preparation and occurs before trainees arrive. Prior to the beginning of instruction, "last-minute checks" are made to ensure that all materials, procedures, tests, and other components of the total training program are ready to implement. These checks are also a quality assessment of the development process.

Instructors and any other personnel who will supervise, tutor, or examine the trainees are trained in the techniques and procedures with which they are not familiar. Although this training is critically important, it is not a substitute for good personnel screening and selection. Without adequate potential, interest, and ability, there is a limit to what such additional preparation can do. The emphasis is on assuring that qualified people (a) are at the right place at the right time; (b) know what they are to do; and (c) have the materials, equipment, facilities, and other resources necessary to do it (NAVEDTRA 106A: Phase IV & V, 1975, p. 1).

Complete training program capability, consisting of learning objectives, criterion-referenced tests, instructional materials, instructional management plan, trained personnel, and adequate facilities, tools, equipment, furniture, materials, supplies, and time should be available at this point. What remains to be done is to conduct instruction in accordance with the procedures and documentation contained in the instructional management plan. This is the "fruit of the labor."

Conduct Instruction (Step IV.2)

In addition to managing the resources, conducting instruction, evaluating trainees, and other activities, instructors need to keep records and collect data. These tangible remnants of occurrences make it possible to reconstruct a credible portrayal of what went on in the course or program. Among the records kept are (a) test and assignment results as well as information on trainee performance for each learning objective; (b) enrollment; (c) attendance; (d) remediation; (e) attrition; (f) scheduling data; (g) circulation files on books, videotapes, etc.; (h) activity or field trip rosters; and (i) accident reports.

A daily log is also maintained in which information such as the following is noted:

(1) Time requirements for instruction and testing

(2) Instructor comments on trainees

(3) Problems with instructional materials and tests

(4) Problems with individuals associated with instruction

(5) Positive and negative incidents, as well as unusual situations

(6) Maintenance and safety experiences

All editorial, procedural, and content refinements that were made also must be documented in order to facilitate a complete and accurate evaluation of the course/program.

Records and data kept on a regular basis support management information needs and are essential for evaluation purposes. At the completion of each training cycle, the collected information is made available as part of the internal evaluation in order to improve instruction for succeeding cycles.

PHASE V, CONTROL

Notwithstanding the care taken in each procedural step, it is still necessary to determine the effectiveness of training operating as a dynamic interrelated entity. The internal and external evaluation steps in this phase provide the information needed to judge the merit of the course or program. More specifically, this comprehensive evaluation process determines whether the training accomplished what it was designed and developed to accomplish in a cost-efficient manner.[8]

Evaluation can also provide a feeling of worth and accomplishment to the personnel associated with the course or program. Everyone needs feedback on how they are doing, and evidence that the training is really worthwhile can be a source of pride and satisfaction.

Conduct Internal Evaluation (Step V.1)

Internal evaluation is the collection and analysis of feedback and management data from within the instructional setting (school, institution, etc.). Sometimes called a course or program review, internal evaluation seeks to determine if instruction is providing trainees with the knowledge and skills necessary to attain the learning objectives (*NAVEDTRA 106A: Executive Summary,* 1975, p. 104). The principal measure of instructional effectiveness is the trainees' performance on criterion-referenced tests. Other measures include (a) instructor evaluations, (b) trainee and instructor opinions concerning instruction and testing, and (c) the amount of time required to complete each learning objective (time on task). In cases where standard licensing or certification tests exist (nursing, cosmetology, barbering, welding, automotive repair, etc.), the graduates' scores on these exams also furnish important evaluative data.

Training records and reports, as well as the notes kept by instructors during the conduct of instruction, provide additional sources of valuable information on course or program operation and management. This is augmented by an inspection of the instructional materials, facilities, tools, equipment, furniture, materials, and supplies to make sure they are adequate and appropriate. Additionally, the operation and maintenance of trainers and audiovisual equipment is checked.

An examination of how the ISD process itself was carried out is also part of the internal evaluation. The purpose is to identify any procedural omissions and ensure the quality of each activity and product. After internal evaluation data are collected and analyzed, deficiencies are corrected in a timely manner in order to receive the greatest benefit from the changes. Since the capabilities and performance of trainees and the manner in which instruction is sequenced and conducted may vary over time, internal evaluation is an ongoing process.

Conduct External Evaluation (Step V.2)

In addition to the internal evaluation, a properly planned and conducted external assessment needs to be completed in order to answer questions such as:

(1) Are graduates employed in jobs for which they were trained?
(2) Can graduates do the job for which they were trained?
(3) Is the job still the same as when it was analyzed?
(4) Do graduates need any instruction they did not receive?

In a sense, the last two questions revalidate the original job analysis and selection of tasks for instruction.

Before beginning the external evaluation (follow-up study), it must be determined (a) who should be contacted, (b) what information is needed, and (c) when and how the information will be gathered. Information useful in assessing the relevance and effectiveness of training will come from three sources:

(1) Records of the graduates' performance during the course or program (internal evaluation data)
(2) Graduates who are working at the job for which they were trained
(3) The employers or supervisors of those graduates

Either by in-person interviews, telephone interviews, or a questionnaire, information is gathered from graduates to determine:

(1) How well they are able to perform the job
(2) How well the training program prepared them for the job
(3) Whether any portions of the training program were irrelevant to the job
(4) What additional training (kind and amount) they have received since graduation
(5) What problems or successes they have experienced as a result of the training
(6) Whether their supervisor gave performance instructions different from those learned during training

The most reliable, but costly, feedback is gained at the workplace by (a) observing and evaluating the graduates' job performance, (b) interviewing both graduates and their supervisors, and (c) administering the job performance measures. Questionnaires completed by graduates and their immediate supervisors provide a valuable and less expensive means for conducting field-based evaluations (*AFP 50-58: Vol. V,* 1978, p. 1-3).

The external evaluation should take place from 4 to 6 months after graduation. This timing is important because graduates may need to find a job, get oriented, and acquire a "feel" for what the job is all about. Further, the graduates and supervisors need time to formulate judgments concerning job preparation and performance. If more than a reasonable settling-in period elapses before the graduates and supervisors are contacted, it becomes difficult to discriminate between knowledge and skills acquired in training and those acquired on the job (*NAVEDTRA 106A: Phase IV & V,* 1975, p. 68). As with internal evaluation, external evaluation is a recurring process which identifies problems and puts forward specific recommendations for appropriate modifications and adjustments.

Quality Control and/or Revise System (Step V.3)

The final function in the ISD approach is that of maintaining quality control. This is done through revisions that keep training relevant, effective, and cost-efficient. There is a tendency for training, once developed, to fossilize. Instead, courses and programs should evolve to reflect changes in job requirements, equipment, procedures, regulations, and so forth.

The repeated monitoring of training outcomes will no doubt result periodically in the identification of needed changes in what job tasks are selected for instruction, learning objectives, learning activities, time allocations, and other similar actions. When made, these revisions should (a) improve course or program relevance and effectiveness, (b) reduce the time required to complete instruction, or (c) obtain the appropriate level of effectiveness at a lower cost.

Since a considerable amount of time and effort has gone into the design and development of instructional courses and programs, revisions are approached with care. Decisions about what to change are based on the findings of internal and external evaluations (*NAVEDTRA 110A,* 1981, pp. 1-5 & 1-6).

The evaluation and quality control steps of Phase V complete the ISD feedback and revision cycle, thereby forming the closed loop instructional system shown in Figure 1. Continual evaluation and quality control are necessary in order to respond adaptively to unforeseen problems or changing conditions. In this way, instruction can be effectively and efficiently conducted to meet job requirements.

COMMENTARY

Today, more than ever, VET courses and programs must provide relevant, effective, and cost-efficient instruction because they are being held accountable for producing "work-ready" graduates. Both employers and trainees are interested in the quality and efficacy of the training provided. Courses and programs based on nothing more than an instructor's notion of what should be taught and how the training should be organized and delivered are in trouble. And well they should be, since the consequences include misplaced emphasis, irrelevant content, omission of knowledge and skills required for success on the job, and unqualified graduates. Such courses and programs will have to change in fundamental ways if they are to satisfy consumers and play a role in technological development and economic growth.

The search for a logical and organized, rather than haphazard, approach to training which will qualify graduates in job performance requirements has resulted in the advancement of ISD. This is because the iterative and derivative character of the methodology assures that instruction will meet job requirements when its procedures are conscientiously carried out. There is empirical evidence that competent use of the ISD approach can improve instruction in distinct ways (*AFH 36-2235: Vol. 1,* 1993, p. 14). Nevertheless, ISD will be worth its cost and considerable effort only to the extent that it is implemented so as to realize its full potential.

The extent to which some will perform all the activities associated with each phase of the ISD model and actually use the products in designing training is subject to question. In practice, steps are omitted at times and the close connection between components, which is essential to make the process truly derivative, is not maintained. Most important, the quality control and revision necessary to ensure the continuing relevance, effectiveness, and efficiency of training may be overlooked. When this happens, ISD becomes a patchwork of parts. Efforts to implement ISD should, therefore, attend to the integrity of the model by guarding against omissions in the process and failure to use its various products.

As this chapter revealed, there is nothing really novel about ISD procedures. They are broadly accepted and have been used by U.S.

government agencies, the Institute of Nuclear Power Operations, the Bank of America, New York City Transit Authority, and multi-national companies such as AT&T and Saudi ARAMCO. Nor is Systems Development a catchword to suggest something new; at most, it is a process for doing something better in deliberately attempting to be systematic, analytic, and comprehensive.

The Department of Defense, America's largest trainer, and other U.S. Government agencies have invested heavily in the development and refinement of ISD. The entire process has been documented and is available through the publications listed in the references.

APPENDIX A

Advantages and Disadvantages of Job Analysis Techniques

Advantages	Disadvantages

Observation of Job Incumbents Doing the Job

Advantages	Disadvantages
• Accomplished directly by observer or indirectly with a motion picture camera or an audio and video tape recorder. Simultaneous recording of personal observations is recommended.	• Safety and security factors may preclude direct observation.
• Best way to obtain an understanding of job context or environment.	• Not able to observe all job tasks, especially those performed infrequently over a long time span.
• Finds out what incumbents actually do, not what they say they do.	• Job tasks not observed must be identified by means of another technique.
• Few individuals involved.	• Expensive and time-consuming to observe and prepare the job analysis schedule.
• Little if any interference with operational activities.	• Presence of observer or recording device may cause stress and/or bias performance. May be perceived as "spying."
• Appropriate for jobs with observable psychomotor tasks, especially when an incumbent, even with assistance, cannot describe what is actually done and how it is done.	• Ineffective for jobs involving considerable personal judgment or mental application.

Advantages	Disadvantages

Observation of Job Incumbents Doing the Job *(continued)*

Advantages	Disadvantages
• Appropriate with incumbents who are deaf, blind, or unable to speak.	• Observations should be checked and verified, whenever possible, by repetition, or by comparison with those of other competent observers. • Requires a trained and knowledgeable observer who is patient and nonthreatening. • Methods oriented and slanted to the incumbent's way of doing things.

In-person Interviews of Job Incumbents and Their Supervisors

Advantages	Disadvantages
• High response rate. • Individuals are generally more willing to talk than to fill out a questionnaire. • Misunderstood questions can be clarified. • Finds out about job tasks performed infrequently over a long time span. • Appropriate for jobs involving considerable personal judgment or mental application (intellectual tasks). • Can be formal or casual, structured or unstructured, or somewhere in between. • Cost-effective when there are relatively few individuals to be interviewed and they are all in the same geographic area. • Yields precise, complete, and comparable information when structured.	• Time-consuming and costly to prepare for and conduct a number of individual interviews and compile the information collected. • Results depend upon the cooperation of those interviewed. • Individuals not able to recall all job tasks, especially those performed infrequently. • Can interfere with operational activities. • Requires a skillful, understandable interviewer with a pleasant personality and the ability to listen. • Individuals tend to say they do what they think they should do, not what they actually do. • Interviewer's bias, demeanor, and appearance can distort responses.

Advantages	Disadvantages

In-person Interviews of Job Incumbents and Their Supervisors *(continued)*

Advantages	Disadvantages
• Additional information revealed through non-verbal messages (body language). • Appropriate with incumbents who are illiterate or have language difficulties. • Responses can be recorded on audio tape or through written notes.	• Requires a quiet, comfortable, and distraction-free setting. • Note-taking may be disturbing and audio-taping threatening to some individuals. • Scheduling interviews with busy individuals may be difficult. • Individuals may give conflicting information which must be reconciled.

Telephone Interviews of Job Incumbents and Their Supervisors

Advantages	Disadvantages
• High response rate. • Individuals are generally more willing to talk than to fill out a questionnaire. • Misunderstood questions can be clarified. • Finds out about job tasks performed infrequently over a long time span. • Appropriate for jobs involving considerable personal judgment or mental application (intellectual tasks). • Comparatively inexpensive. • Information collected on the job or at home in a short period.	• Less sensitive than in-person interviews. • Not able to recall all job tasks, especially those performed infrequently. • Requires a trained, understandable interviewer with a positive attitude and good telephone manner. • Individuals tend to say they do what they think they should do, not what they actually do. • Reaching busy individuals to be interviewed or having them return a call may be difficult. • As the use of telemarketing increases, some individuals will hang up, not taking the time to distinguish between a job analysis and a solicitation.

Advantages	Disadvantages

Questionnaire Completed by Job Incumbents and Their Supervisors

Advantages	Disadvantages
• Useful when large numbers of individuals perform the same job.	• Requires know-how, substantial time, and hard work to (a) develop effective items, (b) write explicit directions, (c) format and pilot-test the instrument, and (d) compile the information collected.
• Appropriate for jobs involving considerable personal judgment or mental application (intellectual tasks).	
• A cost-efficient method of surveying geographically dispersed as well as mobile individuals by mail.	• Places a heavy demand on recall by those completing it.
• Yields large amounts of quantifiable information in a relatively short period.	• Questions may be misinterpreted.
• Questionnaire can be completed, on or off the job, at the individual's convenience.	• Some individuals may be distrustful and decline to complete the questionnaire or not provide honest, thoughtful responses.
• Bias is eliminated on questions that could be sensitive or embarrassing when asked by an interviewer.	• May be returned incomplete or filled in by unintended or inappropriate individual.
• All individuals are asked the same questions in the same way.	• Low response rate, especially when the questionnaire is long or complicated, requiring considerable time to complete, or mailed and there is no monetary incentive or persistent follow-up.
• Responses can be stored, manipulated, analyzed, and reported by a computer.	
	• Address may be incomplete or inaccurate and questionnaire may not be forwarded.
	• Does not facilitate further probing.
	• May require a computer to manipulate the large amount of information collected.
	• Inappropriate for low literacy groups.

Advantages	Disadvantages

Jury or Panel of Job Incumbents and Supervisors (Consensus Group)

Advantages	Disadvantages
• Few people involved. • Misunderstandings can be clarified. • Participants generally find the activity to be a stimulating and rewarding experience. • Appropriate for jobs involving considerable personal judgment or mental application (intellectual task). • Information collected and verified in a short time. • Consensus can be reached on points of disagreement. • Information provided by one individual can serve as a stimulus to others for recalling additional information.	• Full-time commitment, requires time away from the job, can be expensive. • Requires a recorder and a trained, understandable interviewer (facilitator) well-versed in group dynamics. • Requires knowledgeable individuals who are able and willing to communicate and cooperate as a group. • Presence of supervisors may affect job incumbents' participation. • Requires a distraction-free and comfortable setting. • Results depend upon the cooperation of jury members.

APPENDIX B

Job Performance Measure for Replacing a Tire/Wheel Assembly*

Examinee: _____ Instructor: _____

Start Time: ___ Finish Time: ___ Examiner: _____

Results: Pass ___ Fail ___ Examiner's Initials: ___ Date: _____

*Adapted with permission from Instruction Sheets, by C. P. Campbell, in L. G. Duenk (Ed.), 1993, *Improving Vocational Curriculum* (pp. 107–143). South Holland, IL: Goodheart-Willcox.

1.0 TASK STATEMENT
1.1 Replace a tire/wheel assembly.

2.0 PERFORMANCE CONDITIONS
2.1 Setting: Service shop, under actual work conditions.

2.2 Tools: (a) Hubcap tool, (b) Lug wrench, (c) Torque wrench, and (d) Tire gauge.

2.3 Equipment: (a) Full-size pickup truck, (b) Hydraulic floor jack, and (c) Jack stand.

2.4 Materials and Supplies: (a) Work order, and (b) Replacement tire/wheel assembly.

2.5 Safety Considerations: (a) Wearing safety glasses and safety shoes, (b) using downward pressure on wrenches, and (c) lifting with legs.

2.6 References: Service manuals.

3.0 INITIATING CUE
3.1 Receipt of work order.

4.0 ATTAINMENT STANDARDS
4.1 Conical part of lug nuts toward wheel and tightened, every other one in sequence, until all are torqued, to 80–90 ft-lbs. Tire pressure 36+2 psi. and no damage to hubcap. Performed without assistance.

5.0 EXAMINEE DIRECTIONS
5.1 The above referenced tools, equipment, materials and supplies shall be used to replace a tire/wheel assembly. Both the process of replacement and the completed replacement (product) will be evaluated by the examiner. *All steps must be performed safely and in the prescribed sequence. In addition, all performance must meet standards for the test results to be considered a "pass."* Please note: if you are unable to meet the attainment standard(s) for a critical step, the examiner will stop the test at that point.

6.0 ADMINISTRATIVE INSTRUCTIONS

6.1 Examiner directions: The examinee is to demonstrate the ability to replace a tire/wheel assembly on a full-size pickup truck. Both the process of replacement and the completed replacement (product) shall meet the standards provided.

6.2 Prior to the test: (a) insure that the referenced tools, equipment, materials and supplies are available; and (b) perform an operational check of the hydraulic floor jack. Give a copy of Page 1 of 4 to the examinee(s) so they can review the directions while you read them aloud. Invite the examinee(s) to ask questions for clarification. After answering all questions, ask the examinee(s) to return the page before beginning the test. Give the work order to examinee(s).

Do not provide assistance or coach the examinee(s) during the test, but monitor progress to prevent personal injury or damage to the equipment and tire/wheel assembly. Written comments on test administration and examinee performance may be recorded in the Comments section (item 8.0) on the last page of this test.

6.3 Scoring procedure: Unobtrusively observe the examinee's performance of each task element/step. Mark the YES box if the standard(s) were attained, and NO if they were not. Procedural steps in the process are to be rated directly after they are performed. Do not rely on your memory. All standards must be met in order for the test results to be considered a "pass." Enter the start and finish times on Page 1 of 4 and mark the test results, pass or fail; then initial and date your determination. Make all entries and marks in ink. Corrections must be initialed and dated.

7.0 CHECKLIST

7.1 (S) Sequence: This step must be performed only after the preceding step(s).

7.2 (C) Critical Step: Failure to meet the standard(s) for this step will end the test.

Process

Task Elements/Steps	Standards	Yes	No
1. Park truck in service shop	A. Parking (emergency) brake set. B. Automatic transmission in "park," manual transmission in "reverse." C. Wheels blocked.	☐	☐
2. (C) Remove hubcap	A. Wearing safety glasses and safety shoes. B. Using hubcap tool. C. No damage to hubcap or wheel.	☐	☐
3. (C) Loosen lug nuts	A. Each nut loosened approximately 1/2 turn. B. Using downward pressure on lug wrench.	☐	☐
4. (S,C) Position hydraulic floor jack	A. At manufacturer's recommended lift point.	☐	☐
5. (S) Raise truck	A. Tire approximately 2″ above ground.	☐	☐
6. (S,C) Position jack stand; lower truck	A. ±1″ of manufacturer's recommended lift point. B. Truck lowered slowly until weight transfers to jack stand.	☐	☐
7. (S) Remove lug nuts	A. All nuts completely removed from studs and placed in upturned hubcap.	☐	☐
8. (S,C) Remove and install tire/wheel assemblies	A. Dirt or lubricant cleaned from studs and around bolt holes in wheel. B. Stud threads undamaged. C. Lift with legs, holding from bottom of assembly.	☐	☐

Task Elements/Steps	Standards	Yes	No
9. (S,C) Replace lug nuts	A. All nuts replaced. B. Conical part of nut toward wheel. C. Wheel centered on studs. D. Nuts tightened gradually, every other one in sequence, using downward pressure on lug wrench until all are snug.	☐	☐
10. (S,C) Raise truck; remove jack stand	A. Weight removed from jack stand.	☐	☐
11. (S,C) Lower truck; remove floor jack	A. Slowly, with no jerky motions.	☐	☐
12. (C) Torque lug nuts	A. Final tightening with torque wrench, every other nut in sequence. B. All lug nuts torqued to 80–90 ft-lbs.	☐	☐
13. (S) Check tire pressure	A. 36 + 2 psi using tire gauge.	☐	☐
14. (S) Clean and stow tools.	A. Free of dirt and grease and returned to assigned location.	☐	☐

Product

Scorable Characteristics	Standards	Yes	No
1. (C) Road test truck and make final adjustments.	A. Truck driven 1 to 3 miles. B. Tire pressure no less than 36 + 2 psi. C. No misalignment of tire/wheel assembly.	☐	☐

Scorable Characteristics	Standards	Yes	No
2. (S) Replace hubcap	A. Secure on wheel and undamaged.	☐	☐

8.0 COMMENTS

APPENDIX C

Action Verbs

The following verbs, which convey action (performance), provide useful lead words for writing the behavioral action statement of a learning objective. Action verbs express or show behaviors that are (a) observable, (b) measurable, and (c) verifiable. The key to an effective behavioral action statement is a carefully selected action verb.

Activate	Assemble	Bend
Actuate	Assign	Bind
Adapt	Attach	Bleed
Add	Audit	Blend
Adjust		Block
Align	Backwash	Blow
Analyze	Bag	(off, out, up)
Apply	Bake	Boil
Arrange	Balance	Bore

Box
Braze
Build

Calculate
Calibrate
Carry
Cast
Change
Charge
Check (out)
Choose
Chop
Clamp
Clean
Clear
Clip
Close (up, down)
Coat
Collect
Combine
Compile
Complete
Compose
Compress
Compute
Connect
Consolidate
Construct
Control
Convert
Cook
Cool
Copy
Correct
Count
Cover
Crimp
Crush
Curl

Cut

Deenergize
Deflate
Deliver
Demonstrate
Depress
Depressurize
Design
Develop
Diagnose
Diagram
Dictate
Dig
Dilute
Dip (in)
Disassemble
Discard
Disconnect
Disengage
Dismantle
Dispose
Distribute
Divide
Dock
Doff
Don
Drain
Draw (down, in)
Dress
Drill
Drive
Dry
Duplicate
Dust

Edit
Energize
Engage
Erect

Evaluate
Examine
Execute
Explain
Expose
Extract

Fabricate
Fasten
Feed
File
Fill (in, out, up)
Filter
Fire
Fit
Fix
Flush
Focus
Fold
Follow
Force
    (in, on, off)
Form
Frame
Free up

Gather
Give (out)
Glue
Go (to)
Graph
Grease
Grind
Grip
Ground
Group
Guide

Hammer
Hand

Handle
Hang
Haul
Heat
Help
Hoist
Hold

Illustrate
Immerse
Inflate
Inject
Insert
Inspect
Install
Instruct
Insulate
Interview
Inventory
Isolate
Issue

Jack (up)
Join

Knit
Knurl

Label
Latch
Lay (out)
Level
Lift
Light
List
Load
Locate
Lock
Loosen
Lower

Lubricate

Maintain
Manipulate
Manufacture
Mark (off)
Mask
Measure
Melt
Mill
Miter
Mix
Modify
Mount
Move (up,
    down)
Multiply

Nail
Name
Negotiate

Obtain
Oil
Open
Operate
Order
Organize
Originate
Overhaul

Pack
Paint
Park
Patch
Pick (out, up)
Place
Plant
Plot
Plow

Plug (in, up)
Position
Pour
Prepare
Present
Press
    (down, in, on)
Pressurize
Price
Print
Process
Produce
Program
Pull (up, down,
    in, out)
Pump
Punch
Purchase
Purge
Push (up, down,
    in, on)
Put (up, in, on)

Quench

Raise
Reactivate
Ream
Rearrange
Reassemble
Rebuild
Reconnect
Record
Re-do
Regroup
Regulate
Release
Remove
Reorganize
Repair

Replace
Replenish
Reproduce
Reset
Restrain
Retract
Rework
Rig
Rinse
Roll
Rotate

Sand
Saw
Schedule
Screw
Scrub
Secure
Select
Send
Separate
Serve
Service
Set (up)
Shake
Shape
Sharpen
Shave
Shift
Shovel
Show
Shut (down,
   off, out)
Signal
Sit
Sketch
Slice
Slide
Slip
Solder

Solve
Sort
Splice
Spray
Spread (on)
Square
Squeeze
Stabilize
Stack
Stain
Stand
Start (up)
Steam
Sterilize
Stir
Stop
Store
Straighten
Strike
Strip
Subtract
Survey
Switch (off, on)

Tabulate
Tag
Take (in, out, up,
   off, apart)
Tap
Tape
Test
Thin
Thread
Tie (up, down)
Tighten
Tilt
Torque
Tow
Trace
Transfer

Transport
Treat
Trim
Troubleshoot
Tuck (in, under)
Tune
Turn (off, on,
   up, down)
Twist
Type

Uncover
Unload
Unlock
Unpack
Unplug
Unroll
Unscrew
Untie
Untighten

Vacuum
Varnish
Vent
Ventilate

Wash
Water
Wax
Weave
Weigh
Weld
Winch
Wind (up)
Wipe
Wire
Wrap
Write (down)

Vague concept-related words and phrases which describe supposed internal states or mental processes must be avoided when writing learning objectives. The following examples, unlike performance, are neither observable nor measurable. Furthermore, they are subject to considerable differences in interpretation of meaning.

Appreciate	Concern for	Perceive
Accept	Explore	Realize the
Be aware of	Feeling for	importance of
Become acquainted	Gain insight	Recognize
with	Gain proficiency	Satisfy
Become familiar	in	Should be able to
with	Grasp signifi-	Take responsibil-
Become well	cance of	ity for
versed in	Have faith in	Think about
Believe in	Have interest in	Understand
Capable of	Have knowledge of	Value
Cognizant of	Knowledgeable	Visualize
Comprehend	about	Working knowl-
Conceptualize	Learn the value of	edge of

APPENDIX D

Specifying Performance Conditions

Circumstances to Be Considered in a Statement of Performance Conditions	Examples of Conditions
Environment (setting)	1. on deck, in a storm, at sea
	2. under pressure in stressful surroundings
	3. in a confined space (cramped quarters)
	4. inside a factory with distracting noise
	5. in a garage with poor lighting
	6. in a storage tank with poor natural ventilation
	7. during a forest fire

Circumstances to Be Considered in a Statement of Performance Conditions	Examples of Conditions
Tools, equipment, furniture, materials, and supplies	1. using a lug wrench and hydraulic floor jack 2. using a fiberglass extension ladder 3. using a drill press 4. using a Ludlum model 177-145 monitoring instrument 5. given a 1/2-ton pickup truck with a standard transmission 6. given a 33-foot utility boat 7. given 2 × 4's, 8 feet long
Safety considerations	1. wearing burning goggles, a welding jacket, and welding gloves 2. wearing safety shoes, safety glasses, and a hard hat 3. wearing coveralls and gloves 4. wearing an air-purifying respirator 5. wearing chemical-resistant boots 6. wearing sterile gloves and face mask 7. wearing ear muffs
Job performance aids, references, and special instructions	1. using a procedural guide 2. with the help of the American Red Cross checklist 3. given service manuals 4. using a troubleshooting chart 5. given a floor plan 6. given technical order 157-19B
Special physical demands	1. pushing a loaded wheelbarrow 2. while kneeling on a roof with a steep pitch 3. hands and eyes are occupied at all times

Circumstances to Be Considered in a Statement of Performance Conditions	Examples of Conditions
Special physical demands *(continued)*	4. strength in lifting and carrying boxes 5. while climbing a ladder 6. standing for long periods

Notes: In considering the applicability of different items in the statement of conditions, the question to be answered is, "Does it affect task performance?" It is best to specify all important performance conditions. Even though the idea of implied conditions avoids redundancy when the conditions are identical for a set of learning objectives, important information about the performance environment and available resources is necessary for learning objectives to be beneficial in their various roles.

When simulators or other training devices are used in place of actual equipment, they are stipulated in the performance conditions.

The conditions circumstances listed in column 1 are from Manipulative Performance Tests, by C. P. Campbell, in L. G. Duenk (Ed.), 1993, *Improving Vocational Curriculum* (pp. 173–201). South Holland, IL: Goodheart-Willcox. Reprinted with permission.

APPENDIX E

Specifying Criteria for Attainment Standards

Categories to Be Considered in a Statement of Attainment Standards	Examples of Criterion
Quantity, rate of production or amount produced	1. at the rate of 30 units per hour 2. not less than 100 cubic yards of earth must be excavated every hour 3. no less than 15 grams of powder shall be inspected per minute 4. minimum output, 20 pages per day

Categories to Be Considered in a Statement of Attainment Standards	Examples of Criterion
Quality, degree of excellence	1. free from surface imperfections 2. connection firmly seated with no kinks in cord 3. all chipped, cracked, scratched, and pitted tiles shall be replaced 4. all nail heads countersunk below surface of wood 5. all windows and doors plumb 6. engine runs at its smoothest point 7. no customer complaints
Accuracy (precision), within tolerance limits	1. within 1 psi as compared to a calibrated master pressure gauge 2. measurement should be within $\pm.005''$ of actual thickness 3. no more than 12 and no less than 10 feet long 4. floor joists cut $16'\text{-}4''$, $\pm 1/16''$ 5. dressing is $1''$ to $1\ 1/2''$ larger than burn area 6. within 5% of predetermined totals
Number of allowable variations or permissible errors	1. zero production defects 2. not more than one noncritical defect per 10 units of production 3. free from errors in spelling, grammar, and punctuation 4. with less than four errors
Standard(s) and/or criteria in reference documents	1. within inspection criteria as listed in MIL-STD-1042 2. based on the criteria specified in ANSI B4.1-1967

Categories to Be Considered in a Statement of Attainment Standards	Examples of Criterion
Standard(s) and/or criteria in reference documents *(continued)*	3. in accordance with Occupational Safety and Health Standards, part 1910 4. within dimensional tolerances specified on engineering drawings
Time limit, speed	1. completed within 30 minutes 2. ready for return to customer within 2 days 3. minimum speed of 40 words per minute
Amount of supervision or assistance to be provided	1. with close supervision 2. without assistance 3. with assistance as required

Notes: When writing the attainment standards part of learning objectives, it is advisable to make allowance for the fact that trainees are engaged in a learning process. For example, a maximum time limit may be specified in order for trainees to attain the accuracy, quality, quantity, and other criteria. High levels of speed can be achieved on the job, based on practice.

The attainment standards categories listed in column 1 are from Manipulative Performance Tests, by C. P. Campbell, in L. G. Duenk (Ed.), 1993, *Improving Vocational Curriculum* (pp. 173–201). South Holland, IL: Goodheart-Willcox. Reprinted with permission.

APPENDIX F

Vague Attainment Standards

Troublesome Standards	Problem
". . . with at least 90% accuracy."	Tasks may not lend themselves to mathematical attainment standards, for example, lubricating a vehicle. This standard presents a risk. In some workplaces the missing 10% could lead to injury or damage.
". . . to the instructor's satisfaction."	The instructor is keeping the real standards from the trainees, specifically what constitutes "satisfactory." Some instructors may be satisfied with less than others.
". . . performance will be evaluated by the instructor."	The instructor is assumed to be the evaluator, and this does not need to be repeated in the learning objective. The criteria for what constitutes adequate task performance is needed.
". . . in accordance with manufacturer's specifications."	Many manufacturer's "specifications" are only procedural steps in task performance and are not recognized as standards of accuracy, quality, time, etc. Product standards, or key points in the process, should be measured.
". . . in accordance with the procedure sheet."	A procedure sheet may tell only "what" is to be done, not "how well" it should be done. The "how well" ought to be addressed in the attainment standards.

Troublesome Standards	Problem
Words such as "acceptably," "adequately," "appropriately," "completely," "correctly," "properly," and "satisfactorily."	Such words are vague and ambiguous, open to varying interpretation. The criteria must be explicit—unmistakably clear, observable, and measurable, leaving nothing implied so there is no doubt as to the meaning.

ENDNOTES

1 The definitions of *knowledge* and *skill* have changed over time. In Samuel Johnson's eighteenth century *Dictionary of the English Language,* the words were synonyms. He cites their interchangeable use by Shakespeare. However, present definitions and current usage reveal important differences in their meaning. *Webster's New World Dictionary* defines *knowledge* as—being acquainted or familiar with facts and principles, that which is grasped by the mind, learning. *Skill,* on the other hand, is—a great ability or proficiency in art, a craft, or science; expertness involving use of the hands or body that comes from training and practice.

2 Some courses and programs are intended to teach a body of knowledge (for example, psychology). The goal is to "cover the subject" rather than to deal with any particular job applications. In such cases, job analysis is not the best approach to identifying course content.

3 It is explicit in ISD that test items are written for learning objectives rather than from subject matter content, as is the practice in some other instructional approaches.

4 Results for each test item will probably show that some trainees already have relevant prior knowledge and skills while others do not. It is unlikely that everyone tested will either know or not know all of the material. Therefore, in establishing an entry level for a group-paced program, curriculum developers must use their best judgment in determining the exact level of instruction at which to begin.

5 Instruction can be personalized by sequencing, to the extent possible, learning objectives to meet individual trainee needs and interests. Having a set of learning objectives for a course or program makes meeting individual needs easier and more systematic. The time initially spent writing objectives is more than compensated for when an instructor can reorder existing learning objectives for each trainee with a particular need.

6 Group-paced instruction is delivered in a fixed sequence and paced by the progress of the majority of the class. All trainees in the class (group) progress through the instruction at the same rate. Slower learners normally have trouble keeping up with the rate when it is determined by the average learner and faster learners are slowed down. Self-paced instruction enables trainees of different ability, background, and motivation to progress through an instructional program at their own rate. Slower learners can take more (but not unlimited) time; faster learners can finish quickly.

7 It is explicit in ISD that terminal objectives are prepared for every job task selected for instruction and that these terminal and their enabling objectives are the basis for the selection and development of all instructional materials used in the training program. Learning (terminal and enabling) objectives are not derived from subject matter content as is the practice in some other instructional approaches.

8 To assure objectivity, the internal and external evaluation should be conducted by specialists who are not directly responsible for developing or conducting the training. The more independent and impartial the evaluator is, the more useful the data collected will be.

REFERENCES**

AFH 36-2235: Volume 1—Executive summary. Information for designers of instructional systems. (1993, November). Headquarters U.S. Air Force, Washington, DC: Department of the Air Force.

AFM 36-2234. Instructional systems development. (1993, November). Headquarters U.S. Air Force, Washington, DC: Department of the Air Force.

AFM 50-2. Instructional systems development. (1975, July). Headquarters U.S. Air Force, Washington, DC: Department of the Air Force.

AFM 50-2. Instructional systems development. (1979, May). Headquarters U.S. Air Force, Washington, DC: Department of the Air Force.

AFM 50-62. Handbook for Air Force instructors. (1984, January). Headquarters U.S. Air Force, Washington, DC: Department of the Air Force.

AFP 50-58: Volume II—Task analysis. Handbook for designers of instructional systems. (1978, July). Headquarters U.S. Air Force, Washington, DC: Department of the Air Force.

AFP 50-58: Volume III—Objectives and tests. Handbook for designers of instructional systems. (1978, July). Headquarters U.S. Air Force, Washington, DC: Department of the Air Force.

AFP 50-58: Volume IV—Planning, developing and validating instruction. Handbook for designers of instructional systems. (1978, July). Headquarters U.S. Air Force, Washington, DC: Department of the Air Force.

AFP 50-58: Volume V—Conducting and evaluating instruction. Handbook for designers of instructional systems. (1978, July). Headquarters U.S. Air Force, Washington, DC: Department of the Air Force.

Braby, R., Henry, J. M., Parrish, W. F., & Swope, W. M. (1978, October). A technique for choosing cost-effective instructional delivery systems (TAEG Rep. No. 16). Orlando, FL: Training Analysis and Evaluation Group, Chief of Naval Education and Training.

CNTT-A10. Procedures for the planning, design, development, and management of Navy technical training courses. (1976, April). Naval Air Station, Memphis, Millington, TN: Chief of Naval Technical Training.

**It is important to recognize the significant contribution made by those who were involved in producing the original source documents on ISD which are listed in the references. Their sound thinking and effective writing made this chapter possible. To all these individuals, I convey my appreciation, while reminding the reader that I alone am responsible for any errors or omissions.

Handbook for implementation (Interservice procedures for instructional systems development). (1979, January). Washington, DC: Naval Health Sciences Education and Training Command.

MIL-STD-1379A. Contract training programs. (1976, October). Washington DC: Department of Defense.

NAVEDTRA 106A: Executive summary and model. Interservice procedures for instructional systems development. (1975, August). Naval Air Station, Pensacola, FL: Chief of Naval Education and Training.

NAVEDTRA 106A: Phase I—Analyze. Interservice procedures for instructional systems development. (1975, August). Naval Air Station, Pensacola, FL: Chief of Naval Education and Training.

NAVEDTRA 106A: Phase II—Design. Interservice procedures for instructional systems development. (1975, August). Naval Air Station, Pensacola, FL: Chief of Naval Education and Training.

NAVEDTRA 106A: Phase III—Develop. Interservice procedures for instructional systems development. (1975, August). Naval Air Station, Pensacola, FL: Chief of Naval Education and Training.

NAVEDTRA 106A: Phase IV & V—Implement and control. Interservice procedures for instructional systems development. (1975, August). Naval Air Station, Pensacola, FL: Chief of Naval Education and Training.

NAVEDTRA 110. Procedures for instructional systems development. (1978, July). Naval Air Station, Pensacola, FL: Chief of Naval Education and Training.

NAVEDTRA 110A. Procedures for instructional systems development. (1981, September). Naval Air Station, Pensacola, FL: Chief of Naval Education and Training.

Principles of training systems development (Manual INPO 85-006). (1985, February). Atlanta, GA: Institute of Nuclear Power Operations.

U.S. Department of Energy. (1992). *Guide to good practices for developing learning objectives* (DOE Publication No. STD-1005-92). Washington, DC: Author (NTIS No. DE 92017689).

CHAPTER 3

The Content of Instruction

DENNIS R. HERSCHBACH—*University of Maryland*

WHEN an instructor develops a course outline, prepares instructional materials, makes up lesson plans, or assigns instructional activities, decisions are being made about what students should learn—the content of instruction. Strictly speaking, questions about instructional content relate to the effectiveness of instruction, that is, the strength of the relationship between the content taught and the intended use of instruction. In the case of courses or programs that prepare students for work, if there is a strong relationship between what is taught and what the job requires, then the instructional course/program is effective and has high content validity. Courses, however, may not have immediate job placement as an objective. Nevertheless, to achieve a high level of content validity, there needs to be a strong relationship between what is taught and the intended instructional outcome.

Establishing content validity is as important as achieving instructional efficiency. It does little good to have a very efficient instructional course/program if what students learn is not useful. Improving the quality of instruction is partly a matter of improving instructional and organizational efficiency. However, it also involves the capacity of instruction to transfer appropriate skills, whether they are related academic subject matter, manipulative operations, work attitudes, or new technology. Obviously, when designing instruction, the aim is to maximize both instructional efficiency and effectiveness. Furthermore, there is a direct link between the two. By eliminating superfluous content, instructional time can be reduced, and greater emphasis can be placed on the most important content to be learned.

THE SOURCE OF CONTENT

The famous architect Frank Lloyd Wright coined the saying "form follows function." A similar statement can be made about instructional

109

design: content follows function. Vocational and technical instruction can have a number of functions, or purposes. To be sure, the overall purpose is utility, to prepare individuals for useful work. But even within this broad definition, there is room for considerable variation. Instruction can be designed, for example, to retrain individuals who already have considerable skills, to provide initial skills training, to focus on general pre-employment preparation, to impart remedial skills, to relate academic knowledge to vocational and technical skills, or a number of other purposes, depending on what those who are designing instruction intend to accomplish. As in the case of the architect, the instructional designer must be clear about the intended use, or function, of instruction in order to select the appropriate content. There are endless ways that courses can be put together, depending on the intended use of instruction (Engestrom, 1994).

The instructional content itself comes from a number of sources. The most widely recognized is *formal knowledge* from established fields of study, such as algebra, biology, physics, English, or economics. Content also includes *social learning,* such as job attitudes or personal behavior associated with work, and *technical content* specific to a particular field or technical activity. Most vocational and technical instruction includes a combination of formal knowledge, specific applications of formal knowledge and social learning, and technical content specific to the field. Regardless of the combination, however, the technical activity itself constitutes the basis for the selection of content (McNeil, 1990). If certain formal, factual knowledge or concepts are included in instruction, for example, it must be because they relate directly to the technical activity, not because they make up part of a formal body of knowledge. The same is true of social learning. Certain behaviors are taught because they are a part of job activity. The technical activity, in other words, determines what is selected. This is what sets vocational and technical education and training apart from academic instruction.

Linking with Employment

The technical activity, then, is the means through which instructional content is identified and selected. For this reason, contact with the workplace should be established at the initial stage of course or program design and should be continued periodically, with revisions based upon changing work requirements. The consequence of not maintaining a link with potential employers is instruction characterized by low content validity, that is, the teaching of inappropriate or unnecessary content.

The flow of information can be maintained in several ways: the formation of advisory committees or employer groups, the use of placement or development officers, and systematic feedback from job placement. Cost is a factor, however, regardless of which method is used, and few individual educational or training organizations systematically address employment-related information needs.

Analyzing for Content

Well-designed job and task analysis procedures have been developed to effectively identify instructional content after the initial decision is made to train in a specific job or occupational category (Melching & Borcher, 1973; Norton, 1985). These procedures can also be used to identify content for courses and programs with more general functions, such as pre-employment preparation. The procedures are straightforward, and incorporate some type of validation process. Job and task analysis procedures, however, can be used to identify a broad array of instructional content, including related academic knowledge, a fact often overlooked by program developers. When task analysis procedures are not used, or when inappropriate tasks are sampled, the resultant training usually lacks content validity.

Standardized task lists, which appear to provide a short-cut to instructional development, are often available. These listings, however, are often not applicable to local conditions, and rarely consider the variety of purposes which technical instruction can address. Such material, although providing an initial, basic task listing, should serve only as a beginning point. Additional steps are necessary for specifying relevant content.

Job and task analysis procedures are most commonly applied to identifying job-specific content. By the use of clustering techniques, occupation-specific and basic academic skills can also be identified, but this is often not done—even when the purpose is to provide more generic training. Courses and programs can be designed to emphasize different "skill mixes," depending on their function and the characteristics of the population being served.

DIFFERENT KINDS OF SKILLS

Formal vocational and technical programs are often equated with specific skill training. As suggested, however, work involves not only the application of strictly academic, cognitive skills, but also special uses of academic skills common to a particular occupation, in addition to specific job skills—the particular techniques and processes applied to work. There are also attitudes and habits, that is, affective behaviors, associated with work. Different training alternatives are more or less successful in their capacity to transfer these skills. In general, formal vocational and technical education and training (VET) is conceived too narrowly when the instructional focus is limited to specific job skills.

Cognitive Skills

Cognitive behavior is present in almost all job activity and relates to the knowledge and intellectual abilities involved in performing the job. There is sometimes a tendency to undervalue the extent of cognitive behavior present in task performance, but very little job activity can be carried out without grounding in a cognitive structure. For some job tasks, complex levels of behavior are required, such as when diagnosing an engine malfunction without sophisticated test equipment. This is especially true in technological fields and cannot be overlooked when designing instruction. Unless the higher levels of behavior are recognized and instruction is structured accordingly, students cannot be expected to adequately perform the job tasks. Of course, some tasks include only lower-level behaviors. It is also important to guard against unrealistic instruction in light of job requirements.

Basic Academic Skills

Proficiency in basic academic skills is important to training and work, since it establishes the foundation for successful skill development. Many job skills are merely adaptations or extensions of academic skills. As the technology incorporated into work becomes more complex, academic skill requirements tend to increase. Probably the greatest contribution to human resource development that can be made by formal education and training institutions is the assurance of a sound grounding in academic skills and special vocational uses of academic skills. Many students, however, do not possess sufficient basic skills to enable them to profit from VET or to realize their full work potential. It is this deficiency in basic skills that inhibits vocational development, within school and at work.

Jobs that require significant uses of cognitive skills are probably best learned in formal courses and programs; similarly, the academic skill component of many jobs is best learned in a structured, classroom environment, in either public or private settings. Few employers, however, have the capability or inclination to instruct in formal knowledge. The inclusion of basic academic education is one reason why formal VET is often less job-specific than some critics would like it to be.

Stasz, McAuthor, Lewis, and Ramsey (1990) distinguish between basic skills, such as reading and simple mathematical calculations, and complex reasoning skills, such as critical thinking and problem-solving. Complex reasoning skills are thought to include higher-level cognitive processes and, for this reason, they are considered to be more desirable to teach. Basic skills are considered by the authors to be only the minimum skills that a person brings to the job, in contrast to complex skills which are considered to make up the performance repertoire of an expert. Research in cognitive processing shows that experts make more use of higher-order learning and metacognitive strategies than they do of low-level subskills or abstract conceptual and factual information (Johnson, 1989).

However, one should be cautious when distinguishing between the relative instructional value of different skills. As previously suggested, all skill levels have to be taught if they are part of task performance. Complex reasoning skills cannot be easily separated in a meaningful way from the cluster of skills which are combined in a task. It is difficult to teach problem-solving, for example, in an abstract form separate from its application to a specific technical problem. The technical problem may, in fact, involve the use of a number of discrete skills, many of which are simple, basic skills. Some learning theorists contend that general, complex reasoning skills, such as critical thinking, cannot be effectively taught in isolation from their application (Resnick, 1987). The opposite is also true. Even an apparently simple basic skill, such as reading, is cognitively complex. To ignore basic skills and focus only on what appears to be complex reasoning skills results in incomplete and distorted learning.

There is considerable recent interest in the integration of academic with technical instruction. The inclusion of more applied math, communication, science, and other similar academic content is thought to provide students with a broader educational background. In this way more "rigor" is introduced into VET while, at the same time, the individual is thought to have greater flexibility in the workplace. The high-tech fields, in particular, require solid academic preparation.

Greenan (1982, 1983) identifies what he terms "generalizable skills," which are generic to a broad range of occupations. His four skills categories of mathematics, communication, interpersonal relations, and reasoning (see Appendix A) are a combination of basic academic skills as well as more general intellectual processes, such as problem-solving. The generic skills identified in Appendix A are thought to be basic to a wide range of occupational fields.

The Secretary's Commission on Achieving Necessary Skills (SCANS, 1991) identified thirty-six skill clusters considered necessary for effective job training. These skills are grouped into three foundation skill categories (see Appendix B) and five competencies (see Appendix C) thought to be needed for employment. Research by others identified similar skill classifications. Additionally, a job analysis was conducted in order to identify the use of the skill clusters on the job, and to establish skill levels. The research and job analysis were all attempts to conceptualize VET in broad terms. Instruction too narrowly conceived is considered inappropriate to the challenges of workforce preparation.

Psychomotor Skill Development

Some jobs consist mainly of applications of psychomotor skills, such as the manipulation of tools, machinery, and equipment. In general, psychomotor skills can best be learned at high proficiency levels within the actual work setting. Relatively long periods of practice are often required and the business's actual machinery and equipment can be used. Combinations of classroom instruction and work experience may work best, with classroom instruction focused on the cognitive job skills and familiarization with manipulative skills. Supervised work experience is used to bring the trainee to required proficiency levels.

Formal school-based programs tend to concentrate too heavily on psychomotor skill development; whereas, workplace-based instruction tends to spend too little time on related cognitive skill development.

Affective Skills

Affective skills relate to the work habits and attitudes, values, and beliefs one exhibits at work. There is often reluctance on the part of instructors to identify and teach affective content. One reason for this hesitancy is the fear of imposing values upon individuals and of being susceptible to the charge of indoctrinating students. Affective behavior is often considered "right" or "wrong," depending on the context of a specific value system. Should instructors try to teach a predetermined set of values?

When affective skills are identified directly from job activity, however, the argument can be made that these skills are no less important to performance than cognitive or psychomotor skills, and that affective skills are not just the reflection of a set of personal values. In many occupations, affective behaviors are highly important and cannot be overlooked. For example, individuals such as receptionists, salespersons, clerks, dentists, and cosmetologists must maintain a rapport and credibility with the public they are serving. When preparing for such fields, it is essential that the required affective skills are identified. Moreover, the failure to succeed in many jobs is often due more to the lack of attaining the necessary affective skills than to the ability of individuals to perform psychomotor or cognitive functions. Affective behaviors which constitute job skills can be identified, and these should be part of instruction.

Failure to identify and teach the requisite affective behaviors may also be due to the fact that they are not always an obvious part of the job sequence. Affective behaviors, nevertheless, can be identified through job and task analysis procedures, but it may take considerable probing and initiative on the part of the investigator. While cognitive and psychomotor skills are more obvious and are organized in different levels from the simplest to the most complex, affective skills represent internalized responses. The instructor should aim to achieve at least low levels of internalization for most job functions, and for critical tasks, such as those involving safety or complex job performance, high levels are essential. However, because most formal courses and programs are of relatively short duration, it is probably unrealistic to expect that a high degree of response internalization can be achieved. Combinations of school-based and workplace-based experiences may be the best alternative.

PROGRAM DESIGN OPTIONS

As previously discussed, content follows from program function, or purpose. There are a variety of possible program designs, each with its relative merits and limitations. They vary in cost and with the type of training provided, depending upon what the instructional designer wants to accomplish within the range of available resources. The different potential skill combinations are the building materials that the instructional designer uses. Following is a brief review of different program design options.

Job-Specific Training

Job-specific, or skill-specific, training focuses on a clearly defined and limited set of useful skills. The purpose is to prepare individuals for immediate job placement. Instruction tends to be narrow in scope, but depth of coverage is provided. Upon completion of training, the individual is expected to be proficient in the skills covered and able to perform satisfactorily in the job setting. Training is often provided in only one job category, so only limited training resources are needed. The direct relationship between training and job placement is the attractive feature of job-specific training.

Careful selection of instructional content is essential, since job-specific training is only effective to the extent that the instruction is directly related to job requirements. Skills not directly related to job performance are not taught. Students are taught skills to the required performance level, and their performance is evaluated to determine if, indeed, requisite skill levels have been reached. Reteaching follows, if necessary. Feedback from placements is essential for assessing program effectiveness (see Figure 1).

Job-specific training is used extensively by industry to provide entry-level training, retraining, or upgrading. The training is skill-specific since its purpose is the development of immediately marketable job skills. What is taught can be carefully controlled, high performance levels can be achieved, and limited resources are required. On the other hand, when the objective is not immediate job placement, or the student's occupational choice has not yet crystallized, job-specific training may not be the best option.

Occupation-Specific Training

Occupation-specific training provides a basic technical and theoretical background, but few graduates are prepared to enter directly into work without additional, short-term training, either just prior to employment or on the job. The purpose of occupation-specific training is to provide

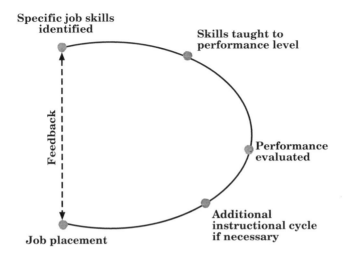

Characteristics
- Clearly defined set of skills taught
- Scope of instruction narrow
- Depth of coverage provided

Advantages
- Specialized training
- High performance levels
- Cost less than comprehensive training

Application
- Retraining or upgrading
- Immediate employment follows training
- Definite student career choice
- Limited resources

FIGURE 1 Job-specific training.

exposure to a representative sample of skills relating to one occupational field or related fields. Instruction centers around a core of representative skills common to a range of specific jobs within an occupational field, rather than around the individual skill requirements of a single job. Broad coverage is traded for depth of instruction, and skills are not always taught to high performance levels.

Occupation-specific training is most appropriate in cases where the occupational goals of students are not yet clearly defined and/or where job placement does not immediately follow training. The foundation is developed for later skill development, occupational mobility is enhanced, and variations in student interests, backgrounds, and ability can be accommodated (see Figure 2).

To be most effective, however, occupation-specific training must be complemented with specific and focused training prior to or at the time of employment. More specific, short-term training can be obtained in a

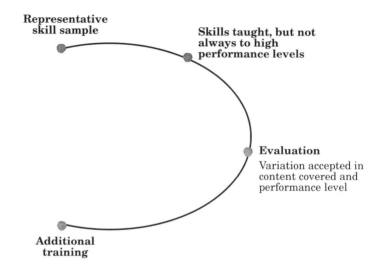

Characteristics
- Representative sample of skills identified
- Proficiency level may not be high
- Broad training provided

Advantages
- Increased occupational mobility
- Comprehensive coverage
- Variation in student background, ability, and interest accomodated

Application
- Where job placement unknown or not immediate
- Where additional training is available
- Not clearly defined student occupational goal

FIGURE 2 Occupation-specific training.

number of ways, either through public-supported programs or by direct links to private industry. The combination of occupation-specific training coupled with short-term job-specific training capitalizes on the strengths of both alternatives.

Public VET is often equated with skill-specific training, particularly when the employment community's support is needed—the program is "sold" on the claim that it can, indeed, address the immediate skill needs of specific employers. "Conventional" formal VET programs, however, are limited in their capacity to provide skill-specific training largely because of their inability to rapidly upgrade machinery and equipment, adjust curricula, and focus on the varying skill needs of specific employers. Also, occupational choices are generally not well-defined. For these reasons, formal VET courses and programs best provide "generic training" in occupation-specific skills. Individuals build the necessary foundation skills for employment, but additional short-term, skill-specific training is needed. Trainees' mobility is enhanced since they are prepared to enter any number of related jobs with a number of different employers. The instruction itself is less costly because it teaches a core of common skills to large groups of students, making better use of equipment and requiring only a limited range of instruction. Occupation-specific training develops the general ability to assimilate additional training, a capability that is not necessarily an outcome of job-specific training.

Integrated Programs

Until recently, a less-common curriculum option was the integrated program: technical training directly coordinated and integrated with supporting academic and theoretical instruction. Integrated programs developed from the recognition that science, mathematics, and communication skills are an increasingly important aspect of work. Integrated programs are most common in high technological fields requiring a firm foundation of academic preparation. As in the case of occupation-specific training, the purpose of integrated programs is to provide a foundation for additional training, either in the form of advanced school-based instruction or through job entry training at the workplace. It should not be expected that an integrated program graduate will be prepared to go directly to work without some skill-specific training.

Academic skills are directly integrated with technical skills and instructional sequencing is correlated through cooperative planning. Science, mathematics, and language instruction, for example, typically occur concurrently with instruction in technical skills, with all instruction linked through coordinated planning and course sequencing.

In the case of job-related models, instructional content is identified through an analysis of job activity in the field. Theoretical and academic instruction make use of practical examples, and technical instruction fully integrates theory (see Figure 3).

There are several patterns of integrated training (Grubb, Davis, Lum, Plihal, & Morgaine, 1991). The simplest is to provide more academic content in technical instruction. Academic skills and their specific technical applications are given greater emphasis. The academic instruction is either provided in separate courses or included as part of a specific technical course.

Another variation is to modify academic courses by including techni-

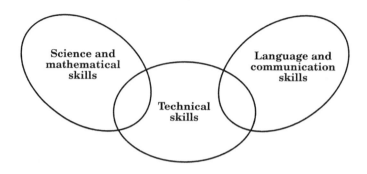

Characteristics
- Parallel, correlated, or direct integration
- Integrated planning

Advantages
- Depth and quality of training
- Preparation for additional training
- Future occupational growth and mobility

Application
- In high-tech fields
- Where academic skills are important
- Where additional training follows

FIGURE 3   Integrated curriculum.

cal content. This is done either by modifying "traditional" subject-centered courses, or by developing new "applied academics" courses. In both cases, the general idea is to use standard academic content in combination with occupational examples and applications.

The inclusion of instructional units of academic content in vocational and technical courses is yet another integrative pattern. While examples of technical applications are used, the formal structure of the academic content is retained. The academic content is, essentially, inserted in an unaltered form into the instructional sequence.

Yet another integration pattern is to offer both occupational and academic courses sequenced in tandem. Students simultaneously take both kinds of courses, which are designed to complement each other. All of these patterns are relatively unobtrusive forms of integration.

A more complete form of integration is achieved through combining academic and technical content into a new multi-disciplinary structure. These "hybrid" courses make use of the content and methods of inquiry associated with the formal disciplines, but the disciplines lose their formal subject-matter identity. The content is organized around issues, problems, and concerns which are distinctly technical and occupational, and instructional content is drawn from a number of the formal disciplines, reflecting the fact that technology itself makes multi-disciplinary use of knowledge.

The potential of the SCANS model for organizing integrative programs has not been sufficiently explored. The eight categories (three foundation skills and five competencies, detailed in Appendices B and C) provide a coherent framework for identifying and organizing instructional content. A mix of behaviors is included, ranging from basic reading and writing skills to higher order learning and affective behaviors which probably more closely mirror job requirements than do formal subject-matter classifications. Similarly, Greenan (1982, 1983) provides a functional way to relate academic and vocational content, based on the actual use of academic skills. The academic, intellectual, and interpersonal skills which clearly relate to job performance can be identified.

Integrative programs are best used in high technological areas where the supporting academic skills are important to job performance and mobility. The academic depth of training achieved is an advantage. However, because instruction tends to be "general," more skill-specific training usually is required before the student is ready to obtain a job. Nevertheless, a sound foundation is constructed for additional classroom or on-the-job instruction.

The Cluster Concept

Programs based on the cluster concept prepare individuals to enter a family of occupations rather than a specific job (Maley, 1975). Representative skills from a number of related occupations are taught, so that the trainee is prepared in a broad range of entry skills, but does not acquire depth in any one job. Five criteria are used to determine which occupational areas should be the focus of instruction:

(1) Favorable long-term employment outlook
(2) Opportunity for job entry upon program completion
(3) Opportunity for advancement through further instruction, such as apprenticeship or on-the-job training
(4) Commonality of the skills and knowledge of individual jobs with the other jobs in the cluster
(5) The capability of being implemented in a school-based program

Job and task analysis procedures are used to identify instructional content and to group jobs into clusters which share common characteristics. Typical clusters, for example, might include the following:

(1) Electro-mechanical installation and repair
- business machine service
- home appliance service
- radio and television service
- air conditioning and refrigeration service

(2) Metal forming and fabrication
- welder
- machinist
- sheet metal worker
- assembler

One outcome of programs based on the cluster concept is that participants have a broad, basic background which can form the foundation for further training. In addition, trainees have increased mobility within occupational areas, facilitated by the transferable skills developed.

Core Program

The core program is based on the idea that there are skills common to a number of related technologies (Schill & Arnold, 1965). These skills can be grouped, forming a basic instructional core. Subsequent skills, common to fewer technologies, are also identified, forming a less common core, and so on. The result is that a curriculum can be organized around skills which have the greatest common application, those that have the next evident application, and eventually, those that are most relevant to only one occupational field or job.

Standard job and task analysis procedures are initially used to identify the skills in each technological area. The skills are sorted on the basis that they are closely related, somewhat related, or totally unrelated to the technology. Common skills are identified across different technologies.

A major advantage of the core program is economy. Common skills can be taught in large instructional groups using the same equipment and machinery. Trainees eventually specialize in one area, but this specialized training includes only a limited number of skills not common to other technologies. Specialized skills also can be acquired through on-the-job training or through other combinations of training. However, specialized training is required prior to, or at the time of, employment.

Besides economy of instruction, core programs offer greater occupational flexibility. First, the trainee can delay a specific occupational choice until after core skills are learned. Choices can then be narrowed to one or two technologies, and then to one. The trainee also has the potential to shift to other technologies with only limited training required. In sum, entry-level training is provided, but the foundation is also established to address a number of employment opportunities and to build additional competencies. The flexibility of planning is increased, and the negative effects of inaccurate labor market forecasts reduced.

The foregoing has been a brief review of a number of different program design options. The various content components of a program are the building blocks with which the instructional designer works. Combinations of academic knowledge, technical skills, and affective behaviors are used to achieve particular program designs. The kinds and range of skills selected, the scope of coverage, and the level of proficiency achieved all relate to the instructional designer's particular purpose.

While the overall purpose of VET is job preparation, programs can range from the narrowly conceived and highly specific, designed for immediate job placement, to the more general, intended to provide broad occupational preparation.

HOW MUCH TO TEACH

Perhaps the most common error made when designing VET courses and programs is the inclusion of too many instructional tasks. This error is particularly common when the actual job has not been adequately analyzed.

Selecting Content

The matrix in Figure 4 provides one way to conceptualize content selection, and illustrates the importance of selecting and prioritizing tasks.

Jobs are made up of many tasks, some of which all employees need to know how to perform. These tasks comprise primary job tasks. The ability to perform primary tasks means that the individual will be successful on the job. There are also secondary tasks, which are not basic to the job. Secondary tasks are usually more specialized and are outside

	Primary tasks	Secondary tasks
Formal instruction required	A	C
Taught on the job	B	D

FIGURE 4 Task classification matrix.

of the normal range of daily work activity. They are assigned on the basis of prior experience, seniority, or demonstrated ability to perform. The individual can obtain and hold a job without being proficient in the skills needed for secondary tasks.

There is also a distinction between tasks which require formal (school-based) instruction and those that can be learned on the job. Some tasks are better mastered on the job and need little or no formal instruction prior to job placement. A specialized piece of equipment may be involved, or the employer may prefer to teach the task only after the novice has demonstrated the ability to perform primary tasks. Of course, the opposite may also be true. Some job tasks must be taught prior to job placement, for example, a primary task which the employer cannot take the time to teach. Some tasks cannot feasibly be taught on the job because they require extensive periods of close supervision or are needed immediately upon job placement.

In any case, employers do not generally expect new employees to be able to perform all of the tasks associated with a job. Legere (1978), for example, suggests that the typical range of work activity is limited to between six and nine different skill clusters.

The simple matrix classification scheme shown in Figure 4 provides a way to establish instructional priorities. Tasks in category A must be given primary instructional emphasis. They are fundamental to job performance and cannot be learned on the job. These tasks should form the basic core of the instructional program. Tasks included in category B are less important to teach since they can be learned on the job. However, trainees should become familiar with these tasks in order to know what to expect on the job; they are, after all, primary tasks. More important, trainees need to master the prerequisite skills required to learn tasks on the job. If a task requires computation, for example, then it is essential that the trainee know how to compute.

Category C tasks are optional. They should not be taught until the trainee has learned the tasks included in category A and the prerequisite skills associated with category B. Perhaps all that is needed is to inform the trainee that category C and D tasks are a part of the job functions of some employees.

Some skills need to be formally taught and some do not. By making a judicious selection of instructional content, instructional time can be considerably reduced, and, equally important, resources and time can be concentrated on the knowledge and skills which are most essential for students to learn.

Establishing Instructional Priorities

It is useful, then, to view the instructional design process as concerned with two essential conditions. One is the selection from the total universe of potential skills only those which require formal instruction, thus reducing the scope of instruction. All instructional programs must select content. What is important is that this be done objectively and systematically, resulting in high content validity. As suggested previously, clearly establishing the program purpose is the first, and most crucial, step.

The second condition is the identification of instructional priorities. Not all content needs to be taught to the same level of mastery. As the simple matrix in Figure 4 illustrates, familiarization is sufficient for some tasks, while for others a high proficiency level is desirable.

In general, tasks which are (a) critical to job performance, (b) performed immediately at the time of placement, and (c) not easily mastered on the job should be taught to high-performance levels. Those tasks which can be taught on the job, are less critical to performance, and are not performed immediately require considerably less instructional emphasis. In any case, instructional priorities should be established, thereby reducing instructional time. In many programs there is considerable latitude for reducing the competency levels established for instruction.

SUMMARY AND IMPLICATIONS

There is a direct relationship between content selection and the quality and cost of instruction. An instructional program may be efficiently organized and taught but include an excessive amount of unimportant content. Quality can be improved and cost reduced by judiciously selecting content based on a systematic analysis of job requirements. Then again, there is a considerable difference between what has to be formally taught and the universe of job skills in an occupational field. Some skills can be taught as well or better and at less cost on the job.

Instructional design should be conceived as a systematic, ongoing process which makes use of job and task analysis procedures and establishes functional links with employment. But the potential "skill mix" of instruction should also be broadly conceived and include basic academic skills, special applications of academic skills, specific job skills, and affective skills when appropriate to the purpose or function of instruction. In general, formal programs should concentrate on occupation-specific training in contrast to job-specific training, which can best be carried out in workplace-based forms of preparation. Formal training programs should emphasize the development of basic and cognitive skills. High levels of psychomotor skill development can best be attained on the job.

Many skills do not have to be taught formally to high levels of competency. Considerable instructional time and cost can be saved by establishing minimum competency levels. Greater instructional effectiveness results because instructional time is focused on what is most essential to learn.

APPENDIX A*

Examples of Generic Skills

Mathematics

Read, write, and count whole numbers; add and subtract whole numbers; multiply and divide whole numbers; solve word problems with whole numbers; round off whole numbers; read and write fractions; add and subtract fractions; multiply and divide fractions; solve word problems with fractions; compute dollars and cents; read and write decimals;

*Adapted from "The Development of Generalizable Skills Instruments for Identifying the Functional Learning Ability of Students in Vocational Education Programs," by J. P. Greenan, 1982, *Journal of Industrial Teacher Education*, 19, pp. 19–36.

round off decimals; multiply and divide decimals; add and subtract decimals; solve word problems with decimals; read and write percents; compute percentages; convert fractions to decimals, percents to fractions, fractions to percents, percents to decimals, and decimals to percents; solve problems using correct order of operations.

Communication

Understand the meaning of words in sentences; use books to find information; understand spoken communication; interpret or give your explanation to spoken communication; pronounce words correctly; use good word choice; talk fluently; organize ideas while speaking; ask and answer the six "w" questions given a reading or speaking situation (what, where, why, when, who, and which); give directions or information; use the telephone by finding names and telephone numbers in a telephone directory and yellow pages, and make local and long distance calls; understand the word-for-word meaning in a reading passage; interpret or give your meaning to a reading passage; read short notes, memos, and letters; read charts and tables; read manuals; write statements or phrases on forms; write sentences on forms; write sentences; write memos; take notes.

Interpersonal Relations

Use eye contact, attentive posture, gestures, while listening and speaking, and appear relaxed; identify behaviors which prevent good verbal communication; understand the main idea in another's communication; distinguish between fact and opinion in another's questions; restate what was said in a conversation; confirm one's own understanding of a conversation; pay attention to others' non-verbal cues; appear self-confident while communicating with others; maintain task-focused conversation; state a point of view; maintain friendly conversation; join in group discussion; follow instructions or directions; give instructions or directions; demonstrate a skill; identify people's need for instruction by asking or watching their performance on the job.

Reasoning

Locate information about job tasks, materials, and equipment; locate information about job methods; locate information about the proper ordering of procedures to perform a job task; recall ideas; sort objects; estimate the time required to perform regular tasks on the job; estimate weights of various objects of different shapes, sizes, and makeup; estimate length, width, height, or distance between objects; put work duties in proper order to complete a job; set job priorities for doing work; set job goals; determine activities to reach goals; decide about ways to achieve goals; set standards to measure the activities to meet goals; set the order in which work must be done to reach a goal; determine how a work activity will assist in reaching a goal; select the materials, tools, equipment, and methods to perform job tasks; relate causes to problems in a simple work situation; identify potential problems given a specific set of facts; carefully examine possible methods to solve a simple problem situation; ask questions to identify the problem; use the senses to touch, see, smell, taste, and hear; determine important information for problem-solving; arrive at several possible information statements or descriptions of a problem; select the best statement or description of a problem; determine several possible solutions to a problem; select a possible solution to a problem from a set of alternatives; given a written plan, update or revise it using information or events that have occurred.

APPENDIX B

A Three-Part Foundation

Basic Skills: Reads, writes, performs arithmetic and mathematical operations, listens, and speaks

A. *Reading*—locates, understands, and interprets written information in prose and in documents such as manuals, graphs, and schedules

B. *Writing*—communicates thoughts, ideas, information, and messages in writing; creates documents such as letters, directions, manuals, reports, graphs, and flow charts

C. *Arithmetic/Mathematics*—performs basic computations; approaches practical problems by choosing appropriately from a variety of mathematical techniques

D. *Listening*—receives, attends to, interprets, and responds to verbal messages and other cues

E. *Speaking*—organizes ideas and communicates orally

Thinking Skills: Thinks creatively, makes decisions, solves problems, visualizes, knows how to learn, and reasons

A. *Creative Thinking*—generates new ideas

B. *Decision Making*—specifies goals and constraints; generates alternatives; considers risks; evaluates alternatives and chooses best alternative

C. *Problem Solving*—recognizes problems; devises and implements plan of action

D. *Seeing Things in the Mind's Eye*—organizes and processes symbols, pictures, graphs, objects, and other information

E. *Knowing How to Learn*—uses efficient learning techniques to acquire and apply new knowledge and skills

F. *Reasoning*—discovers a rule or principle underlying the relationship between two or more objects and applies it when solving a problem

Personal Qualities: Displays responsibility, self-esteem, sociability, self-management, integrity, and honesty

A. *Responsibility*—exerts a high level of effort and perseveres towards goal attainment

B. *Self-Esteem*—believes in own self-worth and maintains a positive view of self

C. *Sociability*—demonstrates understanding, friendliness, adaptability, empathy, and politeness in group settings

D. *Self-Management*—assesses self accurately; sets personal goals; monitors progress; exhibits self-control

E. *Integrity/Honesty*—chooses ethical courses of action

APPENDIX C

Five Competencies

Resources: Identifies, organizes, plans, and allocates resources

A. *Time*—Selects goal-relevant activities, ranks them, allocates time, and prepares and follows schedules

B. *Money*—Uses or prepares budgets, makes forecasts, keeps records, and makes adjustments to meet objectives

C. *Material and Facilities*—Acquires, stores, allocates, and uses materials or space efficiently

D. *Human Resources*—Assesses skills and distributes work accordingly, evaluates performance and provides feedback

Interpersonal: Works with others

A. *Participates as Member of a Team*—contributes to group effort

B. *Teaches Others New Skills*

C. *Serves Clients/Customers*—works to satisfy customers' expectations

D. *Exercises Leadership*—communicates ideas to justify position, persuades and convinces others, responsibly challenges existing procedures and policies

E. *Negotiates*—works toward agreements involving exchange of resources, resolves divergent interests

F. *Works with Diversity*—works well with men and women from diverse backgrounds

Information: Acquires and uses information

A. *Acquires and Evaluates Information*

B. *Organizes and Maintains Information*

C. *Interprets and Communicates Information*

D. *Uses Computers to Process Information*

Systems: Understands complex inter-relationships

A. *Understands Systems*—knows how social, organizational, and technological systems work and operates effectively with them

B. *Monitors and Corrects Performance*—distinguishes trends, predicts impacts on system operations, diagnoses deviations in systems' performance and corrects malfunctions

C. *Improves or Designs Systems*—suggests modifications to existing systems and develops new or alternative systems to improve performance

Technology: Works with a variety of technologies

A. *Selects Technology*—chooses procedures, tools, or equipment including computers and related technologies

B. *Applies Technology to Task*—understands overall intent and proper procedures for set-up and operation of equipment

C. *Maintains and Troubleshoots Equipment*—prevents, identifies, or solves problems with equipment, including computers and other technologies

REFERENCES

Engestrom, Y. (1994). *Training for change: New approach to instruction and learning in working life.* Geneva: International Labour Office.

Greenan, J. P. (1982). The development of generalizable skills instruments for identifying the functional learning ability of students in vocational educational programs. *Journal of Industrial Teacher Education, 19*(4), 19–36.

Greenan, J. P. (1983). Identification and validation of generalizable skills in vocational programs. *Journal of Vocational Education Research, 8*(3), 46–71.

Grubb, W. N., Davis, G., Lum, J., Plihal, J., & Morgaine, C. (1991). *"The cunning hand, the cultured mind": Models for integrating vocational and academic education.* Berkeley, CA: National Center for Research in Vocational Education.

Johnson, S. D. (1989). A description of expert and novice performance differences on technical troubleshooting tasks. *Journal of Industrial Teacher Education, 26*(3), 19–37.

Legere, C. L. (1978). Occupational analysis for training. *Educational Technology, 18*(4), 27–35.

Maley, D. (1975). *Cluster concept in vocational education.* Chicago: American Technical Society.

Melching, W. H., & Borcher, S. D. (1973). *Procedures for conducting task inventories.* Columbus, OH: The Center for Vocational and Technical Education.

McNeil, J. D. (1990). *Curriculum: A comprehensive introduction.* New York: Harper Collins.

Norton, R. E. (1985). *DACUM handbook.* Columbus, OH: The National Center for Research in Vocational Education.

Resnick, L. (1987). Learning in school and out. *Educational Researcher, 16*(9), 13–20.

Secretary's Commission on Achieving Necessary Skills (SCANS). (1991). *What work requires of schools.* Washington, DC: U.S. Department of Labor.

Schill, W. J., & Arnold, J. P. (1965). *Curriculum content for six technologies.* Urbana, IL: Bureau of Educational Resources, University of Illinois.

Stasz, C., McAuthor, D., Lewis, M., & Ramsey, K. (1990). *Teaching and learning generic skills for the workplace.* Berkeley, CA: National Center for Research in Vocational Education.

CHAPTER 4

Employability Skills

GREGORY C. PETTY—*The University of Tennessee*

MANY factors affect the job success of those workers prepared by vocational and technical education and training (VET) courses and programs. However, it is general employability skills (work habits, attitudes, and values), not occupational knowledge or skills, that are most frequently cited by employers as reasons for success or lack of success on the job (Yankelovich & Immerwahr, 1984). These employability skills are often perceived by instructors as important and are assumed by many to be acquired alongside psychomotor behaviors. Unfortunately for students, these skills are often interpreted differently by instructors and practitioners (Petty & Campbell, 1988).

VET instructors are challenged with how to effectively teach occupational knowledge, skills, and attitudes. Most of the literature and research has focused on the teaching of knowledge and skills, while ignoring the teaching of attitudes, probably because so little is known about the affective domain. Yet, employers and personnel directors remind instructors that it is the workers' attitudes or employability skills that are most apt to make or break their future (Naisbitt & Aburdene, 1990).

VET instructors must know the specific employability skills of the occupations they teach, and be familiar with the attitudes and values of the different cultures and backgrounds of their students. They also need to better understand components of the affective domain if they are to effectively prepare skilled workers.

This chapter focuses on employability skills required for work readiness. Particular attention is paid to affective work competencies, work habits, attitudes and values, and the work ethic. Background information on general employability skills is included to provide a sociological perspective of these skills. The impact of the economy and other issues are also discussed to reveal the myriad of factors impacting an individual's development of employability skills.

BACKGROUND INFORMATION

According to the Commission on the Skills of the American Workforce (1990), the U.S. economy has essentially been at a standstill for 20 years. Moreover, the state of the nation's economy directly affects employability, and thus, employability skills. The Commission report, *America's Choice: High Skills or Low Wages,* indicates that the United States experienced a burst of productivity in the 1960s. However, since 1973, the productivity growth rate has slowed to less than 1% per year. The report states that "it now takes three years to achieve the same productivity improvement we used to achieve in one year" (p. 14).

Mangum (1976) explains that all production of goods or services requires some combination of natural resources (raw materials), capital resources (plant and equipment), and human resources. He emphasizes that it is the latter, the human resources, that are essential to every productive activity. And the human resource differs from other factors of production because it is both means and ends. He explains that "the efforts of human beings are essential to every form of production, but any form of production has no other purpose than to enhance the welfare of some human beings" (p. 93). Being a productive worker, productivity, and employability are, therefore, inextricably related.

An employable individual (one who possesses employability skills) has many options for employment, while individuals with few employability skills have few options. This is because workers with employability skill problems often exhibit low motivation and low productivity. When a large number of workers have low motivation and low productivity, working conditions become dangerously self-fulfilling. During times of technological change, such as after the beginning of the industrial revolution, too many discouraged workers can lead to high unemployment rates, recession, or a widespread economic depression, such as the U.S. experienced in the 1920s and 30s.

Policy makers were among the first to recognize the need for training in employability skills. The Manpower Development and Training Act (MDTA) of 1962 and the Job Corps centers were among the earliest federal efforts to focus on basic employability skills training.

THE ROLE OF EDUCATION IN WORK ATTITUDES AND VALUES

In an article promoting Tech-Prep programs in public schools, Scott (1991) argues that we should realize that education in general and work-related education and training, in particular, are lifelong endeavors. He also points out that, in only one decade, a dramatic change has occurred: the factories of the 1990s are filled with microchips, fiber optics, desktop computers, and assembly-line robots requiring multi-skilled workers capable of performing a number of high-tech tasks. Those working with a variety of new technologies in new organizational structures also need employability skills to cope with the important interpersonal relationships required by self-directed/managed work teams.

Katzell's (1979) studies led to the assumption that a person's fundamental attitude toward work and their work role are central to their persona, and "who [a] person is has been defined pretty much by what he or she does for a living" (p. 36). A part of this working persona is the educational level, which can become a central focus of a person's life. Personal status is determined as much by educational accomplishments as by occupation. The attainment of a college degree is a source of personal and parental pride and a source of motivation to many people in the workforce who return to college to achieve that pinnacle of success and status.

Education plays a key role in many other aspects of our lives as well. Cherrington (1980) suggested that work attitudes and values are influenced by education (p. 15). While people have a host of motives for seeking further education, the effects of the learning experience have not been fully perceived in terms of the factors of intrinsic work attitudes, values, and habits. A person may gain more from further education than merely enhanced job opportunities. Job success and positive job attitudes (employability skills) may also be a component of the educational experience.

Salient differences in work attitudes by workers' educational level can also affect the type of training they should receive (Hall, 1990). Counselors and educators need to recognize the effects of educational levels on workforce behavior (occupational work ethic). This knowledge can be useful to more effectively counsel, advise, and deliver further education to students.

As the "baby boom" (born in the 1940s and 50s) generation moves age-wise through the workforce, they develop different expectations from life and from their workplaces (Nirenberg, 1993). Some of these changing expectations were outlined by Havighurst (1972) in his studies of adult learners and the stages they progress through as they age. Workers are demanding more from their jobs in terms of intrinsic rewards (Nirenberg, 1993) than was ever expected in the 1960s and 70s, when many of the educational and development theories used today were being proposed. Changing employability skills require that human resource development (HRD) professionals, who train and retrain America's workforce, be cognizant of the intrinsic or affective needs expressed by adults.

RATIONALE FOR THE STUDY OF EMPLOYABILITY SKILLS

VET instructors often attempt to teach employability skills alongside psychomotor skill development. However, information regarding work habits, values, and attitudes warrant a separate component of curriculum development (Hall, 1990). Assumptions that all workers should or do have the same employability skills are as superficial as saying that all occupations should be taught in the same way. Accordingly, instructors must be aware of the affective worker characteristics required for success on the job. Otherwise, they cannot be sure that affective skills are being taught and practiced.

Attributes for Success in the Workplace

According to Law (1994), the goals of a formal education are the ability to communicate, reason, solve problems, obtain and use information, and continue to learn. Other attributes listed as necessary for success in the workplace are (a) a willingness to take initiative and perform independently, (b) the ability to cooperate and work in groups, (c) competence in planning and evaluating one's own work and that of others, (d) understanding of how to work with persons from different cultures and backgrounds, and (e) the ability to make decisions. These attributes were included, using somewhat different wording, in a comprehensive report by the U.S. Secretary of Labor's Commission on Achieving Necessary Skills, known as the SCANS report (Secretary's Commission, 1991). The report identifies three skill areas which the Commission considers essential for employment success:

(1) *Basic skills*—reading, writing, mathematics (arithmetical computations and mathematical reasoning), listening, and speaking

(2) *Thinking skills*—creative thinking, making decisions, solving problems, visualizing things in the mind's eye, knowing how to learn, and reasoning

(3) *Personal qualities*—individual responsibility, as well as self-esteem, sociability, self-management, and integrity

The SCANS report further specifies that, upon graduation from high school, all potential workers should possess the ability to (a) manage resources, such as money and time; (b) work as a team (member) and negotiate; (c) acquire and use information; (d) understand complex systems; and (e) use technology.

Berryman, Knuth, and Law (1992), in their review of the SCANS report, list generic workplace skills as

(1) Identifying, organizing, planning, and allocating resources, including time, money, material, facilities, and human resources

(2) Working with others (interpersonal skills) by participating as a member of a team, teaching others new skills, serving clients as customers, exercising leadership, negotiating, and working in a heterogeneous workplace

(3) Acquiring and using information, including skills of evaluation, organization, maintenance, interpretation, communication, and computer use

(4) Understanding complex social, organizational, and technological inter-relationships (systems), and working and operating effectively with them; improving or designing them; and monitoring and correcting performance

(5) Working with a variety of technologies, including their selection, application to tasks, and maintenance and troubleshooting

The attributes identified under this heading as necessary for success in the workplace provide insight on the knowledge, skills, and attitudes required for employment. However, much of this is not new to the informed VET instructor.

Employability from a Policy Perspective

Manpower policy at the national level has traditionally focused on enhancing the employability and employment opportunities of individuals who face difficulties in job market competition (Mangum, 1976, p. 18). From a policy perspective, employability is defined as an individual's personality, motivation, skills, education, and health. The key to employability, according to policy makers, is that it must be taken into perspective with income (earned income, investment return, and transfer payments) and employment (economic development, purchasing power, and job creation) (Mangum, 1976).

The beliefs of policy experts with regard to human resource development are that public expenditure on behalf of an individual can significantly increase that individual's employability and productivity. These increases can improve a standard of living through rising income and result in a payback of the training investment.

Other rewards can come from the development of potential talents and skills (employability factors). Still others result from the self-satisfaction and increased self-worth that naturally flow from receiving positive recognition from others. The whole hierarchy of human needs—subsistence, security, social recognition and belonging, self-esteem, and self-actualization—is enhanced (Maslow, 1954).

Forces Affecting Change

American workers, businesses, and industries are facing changes as dramatic as the industrial revolution. The challenge for VET instructors is to both deal with technological shifts and help workers cope with the personal and cultural changes occurring in the workplace.

Demographics

The gender and age of the workforce is rapidly changing. Some futurists and sociologists forecast that there will be increasingly more women in the workplace. Already, there are fewer 18–24 year olds and a declining number of these are white males. The workforce is growing older. The average age of today's worker is 36; by the year 2000, it will be 39 (Commission on the Skills, 1990). It is expected that by the year 2005, 83% of America's new workers will be women, minorities, and immigrants (Hodgkinson, 1992). These demographic changes will forever alter the perceptions between employers and workers.

Employee Interrelationships

Compounding changing demographics in the workplace is the increased focus on team work and employee interrelationships. The whole idea of empowerment is based on the premise that people will work together toward a common goal. Members of self-directed/managed work teams need new skills to overcome barriers created by new relationships with co-workers and employers. The changing workforce composition and structure, along with other cultural and societal changes, will cause job obsolescence, requiring workers to possess more employability skills.

Work Attitudes

Katzell (1979) suggested that rapid innovations in technology have dramatically changed work roles, with significant changes in work attitudes. The redefining of women's work roles may be accomplished by associated changes in their work attitudes, as well as in the attitudes of men. Trends likely to affect work attitudes include

(1) Revised definitions of success, with less emphasis on material achievement and more on personal fulfillment
(2) More flexibility and equal division of work roles between the sexes
(3) Greater social acceptance of ethnic minorities
(4) Growing conviction that there is more to life than working (pp. 48–49)

By projecting changing patterns of behavior, values, and beliefs, the work attitudes of a population can, to some extent, be estimated. Many Americans consider "important and meaningful work" an important job factor. The feeling of contributing to meaningful and important work helps to build positive work attitudes which, in turn, can help establish a stable and successful employment career. Studies regarding workforce cultural change (including gender) suggest that the employability skills needed to cope with these changes can be learned.

Acquiring Employability Skills

The acquisition of employability skills may offer the greatest challenge and opportunity for refinement of best practices for delivering VET. Of particular importance is the research on vocational thoughtfulness. The definition of thoughtfulness, according to Schell and Rojewski (1993), goes beyond basic academic and communication skills and encompasses critical and creative thinking, problem solving, exercising judgment, and learning new skills and knowledge throughout one's lifetime (pp. 46–47).

Schell and Rojewski (1993) contend that learning cannot be assumed to transfer from non-application to application situations. They further point out that "[learning] transfer and the situations where learning takes place are quite interrelated and not isolated easily" (p. 52). They also argue that simulated learning activities conducted in laboratories do not "automatically result in the activation (i.e., transfer) of advanced vocational skills" (p. 53). This "situated learning," they continue, is influenced greatly by the role played by subject matter experts.

Vocational thoughtfulness, therefore, describes a person's level of ability to "apply a host of advanced cognitive skills to ill-structured problems in a variety of contexts" (Schell & Rojewski, 1993, p. 55). The basis of this "vocational thoughtfulness" definition comes from the basic tenets of transfer learning, situated cognition, and expert behavior. For many people, employability skills must be learned in much the same way as cognitive and psychomotor skills.

TRANSITION TO THE WORKPLACE

"The school-work transition links three different parties (youth, schools and employers), and problems can arise from shortcomings in one or more parties, from problems of information flow between them, or from problems in their relations" (Rosenbaum, Kariya, Settersen, & Maier, 1990, p. 264). Schools may offer erroneous preparation or too little help in their graduates' job searches. Youth may either fail to learn necessary skills or have faulty work behaviors. Employers may not give youth a fair chance for full-time career jobs, or may even belittle their work ethics. While employers' needs and school curricula are constantly changing, evidently, a communication gap exists or there is inadequate incentive for action.

Employers need applicants with basic skills in such areas as reading, writing, and math. However, grades and test scores in these areas have little influence on which youth get jobs, better jobs, or higher wages. "Aptitude, class rank, and other school information have small and often insignificant effects on employment and job attainments of high school graduates who directly enter the workforce" (Rosenbaum et al., 1990, p. 269). Graduates with better grades would be assumed to be more productive and to fall into the more valuable category, thereby receiving better jobs and higher pay. It has been found, however, that class rank has little effect on wage rates two years after graduation and even less effect four years after graduation.

Separating "Knowing" from "Doing"

Many would agree that a major problem with American education is that we have too long perpetuated a system that keeps *learning for knowing* separate from *learning for doing*. America must be prepared for competitiveness in a global economy. With the fall of communism in eastern Europe and the lowering of trade barriers in the European Union, these changes point to new standards and new competition. According to Williford (1989), "[when] more than half adult Americans can't find England or France on a map and the average American MBA knows as much math as the average eighth grader in Japan, we're not yet ready to prosper in the coming international economy" (p. 7).

Workplace Skills

The world's labor markets are changing, and these changes are influencing every classroom in America. Law (1994) suggests that the nature of educators' jobs insulates them from the realities of the world of work outside their classrooms. Potential employers of today's students have real needs, and educators must respond to these needs (p. 63).

Jobs are changing, as well, and forcing a change in required workplace skills. Low-skill jobs are disappearing due to automation and third-world competition (Commission on the Skills, 1990). The American-dominated world economy was based on an industrial manufacturing model that required minimal worker control, limited worker discretion, high levels of inventory, sophisticated quality control systems, and specialized personnel. This system works best when there are few changes in products and services, production systems, and technologies.

Higher levels of skills are required for the Information Age model of the new economic environment. Integration of traditionally separate roles, the flattening of organizational hierarchies, decentralization of responsibility, and greater employee involvement at all levels are yielding a system that is more responsive, flexible, and receptive to continuous innovation. However, low-skill and low-paying service jobs, such as fast food and clerical jobs, will continue to be the primary opportunities available to many first-time employees in the foreseeable future.

For most workers, low-skill, entry-level jobs offer no opportunities to earn wages sufficient to sustain a family (Berryman, Knuth, & Law, 1992). Consequently, workers who desire to earn higher wages must acquire the skills needed for middle- and high-skill jobs. The employability skills concepts that were practiced by employment and training policy-makers in the 1970s and 80s, and that were transferable to higher-paying jobs, will not be valid for workers of the 21st century.

MEASUREMENT AND EVALUATION OF WORK COMPETENCIES

A report by Kazanas (1978) lists several components of affective work competencies necessary for VET students. Petty (1979) described a linkage of affective work competencies between the worker, VET instructor, and work supervisor. A review of these competencies reveals interesting insights into employability skills.

The Affective Work Competencies Inventory (AWCI) is an inventory of 95 indicators which describe 15 different affective work competency clusters. The inventory and clusters were developed from an exhaustive review of literature related to affective work competencies. Sixty-three affective work competencies were identified from industrial and educational literature. A panel of experts grouped the 63 competencies into the 15 clusters by similarity of their behavioral characteristics. Each of the clusters is representative of several indicators which are descriptive statements regarding work behaviors. The clusters and their behavioral characteristics are listed in Table 1.

Table 1. Clusters of the affective work competencies inventory (AWCI) and associated behavioral characteristics.

Clusters	Behavioral Characteristics
1. Ambitious	Shows great effort; aspiring; demonstrates strong desire to succeed or to achieve something
2. Cooperative Helpful	Willing to work with and/or give assistance to others
3. Adaptable Resourceful	Able to deal promptly and effectively with problems, difficulties, etc.; able to change without difficulty, so as to adapt to new or changed circumstances
4. Independent Initiative	Self-sufficient; self-reliant; originates action
5. Accurate Quality of work	Free from avoidable errors; precise and exact; displays a degree of excellence

Table 1. (continued).

Clusters	Behavioral Characteristics
6. Pleasant Friendly Cheerful	Neighborly; marked by pleasing behavior—joy, good spirits, and hope
7. Follows directions Responsive	Acts in accordance with, or reacts readily to, suggestions, instructions, and regulations
8. Careful Alert Perceptive	Watchful; cautious; wary; conscientious
9. Considerate Courteous	Has or shows regard and/or concern for others and their feelings; good manners
10. Emotionally stable Non-judgmental Poised	Not easily aroused by emotion; good sense; understanding
11. Persevering Patient Enduring Tolerant	Persistent in effort or purpose; uncomplaining
12. Neat Orderly Personal appearance Manner	Tidy; clean; well-arranged
13. Dependable Punctual Reliable Responsible	Trustworthy; on time, punctual
14. Efficient Quantity of work Achieving Speedy	Productive with a minimum of time; swift
15. Dedicated Devoted Honest Loyal Conscientious	Gives or applies attention or time to some activity or purpose; acts honorably or justly

Work Attitudes Inventory

The Work Attitudes Inventory (WAI) instrument was developed from a factor analysis of data previously collected through the AWCI. Factor analysis is a technique for identifying the smallest number of descriptive terms to explain the maximum amount of common variance in a correlation matrix. The factor analysis identified five factors that accounted for most of the variance, while using only about half of the original 95 items (Brauchle, Petty, & Morgan, 1983). The resultant WAI contained 45 variables, to be ranked on a five-point scale, and five indices or measures of work attitudes:

(1) *Ambition*—set personal job and work goals, improve self, learn new skills to advance on the job, participate in group activities

(2) *Self-control*—be tolerant, cool, stable, and positive toward others

(3) *Organization*—be clean and organized, keep supplies arranged, keep records and files in order

(4) *Enthusiasm*—work toward new goals, take pride in accomplishments, accept challenging assignments, complete the job, adjust to change

(5) *Conscientiousness*—be diligent, mind your own business, be a self-starter, stick by your word, be on time

The extraction of the five factors was based on a study involving 798 workers, 567 industrial supervisors, and 120 VET instructors. The resulting 45 of the original 95 items accounted for 76.3% of the total variance and were grouped on the five factors listed above. The instrument was highly reliable and the respondents' selections loaded on these five factors.

This study offers some insight into important factors of employability. The importance of these factors is verified by other studies of industrial personnel managers and training directors (Cherrington, 1980; Naisbitt & Aburdene, 1990; Yankelovich & Immerwahr, 1984). Incorporating these components of job success could improve the employability of vocational education program graduates.

Work Ethic

Another instrument, the Occupational Work Ethic Inventory (OWEI), was used to measure work ethic, a component of employability skills. It was developed as part of a research project at the University of Tennessee (Petty, 1991) and was an extension of Petty's earlier work (1979) with affective work competencies and work attitudes. Items for the OWEI were selected from a list extracted from a review of literature regarding work attitudes, work values, and work habits. These items were reviewed for appropriateness by a panel of experts. The 50 descriptors selected for the final instrument were listed alphabetically and a random number table was consulted to sort the items into a random order. The OWEI subscales and descriptors are listed in Table 2.

To establish factorial validity, exploratory factor analytic procedures were used to identify the appropriate explanatory concepts. These procedures yielded an objective, statistically-based assessment of the items. Extracted factors were examined using a content analysis to find the most concise list of items representative of the data collected.

The factors identified were working well with others, striving for advancement/success, being dependable, and accepting duty/responsibility. Collectively, these factors explained 37 of the 50 items contained in the OWEI. While the ability of a short list of factors was limited in its capacity to embody the meaning of the 50 items in the OWEI, the factors developed did provide a practical focus for efforts to assess key work ethic characteristics. The 37 characteristics identified as being associated with the four factors are presented in Table 3 and are discussed in the following sections.

Table 2. Occupational work ethic inventory (OWEI) subscales and associated descriptors.

Subscales	Descriptors
Dependable	accurate, careful, dedicated, dependable, depressed,* devoted, effective, efficient, emotionally stable, honest, loyal, patient, productive, punctual, reliable, tardy*
Ambitious	ambitious, apathetic,* conscientious, enthusiastic, hard-working, independent, initiating, irresponsible,* negligent,* persevering, persistent, resourceful
Considerate	appreciative, cheerful, considerate, courteous, devious,* friendly, helpful, hostile,* likeable, modest, pleasant, rude,* selfish,* well-groomed
Cooperative	adaptable, careless,* cooperative, follows regulations, follows directions, orderly, perceptive, stubborn*

*Negative descriptors (designating undesirable behavioral characteristics).

Table 3. Four-factor solution derived from factor analysis of OWEI subscales and associated behavioral characteristics.

Factors	Behavioral Characteristics
Working well with others	friendly, courteous, pleasant, considerate, likeable, cooperative, helpful, appreciative, patient, emotionally stable, well-groomed, stubborn*
Striving for advancement/success	resourceful, productive, initiating, enthusiastic, perceptive, dedicated, persistent, efficient, ambitious, devoted, persevering, independent, orderly
Being dependable	following directions, dependable, punctual, honest
Accepting duty/responsibility	hostile,* careless,* irresponsible,* devious,* selfish,* negligent,* depressed,* tardy*

*Negative (undesirable) behavioral characteristics.

Factor 1—Working Well with Others

This factor was comprised of items related to those interpersonal qualities which facilitate good working relationships and contribute to job performance in a setting where cooperation is important. Descriptors include such characteristics as friendly, courteous, pleasant, and considerate. One negative item, stubborn, helps to clarify undesirable characteristics for this factor.

Factor 2—Striving for Advancement/Success

The characteristics identified for this factor are those which could facilitate "moving up the ladder" on a job and being dissatisfied with status-quo performance. Some of the descriptors, such as dedicated and persevering, also encompass the concept of sticking with a job situation that is not going smoothly. Other descriptors include resourceful, productive, initiating, and enthusiastic.

Factor 3—Being Dependable

This factor is made up of items which have to do with fulfilling the expectations and implicit agreement to perform certain functions at work. Their combined meaning involves meeting at least the minimum expectations for satisfactory job performance, but does not necessarily include going "beyond the call of duty."

Factor 4—Accepting Duty/Responsibility

No positive descriptive items for this factor were identified on the OWEI. All of the descriptors are negative, for example, hostile, careless, and irresponsible. Careful analysis of the items reveals that they are related to accepting job duties and responsibilities. A worker characterized by these descriptors would probably be either derelict of duty or would exhibit only conditional acceptance of the requirements of the job.

ATTAINMENT OF EMPLOYABILITY SKILLS

Studying human social development is useful in understanding employability skills. It is group expectations and the acceptance of workers' on-the-job superiors and co-workers that make up a worker's sense of what on-the-job behaviors are appropriate. These affective traits are partially learned from parents, partially from peers, and partially from school or work. However, where did it all begin?

As civilization evolved, people developed a sense of what they valued about themselves, life, and their society. The maturation of cultures and the increased complexity of interactions left people with a strong feeling of worth and a perception of what was important. The simple agrarian life of the farmer was being replaced by students of the arts, crafts, and the science of astronomy and philosophy. Occupations and professional identity began a caste system of professional hierarchy that cast a shadow of stigma on certain occupations and skills.

As reported by Kazanas (1978), work was considered a curse to the ruling classes of ancient Greece. Homer reported that the gods hated mankind and, out of spite, condemned man to toil (Mosse, 1969). Tilgher (1958) quotes Xenophon as calling work the painful price that the gods charged mankind for living. In most cases, the meaning of work in early civilizations was derived from two primary sources: social and religious (Wrenn, 1964).

The Romans, conquerors of the Greek civilization, assimilated most of the Greeks' attitudes about the arts, science, and social values into their own culture (Tilgher, 1958, 1962). Cicero, a notable Roman philosopher and statesman, found two occupations worthy of a free man: agriculture and commerce. All other pursuits, including handcraft, the work of artisans, and the crafting of material goods, were held in low esteem (Kazanas, 1978).

The early Hebrews also considered work a painful drudgery. However, while the Greeks could see no reason why man should be condemned to labor, other than at the whim of the gods, the Hebrews felt that work was necessary to expiate the original sin committed by Adam and Eve in their earthly paradise (Parker, 1971).

Primitive Christianity followed the Jewish tradition regarding work as a punishment imposed upon man by God because of man's original sin (Kazanas, 1978). However, to this negative doctrine of expiation was added one positive consideration. Not only was work essential to provide many necessities, but it was a means for accumulating enough to share with one's fellow man (Borow, 1973). Upon work, then, was reflected some of the divine light that stems from charity. Riches shared with the poor were considered to bring God's blessing upon the giver (Tilgher, 1958, 1962).

The concept of charity was carried one step further in the establishment of the Christian work ethic. To work and share the products of work with others was desirable (Kazanas, 1978). Thus, it became the duty of the Christian brotherhood to give work to the unemployed, so that no man need remain idle. A refusal to work resulted in the offender being cast out of the community for the good of both the community and the offender (Tilgher, 1958, 1962).

Early Christian leaders generally held a low opinion of physical labor. Work, as performed in the monasteries, became a means of maintaining the established social order. In the feudal system of the dark ages, most physical work was still performed by serfs (Kazanas, 1978).

Skilled artisans and craftsmen, however, suffered a different fate than did the serfs. The artisans and craftsmen were not tied to the land; therefore, they were free to sell their goods and services to the highest bidder. By keeping the processes and methods of their trade as guarded secrets, they were able to control, to an extent, commerce and the trades. Thus, greater diligence led to a degree of wealth that enabled a middle class to form (Mosse, 1969).

Formation of a middle class and wealth gradually led to the establishment of factories. Here, labor was divided so that semi-skilled individuals could perform repetitive elements of a job using apprentices. A working class was thereby initiated. With the advent of the industrial revolution and vast flooding of the metropolitan areas by the unemployed rural population, many old values (such as landowners exhibiting a degree of kindness and care) were eliminated (Kazanas, 1978). With the money economy, factory lords found a way to get around the traditional burden of responsibility through the payment of wages (Bennett, 1926).

The transition of serfs to workers was complete. A lower class was created, composed largely of laborers, a middle class composed largely of artisans and merchants, and an upper class composed of the landed and titled nobility and the wealthy. This, in itself, was an innovation, in that a person with luck and diligence could move, by virtue of accruing wealth, from the lowest class to the middle or upper class (Kazanas, 1978). This transition from feudal to industrial society, however, required several centuries (Bennett, 1926).

The Protestant movement of Calvinism adopted a new attitude toward work. Calvinism held that it was the will of God for all, including the rich and noble, to work. In addition, none should lust after the fruits of their labor—wealth, possessions, or luxurious living. Mankind, however, was obligated to God to extract the maximum amount of wealth from his work. Therefore, the greater his profit, the more he pleased God, and vice-versa.

Although profit was originally conceived by the Calvinists as a means of promulgating ecclesiastical causes (Parker, 1971), it was soon discovered that the same principles of profit could produce great wealth and position for individuals. Non-Calvinists, in particular, were pleased with these concepts; thus, modern business began. The businessman was created from the Protestant merchant who was strong-willed, active, austere, and hard-working out of religious conviction. Idleness, luxuriousness, prodigality, and other extravagances which resulted in the softening of either the muscles or the soul were shunned. Moderation in all things was practiced (Kazanas, 1978).

Calvinism formed the basis for most other Protestant movements and also laid the foundation for the modern factory (Kazanas, 1978). Although the division of labor was not a direct result of the Protestant movement, the diligent application of man's energy, regardless of the project upon which the efforts were spent, enabled the division of labor to occur within Christian society (Tilgher, 1958, 1962).

Puritanism developed from Calvinism and evolved still further into the obligation to work. Both the Puritan and Calvinist forms of Protestantism considered it no virtue to remain satisfied with the class or occupation into which one was born (Kazanas, 1978). On the contrary, it was a holy duty to seek the greatest possible return from one's life (Parker, 1971).

The New England colonies were settled by Puritans seeking religious and commercial freedom, while the middle-Atlantic states were largely settled by Calvinists seeking religious and economic advantages. Although some colonies were founded by Catholics, most, including the southeastern states, were founded by various Protestant groups who were seeking not only wealth but freedom from persecution for their religious beliefs (Bennett, 1926).

In the western hemisphere, several conditions existed that were beneficial to the establishment and strengthening of the work ethic and employability skills which became a powerful concept in society. First, strong feelings regarding the benefits of diligent work and prosperity were ingrained in both the moral and religious fiber of the colonists. Secondly, the colonies were largely peopled by those who had everything to gain and comparatively little to lose. A third factor was the vast opportunity in land and natural resources that enabled almost anyone to succeed who was willing to put forth the effort. Even the concept of indentured servitude was but a postponement of the probability of ultimate success. It provided a means of getting to the land where success was so probable (Barlow, 1967).

Another factor entered into the evolving work ethic: education and training (Kazanas, 1978). Due in part to the availability of wealth, established Protestant ethics, ingrained social attitudes, regard for diligent work, and the social mobility possible in a culture without distinct and traditional cultural castes, many colonists wished better education and training for their sons and daughters. Colleges, universities, mechanics institutes, and other forms of formal education appeared throughout the colonies. Education and wealth were the means to social ascension (Barlow, 1967). This upward mobility was not possible in other societies, as it was in America. Therefore, the American working class achieved what no other working class in history had achieved. The working class became the middle class and the more they worked, the greater their success.

SUMMARY

Attainment of employability skills must occur in the educational and training environment. Part of this environment—the interactions between individuals—is beyond the control of human resource development specialists. But many of the skills can be modified or taught. Employability skills are simply too complex to be acquired only in the home or from peers. Today's technological society demands skills which are sophisticated, from all members of the workforce. Workers need help in acquiring these skills. The same behaviors that impress or make friends on the playground can result in dismissal from a job.

Additional demands from a more diverse workplace are also increasing workers' stress. To be effective in the workplace today, workers must interact effectively with individuals of all races, cultures, and ethnic backgrounds, and with men and women working in roles that as recently as a decade ago were stereotypically male or female. The pressures to conform are too great to be left to chance. Vocational and technical educators must react proactively to these changes.

This chapter has offered rationale for employability skills. A potpourri of employability skills has been reviewed and listed. While there is no "perfect" list of employability skills for all occupations, knowledge of what does exist and seeking to reveal additional information will enrich the learning environment for future generations.

REFERENCES

Barlow, M. L. (1967). *History of industrial education in the United States.* Peoria, IL: Charles A. Bennett.

Bennett, C. E. (1926). *History of manual and industrial education to 1870 (Vol. 1).* Peoria, IL: Charles A. Bennett.

Berryman, S., Knuth, R. A., & Law, C. J. (1992). *Preparing students for work in the 21st century.* Oak Brook, IL: North Central Regional Educational Laboratory.

Borow, H. (1973, January). Shifting postures toward work: A tracing. *American Vocational Journal, 48*(1), 28–29, 108.

Brauchle, P. E., Petty, G. C., & Morgan, K. R. (1983). The factorial validity of the affective work competencies inventory. *Educational and Psychological Measurements, 43,* 190–194.

Cherrington, D. J. (1980). *The work ethic: Working values and values that work.* New York: AMACOM.

Commission on the Skills of the American Workforce. (1990). *America's choice: High skills or low wages.* Rochester, NY: National Center on Education and the Economy.

Hall, G. S. (1990). Work attitudes of traditional and non-traditional technical community college students. Unpublished master's thesis, The University of Tennessee, Knoxville.

Havighurst, R. J. (1972). Developmental tasks and education. New York: Longman.

Hodgkinson, H. L. (1992). *A demographic look at tomorrow.* Washington, DC.: Institute for Educational Leadership, Center for Demographic Policy.

Katzell, R. A. (1979). Changing attitudes toward work. In C. Kerr & J. M. Rosow (Eds.), *Work in America: The decade ahead* (pp. 35–57). New York: Litton Education.

Kazanas, H. C. (1978). *Affective work competencies for vocational education* (Information series No. 138). Columbus: The Ohio State University, National Center for Research in Vocational Education (ERIC Document Reproduction Service No. ED 166 420).

Law, C. J., Jr. (1994). *Tech prep education.* Lancaster, PA: Technomic Publishing Co., Inc.

Mangum, G. L. (1976). *Employability, employment, and income.* Salt Lake City, UT: Olympus.

Maslow, A. H. (1954). *Motivation and personality.* New York: Harper & Row.

Mosse, C. (1969). *The ancient world at work* (J. Lloyd, Trans.). London: Chatto and Windus.

Naisbitt, J., & Aburdene, P. (1990). *Megatrends 2000.* New York: Morrow.

Nirenberg, J. (1993). *The living organization.* New York: Irwin.

Parker, S. (1971). *The future of work and leisure.* New York: Praeger.

Petty, G. C. (1979). Affective work competencies of workers, supervisors, and vocational educators (Doctoral dissertation, University of Missouri, Columbia, 1978). *Dissertation Abstracts International, 39,* 5992A.

Petty, G. C. (1991). *Development of the occupational work ethic inventory.* Unpublished manuscript, The University of Tennessee, Knoxville.

Petty, G. C., & Campbell, C. P. (1988). Work attitudes of teachers and practitioners in health occupations. *Journal of Industrial Teacher Education, 25*(3), 56–65.

Rosenbaum, J. E., Kariya, T. Settersen, R., & Maier, T. (1990). Market and network theories of the transition from high school to work: Their application to societies. *Annual Review of Sociology, 16,* 263–293.

Schell, J. W., & Rojewski, J. W. (1993). Toward vocational thoughtfulness: An emerging program of research. *Journal of Industrial Teacher Education, 30*(2), 44–64.

Scott, R. (1991). Making the case for tech prep. *Vocational Education Journal, 66*(2), 22–23, 63.

Secretary's Commission on Achieving Necessary Skills. (1991). *What work requires of schools: A SCANS report for America 2000.* Washington, DC: U.S. Department of Labor.

Tilgher, A. (1958). *Homo faber: Work through the ages* (D. C. Fisher, Trans.). Chicago: Henry Regnery.

Tilgher, A. (1962). Work through the ages. In S. Nosow & W. H. Form (Ed.), *Man, work and society.* New York: Basic Books.

Williford, L. (1989, October). Leadership seminar 1989: Workforce 2000. *Proceedings of the American Association of Community and Junior Colleges' and St. Petersburg Junior College's Annual Leadership Seminar* (ERIC Document Reproduction Service No. ED 341 408).

Wrenn, C. G. (1964). Human values and work in American life. *Man in a world at work* (H. Borow, Ed.). Boston: Houghton Mifflin.

Yankelovich, D., & Immerwahr, J. (1984). Putting the work ethic to work. *Society, 21*(2), 58–76.

CHAPTER 5

How Young Adults Learn: Theory and Practice

PAUL A. BOTT—*California State University–Long Beach*

THOUSANDS of years of organized teaching have taught us a number of things about how people learn. We have learned, for example, that what we know about our students dictates how we teach them. Over time, each bit of this knowledge has been verified through research and practice. We now consider much of what we know to be facts, or principles of learning.

This chapter is devoted to an explanation of (a) the principles of learning as they apply to young adult learners, with practical methods for applying these principles; (b) learning styles which are common to young adults; (c) teaching styles which are effective with young adults; and (d) how to create an effective learning environment for young adults.

PRINCIPLES OF LEARNING

Learning is an active and continuous process. We see that learning is occurring or has taken place in students by observing changes in their behavior and the different ways they demonstrate growth of knowledge. When teaching, it is important to remember the active and continuous nature of learning. Learning is facilitated by repeatedly checking on student progress through the use of quizzes, tests, oral questions, and observation of skill development.

Learning styles and rates vary from one student to the next. For example, some students learn better by reading than they do by listening; and some learn faster than others, even among those who learn best using the same style. It is not uncommon to have five or six types of learners in a single class. It is the instructor's job to determine the students' different learning styles and develop teaching strategies that will best help each student to realize his or her potential. This principle will be discussed at greater length in a later section of this chapter.

153

Readiness

Learning depends upon students' readiness to do so. This includes their emotional state, abilities, and motivation or desire to learn. A major portion of the instructor's job is to spark a desire to learn or to enhance an existing desire. This is done by emphasizing the meaningfulness of the subject, exhibiting a sincere enthusiasm for the subject, and by providing incentives to learn. It is important for instructors to know what students want and need out of life and be able to connect this with the learning experiences.

Everyone loves success. Another way to get students ready to learn is to provide them with the opportunity to succeed, and to do so as early as possible. This can be done by having the students produce a simple, usable or "fun" device, or leading them through the solution of a common problem. When applied to teaching, providing opportunity for student success means that learning takes place more effectively in situations where students find satisfaction.

Individuals learn best when they are ready to learn, and they learn little if they see no reason for learning. Getting students ready to learn is usually the instructor's responsibility. If students have a strong purpose, a clear objective, and a well-fixed reason for learning something, they make more progress than if they lack motivation. In addition, student performance is improved and students are more motivated to learn when the instructor's expectations are made clear. When standards are set, student performance tends to rise to the established level, so high expectations lead to a high quality of learning.

Readiness implies a degree of single-mindedness and eagerness. When students are ready to learn, they meet the instructor at least halfway, which simplifies the job considerably. Under certain circumstances, the instructor can do little, if anything, to inspire in students a readiness to learn. If outside responsibilities, interests, or worries weigh too heavily on their minds, if their schedules are overcrowded, or if their personal problems seem unsolvable, students may have little interest in learning. In these situations, instructors have a responsibility to do what they can to provide students with possible resolutions or other options, such as by referrals to agencies that can help them.

Life Experiences

Learning is also influenced by the life experiences of the learner. Imagine trying to teach someone how to tie different knots by referring to tying a shoelace. If the student had never tied a shoelace, the reference would be meaningless. Instructors seldom encounter such extremes, but the point is that some knowledge of the students' backgrounds and past experiences is helpful. Helping students to recognize the similarities and differences between their past experiences and present situation helps smooth the transfer of learning from one situation to another. In addition, relating what is being learned to what students already know makes the new knowledge more personal, or relevant to the students.

Application

Learning is more effective when there is immediate application of what is being taught. Students should be active in terms of thinking, writing, discussing, or problem-solving, as soon as possible after information is presented. No lesson is complete without the application step. Whenever appropriate, the instructor should plan "doing" activities such as practical exercises, return demonstrations, case studies, or group discussions. Application of knowledge facilitates both the reinforcement of skills or knowledge and its retention. Without application or a specific context for learning, much of what an instructor tries to convey may get filtered out.

An important point to remember is that students, particularly those lacking a great amount of life experience, will not transfer learning from one situation to another without assistance. They will not connect what they have learned in one setting to similar situations. Students must be taught, generally just by showing them, how to make the connections to other applications and to use the learning in future situations. If the instructor knows something about the students' background and plans for the future, it is easier to develop relevant applications.

Knowledge of Progress

Another principle is that learning is facilitated when learners have knowledge of their progress toward a goal. Application of this principle serves two important functions: (a) It provides students with a sense of direction, and (b) what students have learned is reinforced by their knowledge of success. The same difficulty some learners have in making connections applies to their need to have knowledge of their progress as well. Students can be doing everything well, but be frustrated because they do not realize that they are doing well. High frustration levels lead to learning difficulties.

Determining the degree of progress toward a goal does not always mean testing students, but it can be a starting point. Testing may consist of regular quizzes over material covered or observation of performance using a checklist. Tests, quizzes, or observations should be designed to determine what the students know—not what they don't know—and results should be shared with the students as soon as possible.

Another related principle is that learning is influenced by the learners' perception of themselves and the situation they are in. Everything the instructor can do to help the students succeed will enhance their self-image and make them more comfortable in learning. Each positive experience builds on the last, creating an ever-expanding fund of knowledge.

Repetition

The adage, "Practice makes perfect," conveys the main idea behind the principle of repetition. For learning to take place, the instructor should provide a sufficient number of exposures to the subject material. Each point made during a class should be summarized before proceeding to the next. Students should be provided multiple opportunities to practice their newly learned skills. Remember, a concept or skill important enough to be taught will surely require practice to be mastered.

This principle also assures us that those things often repeated are best remembered. It is the reason that instructors have students practice and drill in order to learn new skills and acquire new knowledge. The human memory is not infallible. The mind can rarely retain, evaluate, and apply new concepts or practices after only one exposure. Students learn by applying what they have been told and shown. Every time practice occurs, learning continues and is reinforced. The instructor must provide opportunities for students to practice or repeat, and they must see that this process is directed toward a goal. It is also important to note that a great amount of learning occurs through imitation. The unconscious actions of an instructor often convey powerful, but unintended, lessons to the students.

If It Is Pleasant, We Will Remember It

This principle is based on what we know about a learner's emotional reaction to new material. It states that learning is strengthened when it is accompanied by a pleasant or satisfying feeling. The corollary is that learning is weakened when it is associated with an unpleasant feeling.

Any experience that produces feelings of defeat, frustration, anger, confusion, or futility is unpleasant for the student. If, for example, an instructor attempts to teach a complex procedure during the first class, students are likely to feel inferior and be dissatisfied because, without a sound basis in the subject, they will have great difficulty even following the lesson.

Instructors should be cautious. Impressing students with the difficulty of a problem, technique, or job task can make teaching difficult. Usually it is better for the instructor to tell students that a problem or task, although difficult, is within their capacity to understand or perform, and that an instructor will be with them throughout the process to facilitate their learning. Whatever the learning situation, it should contain elements that positively affect the students and give them a feeling of satisfaction.

Primacy

Primacy, the state of being first, often creates a strong, almost unshakable, impression. For the instructor, this means that new material must be taught right the first time. For the student, it means that learning must be right the first time. "Unlearning" and "unteaching" are much more difficult than learning and teaching correctly the first time. If, for example, a student learns a faulty technique for performing a task, teaching the correct technique will be more difficult because the student already has established a strong sense of how to perform (although that way is incorrect). Every student's learning process should be started correctly. The first experience should be positive and functional and should lay the foundation for all that is to follow.

Intensity

A vivid, dramatic, or exciting learning experience teaches more than a routine or boring experience. A student is likely to gain greater understanding of job skills by performing them than from merely reading about them. The principle of intensity, then, implies that students learn more from the real thing than from a substitute. The classroom does impose limitations on the amount of realism that can be brought into teaching. Consequently, the instructor should use imagination in approaching reality as closely as possible. Mock-ups, models, simulators, and other manipulative aids, as well as slides, films, charts, posters, photographs, computer animations, and other audiovisual media add vividness to instruction.

Recency

Those things most recently learned are the best remembered. Conversely, the further a student is removed in time from a learned fact or understanding, the more difficult it is to remember. It is easy, for example, to recall a telephone number used a few moments earlier, but usually impossible to remember it a week later. Instructors recognize the principle of recency when they carefully plan a summary for a lesson, a laboratory period, or a post-lesson critique. The instructor repeats, restates, or reemphasizes important points at the end of a lesson to make sure that the student remembers them. The principle of recency often affects the relative positions of lectures within a course of instruction.

All Students Can Learn

All students, no matter what their background, can learn and succeed. We already know that students learn in different ways and by using different styles; consequently, not all students will learn what is taught in the same way or on the same day. This means that, for every lesson to be taught or point to be made in the classroom, the instructor should have several different ways of presenting the material and insuring its application. A lesson does not end simply because the instructor thinks it is finished and does not bring the lesson plan or materials to a later class. Instructors must be prepared to reteach the same lesson at different times and in different ways as the students' needs call for it.

LEARNING STYLES

A detailed examination of learning and teaching styles is beyond the scope of this chapter, but a few of the more common styles are briefly described in the following paragraphs.

Sensory Learners

Sensory learners rely on one or more of their senses for the meaningful formation of ideas. The *sensory specialist* relies primarily on one sense, such as the visual, while the *sensory generalist* uses several or all of the senses to gather information and gain insight. Very few instructors have time to design instructional materials for or adapt teaching styles to each individual learner; therefore, it is important to incorporate as many of the senses into each learning experience as possible. Put into practice the principle of learning regarding intensity.

Intuitive Learners

Intuitive learners are able to take advantage of sudden insights, unexplained leaps in thought, and generalizations to master concepts and ideas. Their learning process does not follow what is considered "traditional" logic, or any step-by-step sequence. Intuitive learners tend to work faster than others and to make more wild guesses. In the process, they often lose or fail to grasp the evidence that led them to the answer. Instructors can best help intuitive learners by assisting them, through questioning, to retrace their thinking and to specify the evidence that they used to reach a conclusion.

Incremental Learners

For many years, it was thought that all people learned best in a step-by-step fashion, systematically adding information, like the pieces of a puzzle, to gain larger understandings. Many people do learn this way, and a good practice in teaching is to start with small, simple steps and proceed to larger, more complex operations. One needs only to recall how arithmetic was learned, progressing from simple to more complex addition, then on through subtraction, multiplication, and on to higher mathematics. An error commonly made by vocational and technical instructors is to assume that, because they are experts in their subject matter, their students will become experts in one quantum leap. In reality, most students learn an occupation in incremental steps, although some take larger steps than others. Some students, especially those lacking large measures of self-confidence, tend to be lock-step, by-the-number, incremental learners. Those students need to be encouraged, as they gain confidence through success, to try to take larger steps without consulting the instructor. The various types of instruction sheets can serve as road maps for such students.

Emotionally Involved Learners

Different students have varying levels of emotional involvement in the process of learning, ranging between those who are emotionally involved and those who are emotionally neutral. Emotionally involved students obviously enjoy learning; they thrive on open, friendly discussions of ideas. These learners give and receive criticism of their work in non-judgmental ways. They are the students with whom the instructor can joke about their mistakes, and the jokes become a learning experience, not a put-down. On the other end of the emotional spectrum are the emotionally neutral learners. These learners might best be characterized as more comfortable in an "intellectual" environment. Students who are emotionally neutral learners may be distracted at best, or threatened at worst, in an emotion-laden classroom.

Explicitly Structured Learners

We know from the principles of learning that students learn best when they know what is expected of them. The explicitly structured learner needs to have all goals, lessons, activities, assignments, and tests laid out for them to see and agree to. They need to be provided with clear descriptors of acceptable and unacceptable behavior and performance on classwork. These are the students who, despite their instructor's repeated admonitions, continue to ask detailed questions about assignments—how many pages are needed, whether it should be double-spaced, which sources are acceptable, and so on. Explicitly structured learners tend to be, for a myriad of reasons, somewhat insecure in a learning environment. With patience and a string of successes, they can generally be brought into a more open style of learning.

Eclectic Learners

Eclectic learners are heaven's gift to instructors. They can shift between learning styles with little notice. The period between classes in most secondary schools is about 5 minutes, and these students adapt easily to the different teaching styles of their various instructors. Eclectic learners succeed regardless of teaching style, and generally are the students who make it through school with a minimum of trouble. While such students are generally not harmed, they are often not helped to realize their full potential because their individual best learning styles are not addressed.

Determining Learning Styles

Without extensive psychological testing, it is difficult to accurately assess students' learning styles. Since such assessment is beyond the ability of most schools, it becomes the instructor's responsibility to determine, in the context of the course or program, each individual student's dominant learning style. Instructors do this by paying close attention to the reactions of the students, while instruction is proceeding and while students are engaged in observable learning activities.

Everyone knows that it is important for instructors to maintain eye contact. However, few think of why it is important and what it really means. Drivers, motorcyclists, and bicyclists all share city streets, usually without a mishap. Drivers and cyclists both gauge their actions by making eye contact with other drivers and cyclists. Words are not spoken, and gestures are not usually made; yet the parties seem to know what the other drivers/cyclists will do next.

The same process can and does work well in the classroom as instructors teach and students learn. All but the most self-absorbed instructors can see from the expressions on students' faces whether they are learning at an optimum rate. When eye contact is met with quizzical expressions or glazed eyes, the instructor needs to shift to a different method of teaching. If, for example, an instructor is lecturing, without visual aids, and students in the class appear uncomfortable with what is going on, it may be wise to augment the lecture by adding audiovisual media. Using anecdotes or clear examples may also help students understand. In addition, a follow-along set of notes can be provided to free students from the need to write while listening.

In short, instructors ascertain student learning styles by being completely involved in the instructional process and aware of students' reactions. Through this awareness, instructors gain a somewhat accurate sense of the students' learning styles. Teaching methods and media which attend to these styles can then be selected and used.

TEACHING STYLES

Just as there are numerous learning styles, there are numerous teaching styles as well. It is a fact that instructors often teach the way they were taught, despite the obvious disparity between their own learning style and the style of the instructors they had. The corollary to the learning style is the teaching style, and they roughly parallel each other.

Student-Centered Teaching

The student-centered instructor is prone to allow students to pursue whatever they choose by virtue of their interests. A good example of a situation where this style can be used to advantage is the advanced seminar, where students have a deep and firm knowledge base upon which to build through discussion and research. Students who have little maturity and knowledge of a subject may have difficulty succeeding in such an environment, and it, thus, has little utility in a secondary school vocational and technical education or training course.

Task-Oriented Teaching

Task-oriented instructors know what is needed and what they want to teach, and devise ways of attaining their goals. They assign specific activities that students complete en route to the goal. They employ a precise, orderly system of accounting for grades, points earned, absences, and each student's concurrence with what is going on in the course and their progress toward the performance goals.

Cooperative Teaching

Cooperative, in this sense, does not mean easy to get along with. Instead, these instructors plan instruction and learning activities with their students. They lend the students the benefit of their experiences and guide the learning, without giving up responsibility for student progress. Learning in courses taught using this style tends to be quicker and more acceptable to the students because they feel ownership of the subject and the way they learn it.

Subject-Centered Teaching

Subject-centered instructors might best be described as "bean counters." Their focus is on covering the subject to the exclusion of everything else, including the students' needs and feelings. Little learning takes place under such conditions, but the instructors feel good because the subject got covered.

Learning-Centered Teaching

Learning-centered instructors have equal concern for getting the subject covered and for doing it while attending to the needs of the students. These instructors adopt elements of several teaching styles, adapting them to their classes and students as appropriate. Priorities include helping the students learn in as many ways as possible and to the greatest extent possible.

Determining Personal Teaching Styles

Instructors need to be aware of their personal learning and teaching styles. A self-assessment of capabilities and style can be conducted by audiotaping class sessions. Listening critically to the tape can reveal subtleties of voice or inflection that may aid some students and impede others. Once the instructor has listened to the audiotaped lessons and used them to improve instruction, the next step is to videotape lessons and repeat the self-assessment/improvement procedure. The video camera should be placed in the classroom so as to capture the facial expressions of as many students as possible. The final steps are to seek feedback from colleagues and supervisors and incorporate their feedback into the improvement of instruction.

THE LEARNING ENVIRONMENT

Perhaps the instructor's greatest challenge is taking what they know about how people learn, relating that to what they know about how to teach, and then combining all of that knowledge to create an environment that optimizes learning. Instructors would do well to take the Boy Scouts' advice—be prepared. Good teaching and learning do not just happen; they are a result of hard work and perseverance.

Being Prepared

The first step in creating an effective learning environment is to do one's homework. Instructors need to know as much about the subject and the students to be taught as they can, in order to design an environment that will lead to learning for those students. In addition to preparing for subject matter issues, instructors need to determine other responsibilities in the classroom and establish time priorities for dealing with them. For example, attendance-taking is almost always a mandatory task. Instructors can either conduct a time-consuming roll call, or they can devise a system that allows them to observe attendance. Alternatively, they can have students sign in, log on, or otherwise make their presence known.

Generally, after an instructor has taught a subject, student questions and problems can be anticipated. An instructor who heeds the principles of learning invests effort into developing materials that add visual impact to the subject being taught. Students are provided with a variety of ways to "see" the subject being taught.

The last, and perhaps most important, aspect of being prepared is to assume responsibility for all aspects of the classroom, the material being presented, the manner in which it is presented, and the success of students in the class.

While Teaching

Nothing can ruin the learning environment quicker than an unruly, unkempt, unresponsive classroom. One of the first steps for establishing the learning environment in a classroom is for the instructor to "take charge." A good way to do that is for the instructor to tell students in a non-threatening way that he/she is an expert in the area—and has significant knowledge and skill that can be passed on to them. It is important, especially with younger students, to clearly establish the ground rules for behavior and performance in the classroom. By the time students become teenagers, they have internalized all the ways to get around rules and know immediately if a new instructor has missed any rules. New instructors might consider asking those with more experience or school administrators for sample course syllabi that could help cover important health, safety, and behavior rules. When presenting the course "code of conduct," instructors need to maintain a firm tone, but try not to be "preachy." There must be no doubt with the students that the learning enterprise they are embarking on is a cooperative venture; however, the instructor is in charge.

If students are expected to be on time, the instructor should always be on time and should start class promptly at the appointed time. Some students would rather engage in unimportant activities than work or study. A popular pastime of many students, in their effort to keep from working, is to see how long they can keep the instructor distracted from the subject. Instructors aware of this tendency can make every effort to begin class promptly and beware of distractions.

Once the lesson has begun, a lively pace should be maintained. Students' facial expressions let the instructor know if the pace is too fast or too slow. New instructors sometimes talk so fast that they deliver a whole hour's lesson in only a few minutes, or they are aware of the tendency and overcompensate by working too slowly.

Although students learn using different styles and at different rates, it is usually necessary to teach to the "average" student. This is done with full knowledge that some students will need more help, while others are being held back by the "average" pace. Once the range of the students in the class is known, it becomes easier to develop supplemental activities for students at various levels. Faster students can take on larger or more complicated assignments or assist in the instruction, while slower students can work on alternative activities.

All instruction and instructional materials must be clear and thorough. If students are being directed to perform some specific feat, they must be provided with oral and written instructions that specify the type and amount of performance which will be considered successful. Students need knowledge of their progress, so the instructor must be ever-present, observing progress and providing assistance as needed. One often-overlooked element of successful student performance is time. If job requirements include the ability to perform an activity within a certain amount of time, students must develop that ability. If the time element is known in advance, it is simple for the instructor to periodically give the students signals regarding their progress by providing gentle reminders, not hovering over them with a stop watch.

Application and practice activities must be adjusted to meet the needs of students in the classroom. If all students develop a skill quicker than expected, the instructor must be prepared to move on to another lesson or activity. Conversely, if the students are slower than anticipated, more time and practice must be provided and future lessons adjusted or postponed accordingly. Instructors have to be flexible—it is better to be overprepared and have to eliminate something than to be underprepared and try to make substance out of nothing with a classroom full of students waiting.

One of the instructor's biggest enemies is being side-tracked. New instructors are amazed at how adept students are at asking tantalizing questions that they (the students) know will send them down some uncharted lane. One way to avoid this trap is to rephrase the student's question or remark while asking oneself what it has to do with the course content. If the answer is nothing, the student can be let down gently by the instructor remarking on the quality of the question, but deferring it to another class or time. If the question is one which is on subject, but clearly beyond the scope of the lesson, the student should be encouraged to stay after class to discuss the answer. One will be amazed at how many students with those kinds of questions forget them when they have to be answered on their own time. Questions that are on track but will be answered later in the course should be treated just that way—deferring them until later. Making a note of such questions allows the instructor to anticipate and prepare for them when teaching the same course again. Obviously, good, honest questions should be answered as forthrightly as possible. Worth remembering, however, is that many pioneers were bushwhacked by straying too far off the beaten path. Keeping a sense of purpose at all times in the classroom enables the instructor to avoid being side-tracked.

Managing student behavior is also key to establishing and maintaining an environment for effective learning. It is important to remember that overzealous students can be just as distracting and disruptive as under-zealous ones. Both groups and everyone in between have to be brought into the learning process in a fashion which will ensure every student's safety.

Two important adjectives—fair and consistent—should govern the instructor's role in establishing and maintaining a learning environment. Instructors who treat their students with fairness, consistency, respect, and dignity will themselves be treated with respect and dignity. Instructors who expect their students to perform every day, and communicate those expectations to the students, find that most do perform as expected. Students of all ages, but especially younger ones, need consistency in their lives. Behavior that is tolerated one day but punished the next leaves students with the impression that the instructor really does not know what is desired for the class. They make a game of seeing what the instructor's "mood for the day" is. Consistency is worth the effort.

Finally, it is important that an instructor be as succinct as possible. Nothing is more tiring than listening to instructors who seem to talk just to impress someone with their knowledge. Even young students know when their time is being wasted, and they quickly develop resentment. Learning each student group's level of tolerance takes only a few class sessions. Use only as many or as few words as needed to get a point across. Be as brief as possible while providing as much coverage as can be done in the allotted time.

CHAPTER 6

How to Foster High Expectation and Motivation

ROGER B. HILL—*University of Georgia*

THE fall term electronics class was fairly typical. Most of the students enrolled were taking the course because it was a requirement for their program of study. The course had a reputation for being rigorous and some students were concerned about their grades. During the first class, the instructor explained the course requirements, including student projects and assignments.

As the term progressed, two students in the class, Taylor and Kerry, began to stand out from all the others. The instructor observed that Taylor was not performing up to potential. Coming from a well-to-do family, Taylor had the best of everything—nice clothes, a new laptop computer, an elaborate townhouse apartment, and plenty of pocket money. Following the first day of class, everyone gathered around Taylor's new luxury car which still displayed a temporary tag. Taylor's parents had purchased the new car as an incentive for Taylor to go back to school. During the previous year, Taylor had dropped out of school to travel with a country music band. The music venture had been moderately successful, but had not been consistent with Taylor's parents' desires and ambitions. Now Taylor was back in school—Mom and Dad were elated.

Kerry, on the other hand, was the type of student who made instructors glad to be in the profession—interested, alert, and eager to learn all of the material in the course and more. Kerry was stretched thin, however, with two children in elementary school, a part-time job, and a spouse who worked an evening-shift job. Funds were tight—that was evident from Kerry's worn-out clothes, battered book bag, and inexpensive calculator that required extra steps to perform many of the calculations necessary for the electronics class assignments. Although Kerry had supportive parents, a job to help with family expenses had taken precedence over schooling after high school graduation. Then came marriage and a family. It was not until recently that circumstances allowed Kerry an opportunity for continued education. Now diligence and hard work

169

were being committed toward preparation for a better job, and significant sacrifices were being made by all involved.

Efforts were made to encourage all students in the electronics class to master the course content. Consideration of how the material applied to workplace tasks was encouraged through field experiences and laboratory activities. Most of the students, and especially Kerry, became excited and enthusiastic about their learning, but Taylor did not seem interested. Taylor was frequently late to class, assignments were often not completed, and lack of study was evident in Taylor's test performance. Kerry, on the other hand, was always on time, usually did problems beyond those assigned, and somehow managed to juggle studies with family obligations so that Kerry's test performance was among the best in the class.

Ultimately, it became clear that Taylor was in school because of the incentives and pressures exerted by two concerned parents. In Kerry's case, motivation came from within and, even when a weary spouse suggested that it might be better to drop out of school and go back to work full-time, school continued to be a priority. Taylor had all of the tools and resources necessary for success, while Kerry struggled to have the bare essentials. The results with respect to the electronics class, however, were at opposite ends of the spectrum.

The story of Kerry and Taylor is a familiar one to experienced instructors. Although the names vary, most practitioners in education and training settings realize that motivation cannot always be predicted based on resources or opportunity. Motivation is a complex issue involving a mixture of internal and external influences, drives, and expectations. While techniques of encouraging and facilitating high expectancy and motivation cannot guarantee success for every student, a good understanding of these constructs underlies the best practices for enhancing vocational education and training.

UNDERLYING ASSUMPTIONS

As with any construct related to the understanding of human enterprise and endeavor, certain assumptions support this discussion of high expectation and motivation. The following section provides not only a definition of the terms, but a discussion of the theoretical foundation on which efforts to influence motivation are based. Without an understanding of this foundation, appropriate measures to tap the tremendous potential of human motivation are not likely to be effectively implemented.

Motivation Explained

A key element for success in learning as well as for success at work is motivation. Related to motivation is high expectation, defined, for purposes of this chapter, as the anticipation of some future good and desirable outcome. Motivation is a state of tension that originates from some unsatisfied need which, in turn, leads a person to start and maintain action to achieve an identified goal (Bigge & Hunt, 1968; Hoy & Miskel, 1978). High expectation and motivation are collectively considered, in this chapter, to be the force behind efforts to learn and to succeed at work, instrumental to both, and strategically important to the effective instructor.

One of the earliest attempts to develop an explanation of human motivation was the work of Niccolo Machiavelli, the Italian statesman and political philosopher who lived from 1469 until 1527. In his work, *The Prince*, Machiavelli described the motives and tactics used to maintain political power (Webster, 1985). His basic premise was that people are self-motivated by individual needs and wants. This idea is a central factor in most theories of motivation which have been developed to explain human behavior.

A perceived need which results in motivation may be primarily physiological or it may be psychological in nature. In most instances, if motivation originates from a physiological need, a particular objective is being strived for as a person takes action to satisfy the need. In addition, when a particular physiological need is met, motivation tends to quickly diminish, as the drive behind it is satisfied.

Psychological needs can also be focused on specific goals, but often are more generalized and enduring. One of the better-known theoretical models for considering needs and motivation is that of Maslow (1987). While a detailed discussion of this, or other theoretical frameworks, is beyond the scope of this chapter, the range of underlying needs which drive motivation must be considered if motivation is to be effectively sustained.

Most attempts to provide an explanation for motivation include a hierarchical structure with physiological needs placed above psychological needs. Physiological needs, variously labelled primary, survival, or viscerogenic needs, include such factors as hunger, thirst, protection from physical injury, and safety from physical threats. Psychological needs, sometimes called secondary, social, or psychogenic needs, consist of things like desire for affiliation, sexual drives, striving for achievement, and aggression.

Maslow and others categorized the identifiable needs toward which people strive into a prioritized list. Higher priority needs must be met before a person is motivated by those of lesser priority. Maslow (1987) described a hierarchy with levels for physiological needs; safety and security; belonging, love, and social activity; esteem; and self-actualization or self-fulfillment needs. Other theorists have developed additional lists, but their common theme is the necessity of having basic physiological needs, such as hunger and thirst, satisfied before higher order psychological needs significantly motivate a person to action.

A key construct underlying much of the work related to motivational theory is *homeostasis*, the maintenance of equilibrium, or constant conditions, in a biological system. As applied to motivation theory, the optimal state is that of having all needs, desires, and recognized inconsistencies satisfied. People are motivated by a constant quest to reach some optimal level of stimulation. Theorists such as Sigmund Freud, Clark Hull, and Kurt Lewin, have speculated that the optimal state is no stimulation at all, while others, like Daniel Berlyne, have suggested that the optimal state for equilibrium is at some point above zero (Arkes & Garske, 1982). Regardless of the precise mechanism, people usually act to seek relief from pressures or tension when satisfaction is available.

External versus Internal Locus of Control

Two significantly different perspectives of motivation are evident among the approaches implemented in both schools and workplaces. One perspective views motivation as externally controlled. From this vantage point, behavior occurs because of some outside stimulus or pressure. An example would be when a person learns material because a test will be given covering it, and a good grade on the test is needed to pass the required course, which is, in turn, required to qualify for a particular job. Since learning is directed toward the test, once it has been passed, the reason for knowing the tested material is no longer present and retention may be brief. In the case of a task performed at work, this type of motivation is characterized by efforts which are expended at the bidding of someone else who has been empowered to meet a felt need on the part of the worker.

Another perspective of motivation holds that behavior is controlled by intrinsic factors. In this case, learning is accomplished because a person wants to know about something. The learning brings satisfaction regardless of external pressures and tends to be retained longer. Work performed because of internal motivation is driven by the resolution of tension which comes through the completion of the work, rather than from some externally controlled reward.

In most situations, external and internal motivation are not easily distinguished. Motivations for most human activities consist of a complex matrix of both external and internal influences. A young woman, for example, might select a particular career path primarily to fulfill a dream imparted to her by her father. Even though her initial choice was based on her father's influence, she now enjoys her work and feels a deep sense of accomplishment in it. Her motivation is derived from a blend of external (father) and internal (self) forces.

A more distinct separation can be drawn between external and internal motivation as a focus for a particular management style in either the learning enterprise or the workplace. For the instructor, decisions about motivation should be grounded in a conscious selection of either the behaviorist or the cognitive branch of educational psychology. The choice to align educational practice with one or the other of these groups of thought is largely dependent on basic assumptions about motivation, but it also has ramifications for other aspects relevant to the learning process. Among these are discipline, assessment, and other elements of the instructional process. Table 1 contrasts a number of differences between behaviorist and cognitive learning theories.

Although learners may, in reality, be motivated by both external and internal factors as they engage in the learning process, the cognitive approach to instruction, with its emphasis on intrinsic motivation, has several advantages. Retention of instruction delivered under this model is not dependent on the continuation of some external influence. In addition, learning which grows out of internal motivation is more likely to be accurate since the learner is monitoring the process out of personal interest rather than simply meeting requirements for some externally controlled reward.

Motivation in the Contemporary Workplace

Just as different perspectives of motivation play a significant role in determining one's approach to managing the learning enterprise, so also

Table 1. Behaviorist and cognitive learning theories contrasted.

Behaviorist	Cognitive
Motivation	
Achieved by stimuli acting on the sense organs. Instructor motivates learners by using positive or negative reinforcers to obtain correct responses.	Learners are fully motivated but instructor needs to help them clarify what their motives are. Feedback is very important.
Stimulus causes motivation.	Striving toward goals causes motivation.
Controlling. Instructor holds responsibility.	Freeing. Responsibility on learner.
Tries to motivate people.	Removes barriers.
Discipline	
External controls are used as needed to bring behavior into compliance with system standards.	Emphasis on self-discipline. Reason with learners to get good behavior. Values and personal ethics important.
Cognitive Change	
Evidenced by change in behavior. Instructor must constantly reinforce desired responses to appropriate stimuli.	Insight and understanding are stressed. Individual goals set for learners rather than one goal or standard for the entire group. Is learner centered.
Attempts to give a precise prediction of results (behavioral objectives).	Process more important than the end result.
Intelligence	
Generally believes individuals can be taught anything with proper technique and time. Environment is the most important factor.	Learners have ability to see relationships and to function in both abstract and concrete modes of thinking. Intelligence may vary in different areas for any one individual.
Teach everyone alike.	Different approaches for different people.

Table 1. (continued).

Behaviorist	Cognitive
Communication	
Alternating one-way street. Information is organized and presented by instructor. Learners give it back on tests. If not understood, instructor goes over material again.	Is a two-way street. Looks for feedback which indicates understanding. Includes value of information and how it will be employed.
Learners may be involved in the teaching process but activities are instructor-directed.	Individual expression and group discussion directly influence the teaching process.
Questions have a right or wrong answer.	Questions are often open-ended and allow for individual expression.
Creativity	
Is simply a new or different combination of stimuli already received.	Comes from within the inner mind. Generated and created new by the individual.
Relevance	
Instructor decides what is relevant. Learners are simply taught with attitude of it being something they will need later.	Emphasis on learners understanding the relevance and application of material being taught. Learner input is a factor in choice of curriculum.
Instructor plans exact schedule of events to occur during teaching.	Instructor is prepared to provide direction and resources needed by learners, but adapts instruction to learner needs as they become evident through feedback.
Teach in parts. Participants learn before doing.	Teach in context of whole. Participants learn while doing.

do beliefs about motivation shape one's management of the workplace. The trend in recent years has been for the workplace to become less dominated by autocratic models of management which assume that workers are inherently unmotivated, and increasingly characterized by participatory management styles which rely on workers being intrinsically motivated. Total Quality Management (TQM), the use of focus groups, and other forms of empowering workers at all levels of the enterprise illustrate this trend.

Underlying these management strategies are efforts to make work meaningful, to instill a feeling of responsibility for work outcomes in individuals, and to provide channels of communication regarding the quality of work performed. By providing avenues of communication and valuing that communication, people at all levels of an organization can develop a sense of ownership and pride which contribute to internal motivation. One of the challenges within this process is simultaneously considering and managing a wide range of individual needs.

One of the more influential theories used to guide understanding of motivation in the workplace has been the *two-factor* or *motivator-hygiene* theory of Herzberg, Mausner, and Snyderman (1959). This theory states that factors which influence job satisfaction and motivation at work can be divided into two major categories. Aspects such as adequate salary, possibility for growth, and interpersonal relations are classified as *hygienes* and must be provided for a person to be satisfied at work. The presence of hygienes, however, does not assure motivation. *Motivators* consist of elements such as achievement, recognition, and appeal of the work itself, and the presence of these can lead to motivation, although their absence does not necessarily produce dissatisfaction. The objective, therefore, is to provide for basic needs, so that absence of hygienes does not impede job satisfaction, and concentrate on motivators when trying to stimulate worker motivation.

Scrutiny of Herzberg's work has led to an understanding that real motivation occurs when a person finds satisfaction within the context of their work and the work environment, not as the result of some externally controlled reward system (Daft & Steers, 1986). For most workers, the carrot-and-stick approach to controlling work behavior has become an undesirable mode of operation. New approaches attempt to structure work so that the goals of the organization are aligned with the goals of individuals, thus providing a mutually beneficial relationship.

Another theory which provides a framework for understanding and implementing this approach is that of Vroom (1964). Referred to as *expectancy theory*, Vroom's model has three central components: (a) expectancy, (b) valence, and (c) instrumentality. Expectancy is the subjective belief that a particular action or change will result in a desirable outcome. Valence is the relative desirability of an expected outcome. Instrumentality is the perceived certainty that a particular action or change is essential for a given outcome to occur. Together, the strengths of these three determine the level of motivation with which a particular task is approached. Figure 1 illustrates the components and

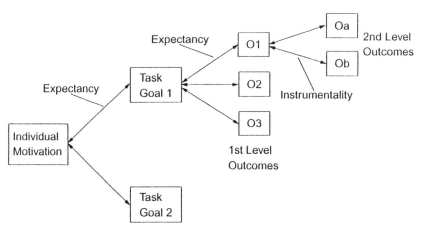

FIGURE 1 Expectancy theory model.

relationships of the expectancy theory model. First-level outcomes are the immediate accomplishments of completing a task. Second-level outcomes are those expected, but more remote, results which are desirable to the individual.

In practice, management strategies based on Vroom's theory provide good communication regarding the expected benefits of particular tasks, maintain integrity by consistently fulfilling obligations to employees, and make conscious efforts to provide a good fit between employees and their assigned tasks. Efforts are made to maximize the valence values of expectancies and to assure that first- and second-level outcomes are being realized.

Numerous other theories and variations of approaches to management and motivation are practiced. In the contemporary workplace, the trend has been toward models which consider the needs and ambitions of the individual worker and which allow a participatory role for the worker to help shape the work environment. Motivation is most effectively applied when it is derived from internally controlled mechanisms rather than from externally imposed influences.

Learning and Motivation

A number of new insights about how people learn have been derived from the past two decades of cognitive research. Traditional practice has often treated people as though the mind was a blank slate. We now know that learners bring much to the learning environment and that prior learning must be considered if new learning is to be effectively facilitated. Where it was once thought that learning best occurred through a didactic encounter between instructor and learner, cognitive research has shown that an interactive exchange between instructor and learner is more effective. Research also supports cooperative learning arrangements, where learners collaborate and work together to gain new insights and understanding. Greater emphasis is being placed on primary sources of data and manipulative materials, where previous practice relied heavily on books and printed materials.

One major concern raised by recent cognitive research is the extent to which learning transfer occurs. Some cognitive scientists are questioning whether transfer happens at all. Some theorists posit that knowledge and understanding are constructed in new situations and that, for learning to be useful and applicable, it should occur within the context in which the knowledge will be used. Constructivism is a term which describes this theory, and situated cognition is a closely related concept. Situated cognition is the term used for a body of theory which emphasizes the relationship between context and knowledge. Research in this area has revealed the importance of providing authentic, real-world activities where learners experience the relevance and applicability of new knowledge being developed (Schell & Rojewski, 1993). Collectively, these theories indicate that learning is enhanced by an environment which is as much as possible like that in which actual practice occurs and where learner-centered instructional experiences, with an appropriate social interaction component, encourage learners to move from prior knowledge to greater depth of understanding about a concept or practice.

KEYS TO A PRODUCTIVE LEARNING ENVIRONMENT

To tap the power of high expectation and motivation in the learning environment, several key ingredients must be in place. If these are not adequately provided, negative expectations and lack of motivation can significantly impair the desired learning outcomes. Among the most important elements for a productive learning environment are (a) an atmosphere of trust, (b) attention to what learners say, (c) a participatory arrangement, and (d) a climate of success. It should be noted that, while these items would support behaviorist as well as cognitive approaches to instruction and learning, they are described here within a cognitive framework since this strategy is more consistent with contemporary practice in the high-performance workplace.

Atmosphere of Trust

For efficient and effective learning to occur, an atmosphere of trust should pervade the learning environment. This trust should typify both the relationship between learners and instructor as well as among learners. Trust between the learners and instructor is necessary for intrinsic motivation to be uninhibited. Learners must feel free to exercise curiosity and interest in aspects of new knowledge which are relevant to their own realm of experience and which can build on prior knowledge. If learners are uncertain of the instructor's real intentions, particularly with regard to testing and evaluation, they will tend to focus on performing to meet the instructor's expectations rather than on developing new knowledge which is meaningful and authentic within their own realm of experience.

An instructor should endeavor to establish an atmosphere of trust from the very outset of the learning experience. If a formal course is being offered, the instructor should clearly communicate requirements and expectations along with a thorough overview of course content. Course experiences should then be consistent with the description provided. If learners discover that a course differs significantly from the advertised or expected content, trust is broken and it is difficult, if not impossible, to restore.

An instructor must also be consistent in implementing other aspects of the course, especially with regard to evaluation. When learners do not understand the basis for critique of their work, they become uneasy and trust is difficult to maintain. This is not to say that instructors should determine all of the details about a course in advance. Learner involvement is critical to shaping the presentation of course content so that new knowledge is connected to prior learning. The basic parameters for the structure of a course, however, should be guided and maintained in a consistent manner by the instructor, in much the same way that an orchestra conductor facilitates a concert. Just as a competent director enables musicians to produce beautiful music, an instructor who is trusted by learners can lead them to achieve the goals established for a class.

Trust among learners is another desirable aspect of a productive learning environment because it promotes individual expression and participation crucial to a productive learning environment. Trust can be facilitated through cooperative learning arrangements and by maintaining an atmosphere which keeps competition in a proper perspective. The mood established by an instructor should emphasize the concept of collective or team success over individual success. Quotas for grades and other systems of forced distribution in evaluating learner work are very destructive of this atmosphere and should be avoided. Group interaction through problem-solving activities or case studies can encourage collaboration, trust, and the development of interpersonal skills essential in the workplace.

Competition is a valued component of the free enterprise system in the democratic world. It can also be useful in a learning environment when used in a non-threatening manner. Competition should be used in a game-like atmosphere, where fun and group support provide insulation from harm to the self-esteem for those who do not win. Whether competing individually or as a team member, the support structure within the learning environment should help learners keep winning and losing in a proper perspective. This aspect is very important for trust to be maintained among learners.

Attention to What Learners Say

While it has long been recognized that adult learners bring to the learning environment a rich repertoire of prior knowledge upon which new learning can be built, cognitive research has shown that prior knowledge should be considered for younger learners as well. For this prior knowledge to be considered in the learning environment, learner dialogue must be encouraged so that existing ideas can be identified. Unless a learner's prior knowledge can be related to new ideas, learning is often thwarted.

Consider, for example, a rate problem of the type that has typically been used in eighth or ninth grade mathematics classes:

A ship sailing at 20 knots travels from point A toward point B. Another ship leaves point B an hour later than the first ship and travels at 15 knots toward point A. If points A and B are separated by 860 nautical miles and the ships travel the same route, how long will the first ship travel before it meets the second ship?

Problems of this type contain concepts which are fundamental to mathematics, physics, and to vocational education and training. The presentation, however, does not consider the interests and prior knowledge of most learners. Few, if any, learners grasp the meaning or have had any experience with ships, knots, or nautical miles. As a result, learning is not relevant to prior knowledge and, without this link, motivation to learn how the problem can be solved is not based on intrinsic interest. If the purpose for the above problem is to facilitate learning about rate, a problem based on the interests and prior knowledge of the learners would be more appropriate. If the objective is to deal with knots and nautical miles, some means of associating the measures with a context familiar to the learners would be helpful. Consider the following alternative problem, which requires the same mathematics skills:

A car travelling at 55 miles per hour travels from city A toward city B. Another car leaves city B an hour later than the first car and travels at 60 miles per hour toward city A. If cities A and B are 500 miles apart and the cars travel along the same highway, how long will the first car travel before it meets the second car?

Students are more apt to be familiar with the units of measure used in the alternative problem.

The central point here is that sufficient two-way communication must be provided between learners and the instructor so that instructional strategies can be structured around prior learning (Brooks & Brooks, 1993). If this does not happen, new learning is impaired and motivation to engage in future endeavors with a particular subject can be dampened.

In addition to guiding the presentation of subject matter, attention to what learners have to say encourages the climate of trust previously discussed. When learners sense that an instructor is taking a personal interest in them, a trust relationship is cultivated. Within appropriate limits, the greater knowledge an instructor has about a learner's individual world, the more adept the instructor can be in his or her efforts to guide the learner toward establishing and achieving meaningful learning goals.

Participatory Arrangement

One of the most effective ways to encourage motivation in a learning environment is to impart a sense of self-control to learners. This can be accomplished through a participatory arrangement where learners have a voice in determining significant course decisions. Bandura (1991) stated that people's beliefs about the level of control they have over their own lives and events affecting their lives has a major influence on their motivation. For learners to really be motivated to learn, they should be encouraged to set specific, challenging, and meaningful goals for their academic work—goals other than merely to get a good grade (McKeachie, Chism, Menges, Svincki, & Weinstein, 1994).

From a practical standpoint, curriculum for educational programs must be designed to meet certain established criteria, and courses of study must cover a specified body of knowledge. Allowing students a participatory role in designing the educational experiences for a course does not mean discarding the requirements and turning content decisions over to persons who have neither the knowledge nor experience to make such decisions. It means enabling learners to consider the content of the course and to participate, with the instructor's guidance, in selecting learning strategies through which they can most efficiently and effectively comprehend the material.

Flexibility should be provided so that learners with different learning styles can succeed in the course. Gardner (1983) has identified at least seven different styles, or *intelligences*, which characterize the ways people best learn. By acknowledging the differences in learning styles present in a particular group of learners, and making some effort to reach a collaborate agreement regarding ways of approaching course content, learners become more motivated through an engendered sense of empowerment.

Climate of Success

An additional element in a productive learning environment is a climate of success. Klein (1991) identified goal setting and expectancy theory as two of the most viable explanations for motivation. These two theories are related in that goals have been shown to mediate the influence of expectancy theory constructs on behavior. For either of these theories to be relevant in a particular instance, however, there must be a belief in the possibility of achieving a desired outcome. For this reason, motivation is enhanced by a climate where success is the norm.

The overall climate of a learning environment should be positive, encouraging, and optimistic. The instructor plays a major role in establishing this climate. From the first day of class, when a syllabus or course outline is discussed, the instructor conveys either optimistic or pessimistic messages. Consider the following excerpt from an instructor's introductory comments.

> You will be allowed to miss this class up to three times during the term, but after that, five points will be deducted from your grade for each

absence. When you are absent on the day of a test, a zero will be recorded for your grade unless you have a physician's excuse. Attendance is very important to success in this course and, when you are absent, you reduce the likelihood of making a good grade.

Implied in this message is an expectation that students will miss class. Rather than presuming that student absence would be unusual, the instructor's anticipation that students will miss class is verbalized, with emphasis on the resultant penalty for absence. A more appropriate statement might be as follows:

Time is a valuable and irreplaceable resource. For that reason, every effort will be made to use our class time wisely. In addition, effective learning is not a passive activity—it requires your personal involvement. Your attendance and participation in every class session is very important. Plans for the learning activities prepared in advance of each class will include a role for your involvement, so it is essential that you let the instructor know if something in your schedule will conflict with your attendance.

Here there is a clear expectation that students will attend class. Attendance is presented as something important to the students' success in the class. It is clear that missing a class may cause more harm than merely having an absence recorded in a gradebook.

Attendance was used here as an example because it is related to the issue of motivation. Students who are not motivated are more inclined to miss class or be tardy than those who are motivated. Numerous other aspects of a course can be communicated in either a positive or a negative tone as well. Messages about expected success on assignments, projects, assessment, and other elements of a course should also be positive, to encourage students to complete them. By establishing a climate of success, students are empowered to set personal goals for a course and expect to achieve them.

FACILITATING THE LEARNING PROCESS

Taking steps to provide an appropriate learning environment is an important consideration for effective instruction. In many ways, this is analogous to a farmer preparing the soil in which crops will be planted. The learning environment should set the stage for high expectation and motivation to develop, based on students' internal control systems. Even after the soil is prepared for planting, the farmer's work is not finished. Considerable work is still involved in planting and cultivating the crops.

In a similar manner, an effective instructor can set a stage for learning to take place, but should still take several proactive steps to facilitate learning and encourage continued motivation.

Focusing Attention and Involving the Senses

A number of guidelines, based on principles of cognitive psychology, should be used to enhance instruction. Included are techniques for calling attention to important concepts and assisting students with identification of critical features. Interaction is encouraged and sensory input is stressed. The following is a list of instructional processes which support effective instruction of concepts.

(1) Explain the goals for studying a particular concept and explain the relevance of desired learning by giving real-world applications.

(2) Discuss any prerequisite knowledge required to understand a concept being studied.

(3) Provide an attention signal when an important point is about to be discussed. This signal might be as simple as saying, "Now listen!" when an important element is about to be explained. If projected visuals are being used, turning on the projector may serve as an attention signal.

(4) Explain and point out the critical features in definitions used.

(5) Point out or highlight the critical features contained in examples and associate them with the corresponding parts of any definition or other explanation given.

(6) Provide opportunities for learners to explain a concept in their own words.

(7) Encourage learners to identify the critical features in a concept as they explain an example or illustration, and encourage them to elaborate on their understanding of the construct.

(8) Provide feedback to learners regarding the accuracy of their perceptions about a concept.

(9) Elaborate on concepts so that alternative perspectives are considered and new ways of looking at a topic are encouraged.

(10) Restate the definition and the critical features of a concept to provide closure to a learning activity, and review the important points students need to remember.

The techniques described above are enhanced when multiple senses are involved in the learning process. Explanations should be supplemented with visuals, since approximately 80% of what people know typically begins with the sense of sight. Seeing an object or diagram that is being explained greatly increases understanding. Hands-on experiences related to instruction further reinforce learning by adding the sense of touch to those of hearing and seeing. This enhancement is pushed even further when a learner demonstrates and explains a process or concept to others. When this is done, use of the senses is involved along with interpretation of personal understanding. The mental reflection about meaning required throughout this process provides a high level of effectiveness for deeper learning of the materials being presented.

Instructional practices which facilitate effective learning form a synergistic relationship with motivation and high expectation on the part of a learner. Motivation increases the ease with which learners become involved in the learning process. Effective instructional strategies help learners sustain motivation as enthusiasm for learning builds.

Enhancing Retention

The test of success in learning is retention. Whether retention is checked through performance or recitation, the learners' ability to recall and apply what has been learned is a desirable outcome of education and training. Strategies which enhance retention and aid learners in having ready access to knowledge needed for application are useful tools. Ability to remember needed information leads to a sense of success and encourages continued learner motivation.

Several significant factors influence learner retention. These include the social aspects of the learning environment, the structure of the content presentation, and the connection of new learning with prior knowledge. One of the most important considerations in efforts to maintain learner motivation and maximize retention are the personal interaction and social environment in which learning occurs. The opportunity to interact and discuss new ideas with others, to argue points of difference, and to explain or have explained complex concepts greatly enhances learning. Effective instructors should encourage social exchange through small group discussion, group problem solving, and other collaborative arrangements to provide an effective learning environment and to enhance retention.

The order and manner in which content is presented by an instructor also affects learner retention. Presentation of a new construct should begin with an overview of the whole and an explanation of how it fits into real-life situations. The instructional sequence in dealing with new content should then provide a guided experience, including explanation, demonstration, and opportunities for hands-on practice where applicable. Care should be taken to check for understanding of critical features so that learners gain knowledge which will be prerequisite to future learning. Careful sequencing of instruction and continual evaluations of learner progress provide assurance of effective learning and increased retention.

Prior knowledge is the foundation on which all new learning is built. Effective instructors assist learners by understanding as much as possible about their prior knowledge and relating new content to that knowledge base. The social interaction previously mentioned provides opportunities to develop insights in this area. Learner involvement in the process is also important because of differences in prior knowledge. In most situations, the instructor's time for providing individualized instruction is limited. When instructional activities employ more knowledgeable learners to help peers with less experience to understand new concepts, efficiency is increased and all learners benefit from the process. The peer experts' motivation is enhanced as they help others to learn and understand. Their own understanding and retention is also improved through the process of reflecting and explaining the concept to another person. Individual or small group instruction gives the peer novice an opportunity to have questions answered and allows more detailed explanations to help the learner relate new learning to prior knowledge.

Metaphor, Analogy, and Mnemonics

To facilitate the learning process, metaphors and analogies provide effective communication tools to enhance understanding and retention. A metaphor is a figure of speech in which a word or phrase is used to describe an object or idea different from its literal meaning. For example, the "ship plowed through the water" or the "engine was purring after the tune-up." The likeness expressed by a metaphor can enhance understanding by comparing a new event or concept with one previously experienced or already understood. Metaphors enhance retention by producing more vivid mental images of a concept or object.

Analogies are also useful devices for effective communication. An analogy was used to introduce this section on facilitating the learning process when a comparison was made between a farmer cultivating crops and an instructor taking proactive steps to encourage learning and motivation. As in the case of metaphors, the object of comparison should be familiar to learners. If the illustration used is outside a learner's realm of experience and understanding, communication will be impaired rather than enhanced. The use of a story or some other form of analogy is often helpful in remembering a related concept. Metaphors and analogies spice the communication of new ideas, help to alleviate bland presentations, and provide an essential part of the recipe for success.

Another common technique for enhancing retention is to associate new learning with prior knowledge. A well-known example is remembering a person's name by mentally associating it with a previous acquaintance of the same name or with some other known word or object.

Mnemonics are another form of a memory aid, which associates a "catchy" or easy-to-remember word or phrase with a more complex concept or idea. For example, a phrase which mathematics students sometimes use to help them remember correct order of mathematical operations in an expression is "My dear Aunt Sally." The first letters of the words in this phrase are the same as the initial letters in the words multiplication, division, addition, and subtraction, which represent the order in which the mathematical operations should be performed. Similar word devices are often used to remember facts or concepts which involve a pattern.

Another memory aid involves using word associations which have some inherent meaning. Resistor color codes, for example, can be associated with things like a yellow dog, a five-dollar bill, and a blue-tail fly. The yellow dog has four legs, and yellow is the resistor color for four. A five-dollar bill is green, and green is the resistor color for five. A blue-tail fly has six legs, and blue is the resistor color for six. Patterns such as these provide a system of direct recall for associated facts without going through a sequence of words and counting to determine the related number.

All of these methods of improving and aiding retention encourage motivation by contributing to ease of comprehension and learning. Just as an expectation of success provides a positive influence on learners, mechanisms through which success is achieved contribute to continued learner interest and participation.

Application and Practice

An essential component of effective learning is application and practice of new knowledge. Opportunities to be personally involved with learning are also key ingredients for maintaining motivation. Particularly when learners are seeking new understanding to fulfill personal goals and satisfy intrinsic needs, opportunities to use what is being learned significantly enhance the process.

Practice should be provided under realistic circumstances and conditions. The context in which practice occurs is a relevant feature of the learning process. When practice is too far removed from real-world conditions, learning may be limited by the artificial nature of the situation. Most significant activity is so influenced by the context of authentic practice that, when it is considered in some other environment, the nature of the experience is much different. Care should be taken to provide practice and hands-on experience under real-world conditions to the extent possible and practical.

Another important element in the practice and application of new learning is to monitor the performance of the newly learned skills. Feedback and correction should be immediately available to remedy mistakes. Otherwise, incorrect performance may be practiced and learned. It is more difficult to relearn something than it is to learn it correctly the first time. Prior learning tends to resurface repeatedly, once it becomes a part of a person's repertoire of experience.

Self-Concept and the Pygmalion Effect

The use of expectation and the influence an instructor can have on the self-concept of learners provides one of the most powerful tools available to facilitate learning. Persons who have a good self-concept are more inclined to be motivated and involved in the learning process. Self-concept is the sum total of the perceptions, ideas, and attitudes a person has developed about him/herself. A healthy self-concept enables a person to more clearly evaluate an idea or position, adapt to experience and change, and more freely accept other people as they are. It contributes to one's ability to interact with others and is an asset to the social elements of the learning environment.

Pygmalion Effect

The instructor's attitude and expectations have a major influence on the learners' self-esteem and performance. This influence is called the "Pygmalion effect," named for a prince in Greek and Roman mythology who carved an ivory statue of the ideal woman. The sculptor fell hopelessly in love with his creation, which then came to life, with the help of the goddess Venus. Numerous other stories, from *My Fair Lady* to *The Little Engine That Could*, inform our culture of the power and influence of self-concept on performance.

As applied to the learning environment, the principle of the Pygmalion effect states that if an instructor believes that a learner will be successful, the learner *will* be successful. When the message, "you can," is communicated to the learner long enough, strongly enough, and consistently enough, the learner believes the message and performance is affected. The primary techniques to implement this tool consist of (a) focusing on learner strengths, (b) verbalizing expectations, (c) listening to learner concerns and ideas, (d) emphasizing the worth of the individual, and (e) having confidence in one's ability to influence learner perceptions and outcomes.

An instructor's use of the Pygmalion effect can be challenging. Communication of expectations involves non-verbal, as well as verbal, communication. Tone of voice, gestures, and eye contact are major components of non-verbal communication. These can be difficult to control if the instructor is not sincere. Efforts should be made to facilitate an accepting, encouraging climate through warm and attentive conversation, smiling and nodding appreciatively in response to others, and providing feedback about existing learner strengths along with suggestions for improvement.

One of the challenges to an instructor seeking to make effective use of the Pygmalion effect involves guarding against unrecognized bias and assumptions about people. Occasionally, an instructor reaches a "first-impression" conclusion about a learner without giving it conscious thought. Consider, for example, the conclusions you formed as you read the first few paragraphs of this chapter. Are Taylor and Kerry male or female? What gender specific stereotypes are involved here? How are perceptions shaped by traits such as race, age, dress, physical appearance, and other individual characteristics? How do these perceptions influence an instructor's ability to encourage motivation and success through use of the Pygmalion effect? The challenge for the effective instructor is to try to facilitate a learning environment where all learners are provided with an opportunity to achieve their maximum potential, where each individual is treated as a person of unique worth, and where high expectation and motivation are expected characteristics of all participants.

TAKING MOTIVATION TO WORK

High expectation and motivation facilitate learning and are desirable elements in education and training for employment. The learning experience, however, should equip learners to make the transition to work so that they remain motivated on the job. Just as motivation is a characteristic instructors appreciate in learners, it also is an attribute employers seek in their associates. Discussion about the importance of motivation in the workplace should be included alongside consideration of employability skills and personal characteristics which contribute to success at work.

Programs which focus on preparation for work should develop awareness of the various management styles likely to be encountered, along with the role of motivation in each of them. While most circumstances are comprised of a unique blend of personalities and belief systems, distinct patterns of management can be distinguished in most organizations. Despite the overwhelming evidence that employee involvement in decision-making processes results in significant benefits to organizations, numerous companies continue to operate in an autocratic manner (Paulsen, 1994).

Expectations for the Workplace

The two primary management modes likely to be implemented in an organization are the *traditional* style or the *participatory* style. The traditional style of management approaches motivation with an external locus of control. Rewards and incentives are used to encourage desired behaviors. Desirable actions are reinforced, while undesirable ones are either ignored or punished. Tools used to influence behavior range from positive feedback to monetary rewards. Decision making is centralized and implemented through a bureaucratic structure. While people within the organization may be self-motivated or driven by personal needs, these may go largely unrecognized as efforts to influence and manage rely on external controls. In some instances, the proclaimed management mode may be participatory or some "in vogue" variant thereof, while the actual practice reflects a more traditional style. Another pattern is for the traditional style of management to be noticeable at a specific level or site within an organization as a result of a particular manager's mode of operation, even though the organization and, in some instances, that manager may verbally espouse a participatory management style.

The participatory style of management is based on a view of motivation with an internal locus of control. Persons are viewed as self-motivated and efforts are made to place people in positions where personal goals can be achieved in conjunction with organizational goals. Vroom's expectancy theory, described earlier in this chapter, is consistent with the participatory management mode. Employees, called associates, are expected to find fulfillment and satisfaction in their work—not as a result of their work. Compensation is important, but pay is not used as an incentive as it is under the traditional mode. People are encouraged to develop a sense of ownership for their work and decision making is decentralized throughout the organization. Few levels of management are needed and bureaucracy is minimized. Particularly in jobs where workers routinely have considerable discretion over use of their time, participatory modes of management are much more appropriate than traditional styles. With the trend toward high-discretion work in the contemporary workplace, participatory management is becoming increasingly prevalent.

Some hybrid forms of management combine elements of participatory management with traditional management styles. One example is the use of gainsharing, a strategy which enables workers to directly benefit from improvements in productivity (McGrath, 1993). In this system, wages are not based solely on time, but are affected by productivity. If weekly profit targets are exceeded due to increased productivity, workers receive a share of the monetary gains. The underlying premise is that employee motivation is governed by a monetary equation. This is more akin to a traditional management mode than to a participatory management mode, but a participatory control mechanism is used to empower workers.

For the learner preparing to enter the workforce, knowledge and awareness of different management styles should be included in the course of study. For the learner pursuing additional training or professional development, consideration of different modes of management is also appropriate. One reason for including a study of management styles in these learning experiences is that management style affects how motivation is implemented in the workplace. The ability to recognize which management system is functioning within an organization can enable a person to implement an effective strategy to achieve personal goals, whatever those may be.

Principles for Staying Motivated

One of the struggles which students in vocational education and training programs should prepare to encounter is that of functioning in a workplace where the management style does not match the expectations of the individual. Sometimes this occurs because one type of management is proclaimed to be in use while, in reality, an alternative style is in operation. In preparing for this contingency, learners should consider in advance how they will cope with problems that may arise as a result. In some instances, a change in employment may be the best solution. In other instances, association with professionals outside the workplace or involvement in community organizations may provide the support needed to maintain motivation.

Learners should be aware of the basic tenets of motivation. They should understand the importance of living within their means, so that their economic situation does not trap them at a lower-level need on the continuum of needs. Efforts should be made to find self-fulfillment in work through relationships with colleagues and associates, whether this appears to be valued by management or not. In some circumstances, the Pygmalion effect may also work in reverse—much of our circumstance at work is determined by what we expect it to be.

Role playing and case studies can serve as effective vehicles for having learners explore the significance of management style to motivation. Such activities give students opportunities to (a) explore their own feelings and personalities, (b) consider what personal goals they will seek in their work, and (c) think about how the climate in an organization might empower or impair their ability to reach these goals.

Making Motivation Contagious

Reviewing the contents of this chapter, a reader may conclude that motivation is a complex human condition. Both internal and external factors have been broadly discussed, ranging from physiological and psychological needs to the context in which a person seeks to find satisfaction. One of the additional observations to be made about motivation, particularly as learners move from education and training programs to work, is that motivation can be contagious. Just as one individual can influence another as a result of the Pygmalion effect, one motivated individual within a business or industry can significantly affect the motivation of others. One of the challenges for instructors is to encourage motivated learners to become motivated workers. Learners should be (a) involved in the learning process, (b) well informed about the work they will do, and (c) eager to apply their knowledge in the workplace. Much of this results from the enthusiasm generated when an instructor is motivated. While numerous psychological and sociological principles are a part of the process of initiating and sustaining motivation, some part of this state of mind is more caught than taught. When an instructor enters the learning environment enthusiastically, works to maintain an optimistic attitude about successful performance by all learners, and sincerely guides the learning process with integrity and consistency, learners are influenced to be motivated themselves. To this end, instructors should strive to encourage and support motivation in all that they do and say.

REFERENCES

Arkes, H. R., & Garske, J. P. (1982). *Psychological theories of motivation* (2nd ed.). Monterey, CA: Brooks Cole.

Bandura, A. (1991). Social cognitive theory of self-regulation. *Organizational Behavior and Human Decision Processes, 50*(2), 248–287.

Bigge, M. L., & Hunt, M. P. (1968). *Psychological foundations of education* (2nd ed.). New York: Harper & Row.

Brooks, J. G., & Brooks, M. G. (1993). *In search of understanding: The case for constructivist classrooms.* Alexandria, VA: Association for Supervision and Curriculum Development.

Daft, R. L., & Steers, R. M. (1986). *Organizations: A micro/macro approach.* Glenview, IL: Scott, Foresman.

Gardner, H. (1983). *Frames of mind: The theory of multiple intelligences.* New York: Basic Books.

Herzberg, F., Mausner, B., & Snyderman, B. B. (1959). *The motivation to work.* New York: Wiley.

Hoy, W. K., & Miskel, C. G. (1978). *Educational administration: Theory, research, and practice.* New York: Random House.

Klein, H. J. (1991). Further evidence on the relationship between goal setting and expectancy theories. *Organizational Behavior and Human Decision Processes, 49*(2), 230–257.

Maslow, A. H. (1987). *Motivation and personality* (3rd ed., with new material by Ruth Cox & Robert Frager). New York: Harper & Row.

McGrath, T. C. (1993). Gainsharing: Engineering the human factor of productivity. *Industrial Engineering, 25*(9), 61–62.

McKeachie, W. J., Chism, N., Menges, R., Svinicki, M., & Weinstein, C. E. (1994). *Teaching tips: Strategies, research, and theory for college and university teachers* (9th ed.). Lexington, MA: D. C. Heath.

Paulsen, K. M. (1994). Total employee involvement: Why are you waiting? *Industrial Engineering, 26*(2), 16–17.

Schell, J. W., & Rojewski, J. W. (1993). Toward vocational thoughtfulness: An emerging program of research. *Journal of Industrial Teacher Education, 30*(2), 44–64.

Vroom, V. H. (1964). *Work and motivation.* New York: Wiley.

Webster Encyclopedia. (1985). Des Moines, IA: Meredith.

CHAPTER 7

Structured On-the-Job Training: Pitfalls and Payoffs

DAVID C. BJORKQUIST—*University of Minnesota*
BRIAN P. MURPHY—*HRD Resource Group, Inc.*

STRUCTURED on-the-job training (SOJT) is first and foremost a means for increasing the productivity of an enterprise. On-the-job training that is structured will more quickly and reliably result in outcomes that contribute to productivity than will on-the-job training that, all too often, is unstructured. The comparative effect of structured and unstructured training is shown in Figure 1.

Productivity goals are frequently expressed in terms of increased product or service amounts and quality, reduced errors, or less waste. Improvements in these qualities make a company more profitable, more effective, or enhance its reputation in some other way. Other goals may relate to a company's place in the community and society, relationships among those in the workplace, and connections between work that is performed and those who do it. The critical understanding is that SOJT is derived from the goals of a company and its outcomes are evaluated against its contribution to the accomplishment of those goals. Training systems based on this logic are fundamental to decision making about the company's operations and less likely to be expendable when organizational resources are tightly limited.

The concept of a company is usually applied to a profit-making enterprise; however, SOJT is used in both profit-making and not-for-profit organizations. SOJT is most often found in the workplace, but its principles are readily applicable to school settings and can help to increase the authenticity of training conducted there.

Some companies have formal strategic business plans. These plans often result from deliberate planning sessions with resultant goal statements. In some cases, strategic business plans are used actively in day-to-day operations and all detailed operational plans are made in association with them, including sales goals, product or service improvements, capital investment, employee training, and so forth. However, the strategic business plan may not be the direction-setting, controlling

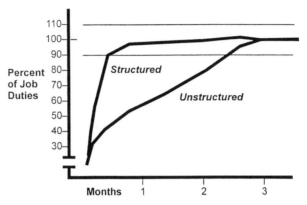

FIGURE 1 Structured and unstructured learning.

documentation of the business. Goal statements may not be in use because they have not kept up with the dynamics of the industry in which the company is engaged. The plan may not have been conceived as a functioning document, or other planning processes may have taken precedence.

Companies that are trying to stay abreast in a rapidly changing environment, for example, often have imprecisely conceived strategic goals, but they almost always have some set of operating objectives, if only in the head of the chief operating officer. Regardless of how these central, functional plans are stated and how they are kept, it is important for the person executing them to take into account training and other human resource development (HRD) activities that relate to the primary business purpose.

Where training is a means for accomplishing business goals, it must be accepted as an element of management practice, similar to production equipment, raw material, or marketing. It is equally critical to realize that training is not the solution for every problem and that it may not address various strategic goals. Decisions about the appropriateness of training require more than the reading of trends, response to training desires, or superficial analysis of needs. Full return on training investments probably will not result from such propositions as "Well, if we need to do that hazardous materials course, let's get it over with," "I guess we should train these folks to correct that problem before it gets any worse," or "Let's offer employees that stress management course to raise their comfort level, given the changes we've made."

In an environment of systematic job training, strategic plans help to define the performance problems and opportunities of the organization.

With a clear identification of objectives and a logical connection of the objectives to a solution based on training, there is confidence that training will produce results that contribute to the accomplishment of strategic goals. For this to happen, there must be a discriminating understanding of the strategic plan, thorough analysis of problems and opportunities growing out of changes in the organization and its environment, and a hard-nosed critique of what can be accomplished by training. These principles apply to manufacturing, retail and wholesale sales, construction, health care, and other goods- and service-producing organizations, whether or not they operate for profit.

Systematic analysis, planning, delivery, and evaluation are important to all forms of training, but especially when training has the purpose of increasing the competency of an employee to perform specific job functions, as in SOJT. Structured on-the-job training is located, physically and conceptually, close to the job. Its content is drawn from the work to be performed, and it is most often taught at the job site by an expert in performing the job. As described here, SOJT is most applicable to facilitating the learning of sets of defined functions within a job where much of the training provided in one job may not be applicable to other jobs. Improved performance in those functions is an expected outcome of SOJT. For these reasons, the purposes of SOJT are identified clearly, the content is precisely described, training procedures are intentional, and evaluation is based on skill performance on the job.

Successful SOJT is founded on instructional methods known to effective trainers and vocational educators since World War I. Therefore, the focus of this chapter is on SOJT as a means for accomplishing business objectives and the justification for its use. More specifically, this chapter describes training's connection to business planning, business risks and opportunities, processes for assessing training needs, as well as the organization and documentation of work.

TRAINING TO FULFILL BUSINESS PLANS

It is not unusual for companies to use banners and plaques to display their strategic goals for all to see. For example, visitors to a plant that manufactures rubber gaskets may be confronted with posters bearing slogans that express the organization's intention to produce quality rubber products. The manufacture of high quality rubber products has been the company's goal for several years, as evidenced by their collection of framed posters. The only variation is in the specific objectives of focus during a given year. In one year, quality was to be achieved through customer satisfaction; in another year, the focus was on reduction of waste; different quality-based objectives were featured in other years. All the posters are displayed to make a favorable impression on visitors, especially customers, and as a reminder to employees that quality is central among the goals of the organization. Consistency is shown by the number of years that quality has been featured as a goal. Selection of this goal, and the attention given to it, appear to be the result of careful planning, not of casual conversation.

A strategic plan focused on quality, for example, may address issues such as the condition of raw materials, manufacturing equipment, systems of inspections, supervision, equipment maintenance, product marketing and sales, after-sales service, and the skill levels of manufacturing employees. Each issue carries risks and opportunities, and each variable must be addressed individually with the intent to achieve a specified level of performance or an optimum advantage. Separate and appropriate actions must be planned for reaching each objective, and resources of the organization allocated as necessary. The diversity of talents within an organization can be used to develop feasible plans for efficiently accomplishing worthwhile objectives. The human resource developer plays an important role in implementing a strategic plan by providing information about the role of training and other related interventions.

When applied in the context of a strategic plan, training becomes more than a generalized approach to workforce development. It becomes a business asset that can be applied to (a) proceed directly toward problems and opportunities presented by the plan, and (b) accomplish specific goals, comparable in purpose to investments in materials, equipment, and facilities. Training is a function of the business, an integral part of the way it accomplishes its purposes, and an endeavor from which a return is expected in the same manner as from marketing, engineering, or product development. As simple as this may sound, it is practiced infrequently. There are reasons, mostly avoidable, why training is often viewed as an overhead expense that does not attain the importance of a strategic investment.

Training can be discredited by some attitudes about its value. When training is believed to be inherently good and without need for justification, it can be considered expendable, especially in a competitive marketplace. For example, when profit-motive businesses see their earnings decline, they often look for ways to cut costs. If training is offered for the enrichment of the workforce because it is "good," and no direct return to the business paying for the benefit is expected, training may be treated as an avoidable expense. By contrast, if training is responsible for maintaining and upgrading the skill level of workers, the cost in productivity to reduce training may exceed the potential savings gain. Training in concert with business plans is not just overhead; it contributes to business outcomes. This applies to profit-making companies, as well as those, such as charitable organizations, that measure their success by other outcomes.

Another reason for failure to link training to business plans and needs of organizations is faulty analysis processes used to identify supposed training requirements. Consideration of the plant that manufactures rubber gaskets can illustrate this point. One troublesome situation in the manufacturing process is in the molding machines used to form the rubber products. A variety of rubber compounds are used to supply different customers with gaskets that meet their specifications for flexibility, hardness, fit, and other qualities. Different rubber compounds respond differently to conditions of humidity and require different heat levels, press times, curing times, and handling for successful formation. With this information, the plant manager has suggested that all molding machine operators should have a course in rubber chemistry.

On the surface, this appears to be an appropriate suggestion. However, analysis of the procedures used by the molders has revealed that they lack knowledge about the forming characteristics of the rubber compounds they are expected to mold. Additionally, there has been no uniform training in molding procedures, so each molder uses his/her own method to adjust molding processes, resulting in not producing enough acceptable parts to meet the production standard. When too many faulty parts are being made, some molders may change the mold temperature while others adjust molding time, for the same perceived malfunction. A course in rubber chemistry may have helped to provide an understanding of rubber compound characteristics but would have been an indirect route to increasing the number of acceptable parts produced by molders.

The molders' productivity could be increased more quickly by providing them with more information about the molding characteristics of each rubber compound as it was delivered for molding. Furthermore, molders need to know the relationship between the molding response of various rubber compounds and ambient conditions, such as humidity, in which the molding is being done. More uniform information about rubber compounds and training for molding machine operators could be offered as a direct contribution to the accomplishment of the company's strategic goal of improving the quality of its products.

There are cases where thorough analysis identifies performance problems and opportunities but the training and other planned interventions are poorly executed. It is inefficient to gather molders who do not know how to adjust molding machines in a classroom to discuss their individual theories on molding. The techniques for adjusting molding machines according to proven principles need to be learned. The best setting for this training would be at a molding machine, where a molder can make immediate application of what is learned. Given the noisy conditions of the factory floor where the molding machines are located, one-on-one instruction would be most effective.

It cannot be assumed that any particular training effort is contributing to the accomplishment of a company's goals. Performance of those who are trained needs to be evaluated against the criteria suggested by the company's goals. When improved quality is the goal, training should result in the improvement of quality, as that improvement is defined. There may be intermediate measures of trainee (a) satisfaction with training, and (b) proficiency in performing tasks. However, ultimately, there need to be measures of actual performance on the job relative to the goals of the organization. These measures can provide the basis for modifications in training and for the justification of training as an element in fulfilling business objectives.

Training is not used just for the correction of problems that stand in the way of achieving goals. It is often a means of taking advantage of opportunities. A company may identify a problem in the intolerable losses occurring because time and materials are wasted on work that has to be redone. These losses can erode profitability and customer satisfaction to such an extent that the company's viability is threatened. Reconsideration of circumstances such as this can recast them as an opportunity rather than a problem. There is an opportunity to strengthen the company's position and make it more profitable by reducing the waste resulting from work that has to be redone. Though there may be little functional difference between problems and opportunities, it is often more palatable to discuss opportunities than to be confronted by a continuous stream of problems.

Training can produce the skills to make an organization more productive and place it in a better competitive position. However, not all training will do this. The problems to be addressed must be clearly identified and the relationship between training and the condition(s) to be changed by training must be logical. Experience documented by evaluation can become a basis for decision making about training choices and can help to assert the training's contributions to the attainment of business goals.

Structured on-the-job training is well-suited to addressing business goals because it originates from those goals and is designed with specific goal attainment in mind. In the next section the establishment of performance expectations and the consequences of not meeting them are discussed.

MEETING PERFORMANCE EXPECTATIONS

Understanding the relationship between a company's productivity, employee skills, and the connection between those skills and training is important. For any job, a range of acceptable performance, from minimal competence to mastery, can be established. This may be based on the performance of incumbents in the job or some more hypothetical analysis. Within the range of performance levels, an optimal or engineered standard can be identified. This is not necessarily the level of performance by the most competent employee but may result from analysis of job descriptions or operating procedures. Experienced workers or supervisors may contribute to developing performance standards.

Performance Gaps

With a performance standard for a job in place, the "performance gap" can be determined, that is, the difference between the standard and any performance below that. Figure 2 illustrates the relative skill level of a new employee as job duties are learned over time in relation to the acceptable performance range.

The period of less-than-desirable performance for a new employee can last from a few days to many months. There also may be a learning curve for an experienced worker. The time required to move an employee to the desired level of performance depends on characteristics of the job, qualifications of the employee, and the amount of support available to develop job skills. The period of time during which an employee is developing the skill to meet the minimum productivity standards represents the time of greatest liability for the company. There is a clear

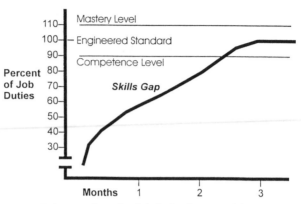

FIGURE 2 Learning job duties for a new job.

advantage in moving a worker to higher performance levels, through the development of skills, as quickly as possible.

Although the focus of the present discussion is on employee skill development, characteristics of the job must also be recognized. The qualities of job elements including the tools, equipment, instruments, and work procedures can enhance or hinder the application of worker skill to the job. When work procedures are unclear or equipment at the work station does not perform to the required standard, it may be impossible for the worker to attain the expected level of performance, regardless of the extent of training.

Some jobs require more learning time than others because of their complexity. Jobs requiring more different skills, problem solving, and decision making, or variable interactions with other jobs, are examples of jobs that require more learning time. Virtually any change in the work setting can lead to skill gaps. This includes new equipment, procedures, processes, standards, and information. Figure 3 shows that, as changes occur, employee skills can fall below the range of expected performance. After a change, a worker must recover through the development of new skills in order to get back to previous performance levels. Anyone can experience a skills gap. The machine operator must close that gap when a new control unit is installed. The accountant must adapt to the latest changes in tax regulations. The supervisor must learn how to use the new computer system.

Some employees have more innate ability than others and are capable of faster skill development. An advantage for others is their experience and its relationship to the job to be learned. With greater similarity between previous experience and present learning, competencies can often be accomplished more quickly. However, there are many instances where the similarity between a previous and a present job results in interference that slows learning. The cues in a new job may be so much like those of a former job that the most likely worker response is appropriate for the old job but not for the new one. The time required by an experienced worker to unlearn old responses and replace them may exceed the time required by a neophyte learner.

Attention is increasingly given to the nature of the support provided to the trainee on the job and the effect of this support on performance. For example, skills are perishable and, if not used, they deteriorate. Therefore, one support mechanism that can be used is to provide the employee with opportunities to use newly developed skills. In some cases, a lapse of only a few hours between training and application can diminish skill levels. Support may also include coaching by a master worker, who can help the beginner apply skills in the correct sequence or avoid common mistakes. A severe lack of support is characterized by co-worker and supervisor attitudes which suggest that procedures learned in training are not appropriate on the job.

Lost Opportunity and Risk

The gap between actual and expected output produces two conditions. One condition is *lost opportunity*, where the planned or potential output is not realized. The second condition is *risk*, where "sub-par" performance leads to mistakes and oversights.

Lost opportunity manifests itself in several forms, including expenses,

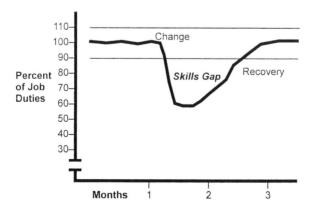

FIGURE 3 Learning new duties for an existing job.

productivity, and quality. For example, operators who lack skills may never reach production quotas, while they may generate excessive scrap and produce parts with too many defects. Below-par output, wasted time and materials, and products that do not meet quality standards represent lost opportunity because the resources of the company have been committed to work activity that does not result in full return as it should. Imagine the differences that could occur if a skilled worker had the same resources. Output quotas and quality standards for products could be met, and waste of time and materials could be reduced. Without any change in employee time, supervisor time, capital equipment, and raw materials, it would be possible to meet all output expectations with a skilled worker. That is lost opportunity!

Risks are evidenced by problems associated with such issues as customer satisfaction and government regulations. For example, dissatisfied customers may discontinue their business before it is realized that their expectations have not been met. Failure to comply with government regulations, such as on the handling of hazardous wastes, exposes the company to fines and penalties. It may not be possible to avoid all risks, but their negative impact can be minimized.

The risk factors associated with employees learning job duties can be approached from different perspectives. One option is to ignore the liabilities or consider them an inevitable cost of doing business. Another option is to minimize or prevent them by shortening or reducing skill gaps. In the majority of cases, it is more cost-effective to attend to the skill gaps than to absorb the costs resulting from the risks.

Every employee experiences skill gaps at some time in their working career. The gaps are often left to close themselves naturally, over time. However, in today's business climate, fewer companies have time to wait. The rate and magnitude of change in the workplace, the shrinking margin of error, and the increasing complexity of jobs all compel companies to actively address skill issues. Employee training presents a viable and reliable method for closing skill gaps. Training simply compresses the time needed to attain proficiency and, when conducted within the company, offers high levels of efficiency and control. The following example explains this concept with dollars and sense.

A new production center is purchased by a manufacturer, and an operator is hired. The new center is estimated to cost $100 per hour to own and operate. The operator's labor and benefit rate is $25 per hour. The vendor of the production center provides two weeks of training for the operator of the new center. After that, it takes the operator about 2½ months to fully learn the required skills. For this first 3 months (13 weeks) the new center and operator are not able to meet output expectations. This 13-week period includes 520 man-hours in each eight-hour shift. Therefore, the direct cost relative to one worker on one machine amounts to approximately $52,000 in machine time and $13,000 in labor, or $65,000 total. In addition to the normal business risks, the new production center brings risks due to the concentration of productive capacity in one center.

The estimation of lost opportunity, in the example, reflects the difference between the output that might have been achieved by the employee, but was not, while learning to operate the production center. Examination of Figure 4 provides a visual estimate of the extent of loss. The shaded section above the curve represents the percent of expected output that the worker is not able to fulfill. The more quickly the worker can reach full productivity, the smaller the shaded area (on the graph) and opportunity loss will be. In manufacturing jobs, for example, it is frequently estimated that employees reach 40 to 80% of job mastery during their first 90 days in a new job or in a job that has had a major change in duties. Seldom does a worker reach mastery within this period. The percentage of expected output below the engineered standard represents the level of loss. Therefore, a worker who is producing at only a 70% level is incurring a 30% loss for the company.

If we estimate that the worker whose output is shown in Figure 4 was averaging 70% over the full 13 weeks of learning, the lost opportunity

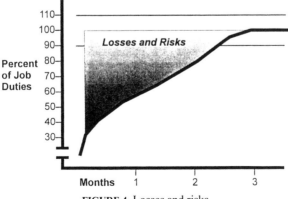

FIGURE 4 Losses and risks.

is $19,500 (30% of $65,000). This estimation of the cost of lost opportunity, based on wages and machine costs, illustrates that on-the-job experimentation is expensive but the potential for significant savings exists if the learning period can be made more efficient by raising output more quickly or by shortening the amount of time required to reach full productivity.

Another approach to estimating the cost of lost opportunity is to use employee wages and benefits and the value of expected output rather than machine cost. For example, a new production center that costs $52,000 to own and an additional $13,000 in wages to operate for 13 weeks may be expected to produce parts that are valued at $100,000. The estimate of lost opportunity may more accurately be 30% of the $100,000 in reduced production ($30,000), because that represents the output that did not occur, even though the machinery and labor costs were incurred. Material costs have not been included in the estimates used but would be expected to parallel the level of output. That is, higher output generally requires higher material costs, although these are offset somewhat by the waste likely to be produced by a learner.

A company can use the form of estimate that best fits its mode of operation to consider the cost of learning by its employees. The $19,500 and $30,000 estimates, however, apply to only a single employee. The estimate must be multiplied by the total number of employees who are engaged in learning new or revised jobs within a given period of time. Even the most conservative estimates of lost opportunities result in dramatically large values. Not-for-profit organizations may prefer to use some value other than dollars, but the estimation process would be similar.

The cost of risk is estimated in essentially the same manner as an insurance company would underwrite a policy. A variety of risks, such as product defects, missed deadlines, and infractions of government laws and regulations, may be associated with an employee learning a job or new job duties. Factors to consider include out-of-pocket expenses such as repairs, rework, attorney fees, and court costs, as well as delayed costs such as loss of future revenue from a customer, worker's compensation premiums, and unemployment insurance experience rates. Since there is less than a 100% chance that the risk will materialize, the estimated amount of the loss is multiplied by the probability of its occurrence.

The potential cost of risks can be made more realistic by considering actual situations. What is the probability that an employee, while learning new job duties, will make a mistake that leads to a customer complaint which, in turn, causes that customer to buy from a competitor?

The probability of that event multiplied by the lost revenue from that customer represents the value of the risk. Other factors of risk include the costs of machine repair and down-time resulting from damage caused by improper operation by an employee. Violation of a government regulation by an inexperienced employee can lead to fines or penalties, not to mention the associated legal fees. Serious injury to an employee learning new job responsibilities can increase the organization's worker's compensation rate by a noticeable percentage of its overall payroll.

Where the estimated costs of lost opportunities and risks exceed the cost of training, training may be an appropriate solution. Training needs to address skill issues, not management problems, and can be most effective if targeted on specific skill objectives. With many available choices for the delivery of training, chances are good that training will prove to be a less-expensive alternative than letting the skills gap correct itself over time. Structured on-the-job training can be one of the least expensive and most effective means of delivering training to meet performance expectations.

ASSESSING TRAINING NEEDS

Training is often contemplated as a solution for problems of employee performance. Whether the issue is one of productivity, quality, communications, customer service, or company policy, training is frequently suggested as a possible remedy. There are cases where periodic training is required for the health and safety of workers. What stronger mandate for training as a solution could there be? However, the potential for training to improve business performance requires closer examination of the variables involved. Training does not solve all business performance problems and it may not produce the intended results.

Changing Attitudes

Training may have some impact in changing attitudes. It can make individuals aware of expectations, perhaps correcting an oversight in providing clear descriptive information about what to do on the job. A supervisor may have assumed that the employee already knew the job or, for some reason, was uncomfortable about communicating job expectations. For example, hospital custodial employees need to maintain a cautious attitude toward the disposal of blood-borne pathogens. This attitude can affect the worker's approach to waste disposal and can be shaped by knowledge of the possible hazards involved. In this case, attitude development would be most effective if employees also were taught the skill necessary to carry out the correct waste disposal practices.

There are cases where employees do not understand the rewards and consequences of their behavior. They may perceive that there is not sufficient benefit to be gained from the correct performance of their work. A breakdown in the enforcement of established work rules and policies can interfere with the achievement of results. Unresponsiveness to rewards and consequences can often be traced to such job variables as pay, job security, accountability, recognition, and the level of supervision present in the work setting. Pay and benefit issues are often based on perceptions about the pay and benefits received by others who are doing comparable work within the company or in other companies. Systems of accountability and recognition need to reward correct behavior while withholding rewards when work performance does not meet expectations. What may appear to be employee performance problems often are problems of supervisor incompetence instead. Problems may be compounded by reliance on supervisors to carry out oversight functions, in cases where the level of supervision has been reduced in the "flattening" of the organization.

Generally, training can solve performance problems only when employees are incapable of performing their duties. The primary question is, "Have the employees ever produced the expected output under the same general conditions?" If the answer is "yes," it is likely that the problem is motivational and not a skills gap. It is important to recognize the qualifier "under the same general conditions." If the conditions under which the work is performed have changed, a skills gap should be suspected.

When performance is below standard and an employee motivation problem (the employee will not perform) has been ruled out, it may mean that the employee cannot perform for one of two possible reasons. Either something is interfering with the work or the worker lacks the necessary skill. These reasons can be separated from each other and are discussed under the following two headings.

Interference

Interference occurs when employees have acquired the needed skills but are prevented from using them in their job duties. Not having the necessary tools, materials, equipment, or information to perform the job are typical causes of interference. In many situations, interference surfaces as the reason for an apparent skill gap. For example:

(1) Pliers are available when box wrenches should be used, leading to damaged adjusting fasteners.

(2) Computer programs have "bugs" that lock up the system, leading to excessive time to access information.

(3) Stock materials are at one extreme of the tolerance range, precluding any variation during production.

(4) Machine tools are worn to the point that they drift past the tolerances specified for the parts they produce.

(5) Operators are utilizing work instructions that are two revisions out-of-date from the current procedures for filling orders.

(6) Other workers are producing low-quality parts in order to meet some incentive goal, resulting in excessive rejects and rework.

Lack of Skill

There are several reasons why employees lack the skills necessary to perform their job duties. They may have never performed the job before or may not have the basic skills needed in the field of work. There are four basic factors to consider when assessing a skill deficiency: underlying skills, number and sequence of skills, related skills, and degree of skill.

Underlying Skills

What level of skill is missing? Is it an underlying skill or a job skill? Underlying skills directly support job skills. They are usually basic skills such as reading, math, computer operation, interacting with others, and following instructions. These skills must be in place before employees can learn job skills. Replacing manual machines with computer numerically controlled (CNC) equipment is a good example of where underlying skill problems surface as a result of technological change.

Number and Sequence

How many different skills does the employee need to perform the job, and in what order? Some employees must master only a few simple skills, while others need to utilize a long list of competencies. Identifying and listing the skills expected of an employee provides the basis for assessing which skills might be missing.

Determining the sequence of skills to perform is sometimes important. Changes in work procedures often contribute to this problem. For example, employees asked to check their own work may not be trained in measurement and inspection techniques.

Related Skills

Are there any related or general skills the employee needs from time to time? Most jobs have primary skills that are used frequently, and secondary skills that are used occasionally. Sometimes the secondary or related skills are overlooked or are learned superficially and become problems only in isolated instances. For example, factory work-cell employees may be expected to interact with vendors even though they have never learned how to conduct a proper business meeting.

Degree of Skill

How well does the employee perform the skill according to established standards of quality and production? Countless employees learn largely through trial and error and, consequently, learn only enough to meet minimum standards. They may never be made aware of the true requirement of the job. Many actual skill problems can be traced to incomplete learning of all aspects of the skill. Comparing the person to the standards can provide evidence as to how close the person is to the established standards of quality and production and how much additional training or guided practice is required.

There are some straightforward questions that can be asked in a logical sequence to help determine whether training is likely to solve a performance problem. In Figure 5, there may be a skill problem if the answer is "no" to any of the asterisked questions. To further define the nature of a skill deficiency and to gain insight into the actual training need, the questions in Figure 6 should be considered.

The need for training is based on skill problems, not management deficiencies. Possible training solutions should be considered concurrently with management actions before concluding that training is the answer. Frequently, the solution to a performance problem lies in a

Work Output Indicators	
Motivation	
Have employees ever produced the expected output?	YES NO*
..........under the same general conditions?	YES NO*
Are employees aware of job expectations?	YES NO
Do employees perceive the rewards and	
consequences associated with the job?	YES NO
Do employees place the same value on the job as	
the organization?	YES NO
Interference	
Is there any interference that prevents employees from	
performing their job?	YES NO
Skill	
Do employees possess the necessary skills to	
perform the job?	YES NO*
* Indicates a possible skills problem. All other "no" responses are management issues.	

FIGURE 5 Assessing job training opportunities.

combination of training and management actions. When interferences are allowed to stand or issues of motivation are not addressed, workers who have received necessary training to develop their skills may not be able to realize the return that the training should produce.

At this point, opportunities and problems that can be addressed by SOJT have been separated from those that cannot be. Next, we turn to

Skill Variables
Underlying Skills
What level of skills are missing—underlying skills or job skills?
Number and Sequence
How many different skills do employees need to perform the job and in what order?
Related Skills
Are there any related or general skills employees need from time to time?
Degree of Skill
How well do employees perform the skills according to established standards of quality and production?

FIGURE 6 Isolating skill variables for job training.

the ways in which work is organized and the impact of that structure on what is to be learned and performed by the worker.

ORGANIZATION OF WORK

The rapid rate of change in work within contemporary organizations no longer allows for lengthy processes in developing and delivering training. It has been common for the identification of content, subject matter analysis, instructional design, delivery of instruction, and initial evaluation to take several months. Because of its focus on the development of well-specified job skills, SOJT is justified on the basis of its capability to deliver instruction of critical content at the time when it is needed and the worker is ready for it. Part of SOJT's success is dependent on the trainer's ability to truncate the processes of preparing and delivering instruction. To do this, an understanding of the composition of work within modern organizations is needed.

Processes and operations within a company change continuously, as do the physical environments where the work is performed, as new technologies are acquired and old equipment is discarded. All of these things affect the work that people perform. Yet the structure of jobs and the skills individuals possess are slow to change. Therefore, it is increasingly helpful to determine the changes to be made to the company and its management systems in the foreseeable future in order to anticipate likely changes to jobs and skill requirements. Changes in the way in which a company accomplishes its work can trigger job training needs which may be analyzed and planned for in advance.

It is important to first gain a view of the "big picture" of how work is organized. This is especially helpful for situations where the same skills may apply to several jobs, processes, or work areas. This broad view makes analysis efforts more consistent and efficient and provides a good indicator of the types of documentation needed. At any given point in time, it is now possible to find new or different work structures for similar functions. Many alternative organizational and management schemes are used. They are related to such characteristics of the enterprise as the type of business and ownership, size of the company, technologies used, products and services provided, geographic location, and applicable governmental regulations. There are three general factors, appearing in numerous combinations, that can be used as the basis for organizing job training: job classifications, organizational format, and skill groups.

Job Classifications

The process of analyzing the work in a company logically begins by examining what the jobs are, for the purpose of identifying what they should be. Regardless of the organizational format, job classifications have been long used as the means to divide the work performed in a company into manageable units, that is, jobs. Typical classifications of jobs are according to crafts or professions, equipment, and work processes. In most cases, job classifications indicate what jobs consisted of at some point in the past. Despite the often anachronistic nature of the available information about the organization of work, it is still a solid place to begin an analysis.

Job descriptions, though often dated, can provide information about the work associated with particular crafts or professions. They include information about qualifications, scope of duties, accountability, and educational requirements. The relationship of one job to those with other skill levels may be indicated. Where a company does not have its own job descriptions, the *Dictionary of Occupational Titles* describes thousands of jobs, and includes required and optional job requirements and alternative job titles, without reference to any particular company.

Some common discrepancies between existing job descriptions and actual jobs are the division of one job into several jobs, the aggregation of multiple jobs into one job, and old jobs taken apart and put back together as new jobs. A strong clue that this has happened is a company reorganization or evolutionary changes, such as a transition to work teams, since the last update of the job descriptions.

A reliable source of information about work can be documentation associated with the equipment used in a company. Equipment can range from personal computers to hand tools to automated assembly centers. Most documentation describes how work is performed on the equipment and often refers to tasks, steps, or procedures. In terms of its application to jobs, several people may be responsible for the same equipment but each person performs different tasks. This is especially true in situations where one piece of equipment, such as a test instrument, is used by maintenance workers for one set of functions and by production workers for separate functions.

Work process information is an additional source of job descriptions and work classifications. Work processes can be the same across equipment, departments, or even different locations, so determining their relative impact on jobs is important. Companies such as food processors and refineries, for example, are strongly oriented to work processes that cut across many jobs. Analyzing work may involve following a process from start to finish and then reexamining how that process applies to various jobs.

Organizational Format

Today, businesses that have only one type of organizational unit are unusual. Typical organizational formats include (a) functions or departments, (b) products lines or business units, (c) work teams, (d) production cells, and (e) focused factories. The same organizational format can be used for a variety of products and services. For example, frying pans or insurance policies may be produced by functional areas, business units, work teams, or production cells. The difference is how management chooses to plan and control the work of employees. The intent of management is usually to enhance the work effort of employees and the output of the business.

Within a manufacturing company organized by functions or departments, the scope of work may include manufacturing, engineering, quality control, safety, administration, and accounting. Within each of these functions there may be several levels of work complexity. The company may also have several products or forms of a product. The functions may be further divided into departments of greater specialty, such as, machining, fabrication, assembly, and shipping, often found in a traditional manufacturing environment. Employees who perform the same or similar job tasks are grouped together and their jobs are arranged according to work levels, steps, or grades. This type of work organization is most effective when the same people do the same work all the time from among a large number of very specific jobs.

Another basis for company organization can be its products or services. Work structures based on product or service lines often contain jobs from many functional areas. For example, employees ranging from assemblers to accountants can all belong to the same unit dedicated to a specific product or line of products. Often, each organizational unit produces its output independently from other units. For each product or service there are usually several levels of work, and the scope of work cuts across multiple functions such as production, marketing, and accounting. This organization can be duplicated, as appropriate, for every other product or service the company offers. However, the levels of work may vary among the business units as demanded by the product or service. This type of organization functions best when the company wants employees to focus on a specific end product. Such an organization fosters improvements in quality, defect reduction, shorter lead times, and other process improvements. Jobs in a business unit organization are more broadly defined, for example, machinist, fabricator, engineering and safety specialist, and administrative assistant. The configuration of responsibilities in these broader jobs results in training needs that are different from those generated in other work classifications.

The concept of working in teams is a relatively new, but increasingly popular, organizational variation. Teams may include any collection of employees logically grouped by the management of a company. Teams may be very specific, existing for a short duration to solve a particular problem or to initiate a new operation. Team organization can also be universal across a company with the intention of long-term utilization. Principal goals of using work teams are flexibility, adaptability, and responsiveness to change. Companies can be more globally competitive by shortening production times and costs while improving quality and customer service. In a manufacturing company, it is not unusual to find "shop floor" occupations organized into teams and "office" jobs structured in a functional format. This has implications for the content and delivery of training to prepare individuals for their jobs.

Other organizational schemes can be derived from those that have been described. For example, a series of products, rather than one, may be produced by a unit identified as a factory that is paralleled by other factories within a company. Serving the factories, in a support capacity, there may be a large team or cell. Again, the work is consolidated into fewer functional areas and job classifications to achieve as much vertical integration as possible.

A company can choose to produce or service using organizations that are structurally different from each other while the essential work activities, in total, remain the same. What occurs at an individual work station may be noticeably different among organizational systems, and a change from one system to another can significantly alter what a worker is expected to be able to do. A good analysis recognizes that the work performed by people may remain constant even though the configuration of tasks, as they are aggregated into jobs, may change. Successful SOJT, therefore, results when it accurately reflects organizational format even though the structure may have little to do with work as traditionally defined.

Skill Groups

A third perspective on the organization of work involves groups of skills that may be found in one or many areas of a company. Scanning the company for groups of skills helps organize them into logical categories as they may apply to multiple jobs or organizational units. Classifying skills in this manner also helps prevent duplication of documentation and training efforts. Determining which skills are common across jobs provides indications of where group training activities may be appropriate. For example, blueprint reading and math skills are very common to many different jobs, from the assembler to the engineer. It is with these types of skills that most group training opportunities are feasible and cost-effective. However, it should be noted that the probability of multiple employees needing to develop the same skills at the same time is quite low. Therefore, conducting SOJT for individuals, even on common topics, may remain the most efficient means of developing employee skills.

Skills may also be grouped according to a particular job held by an employee. In the past, this group of skills was often associated with a trade or craft such as masonry or welding. Today, a job may be a collection of diverse skills combined according to the goals and structure of the company. Job skills are applicable to individual employees performing the same work. For example, all painting operators may need to be able to mix pigment, thinners, and dryer. This specific skill is probably built on a more general skill of measuring volumes that may have been learned in school or at another job before entry into the painting job.

Documentation of the skills needed to perform the work in a company is necessary for developing SOJT. In order to provide training for specific skills, as in SOJT, those skills must be precisely identified in time to meet the need for the utilization of the skill. Understanding the job classifications, organizational format, and skill groups of a company provides a basis for analysis of the work that is and will be performed in that company. This understanding is important to delivering instruction that is timely, to those who need it, for the work that they are to perform.

DOCUMENTATION OF WORK

Existing documentation about work that is performed in a company takes a number of forms. All of these forms can help facilitate understanding of what it is workers need to know and be able to do in order to reach expectations for productive capacity as quickly as possible. Knowledge of needed skills can serve as a basis for designing effective SOJT. The analysis process may use the following sources within the organization to help identify work performed:

- job descriptions
- task inventories
- operating procedures
- equipment documentation
- criteria for quality and workmanship
- specifications and standards
- safety and regulatory requirements

A careful examination of these elements of a company will reveal the many things that workers need to know and the skills that they need to have.

Successful job training must match the way in which the work is organized. In order for job trainers to be effective, they must have adequate documentation to implement instruction on how to perform that work. Accurate and consistent plans and references are necessary to support systematic job skill development in any work setting. The alternative is to leave employees to build skills through random, unstructured experimentation on the job, an option that produces a host of risks and losses.

Work can be documented in a logical and consistent manner regardless of how the work is organized. Figure 7 shows a portion of an actual master skills inventory from a company that manufactures industrial pumping equipment. At one time this manufacturing plant was staffed with traditional craft jobs such as machine operators and material handlers. Now, the company is organized into production cells, where work teams perform a broad variety of work activities. The actual work activities performed in the company have not changed significantly. However, as this inventory illustrates, support functions (such as manufacturing engineering) have been largely merged with production work (such as operating CNC machining centers).

Contemporary organizational formats, such as complex production cells, require employees to more deliberately plan and develop a wide range of skills, some of which may never have been previously grouped into a single job. Figure 7 shows how skills can be combined into a single job made up of entry and core skills. In addition, it shows how an

MASTER SKILLS INVENTORY

	ENTRY SKILLS	Demonstrated?	When?	Verified By

General Skills

Communications
Reading - Engineering Topics

Calculations
Statistics

| | | ☐ | | |
| | | ☐ | | |

CORE SKILLS

Automated Production

Machining Processes

Costing	Establishes accounting methods for variables such as machine time, labor costs and costs of materials and presents costing data to management and engineering personnel.	☐		
Performance Testing	Tests the performance and reliability of automated machining processes including repeatability and process control.	☐		
Technology Transfer	Reviews the utilization of similar automation technologies within the company and at other locations to determine how those technologies can be transferred to the current operation.	☐		

CNC and Specialty Machining

Conversational Controls

620 Multiplex - Attend	Attends the machining center by starting and stopping the machine and loading and unloading parts.	☐		
620 Multiplex - Operate	Operates the machining center and its associated material handling equipment including changing inserts, performing minor control program edits and adjusting feeds and speeds.	☐		
620 Multiplex - Setup	Sets up the machining center for production parts including changing tooling, jaws, collets, fixtures and control programs.	☐		

FIGURE 7 Sample items from master skills inventory.

218

inventory can be utilized to plan and record skill development. This simple approach establishes a map for job training, where both the trainer and trainee can chart their progress. Skills lists of this type have become increasingly useful in companies subject to quality system standards, where management must verify that employees do, in fact, possess the requisite skills for their jobs.

Most job training, however, occurs at a level of detail lower than the descriptions listed in the inventory in Figure 7. Furthermore, job trainers typically require more structure than simple skill definitions to successfully conduct job training. The job training guide in Figure 8 is an example of skills documentation well-suited to SOJT. Stemming from one of the skills listed in the inventory in Figure 7, this guide provides sufficient detail to support consistent and reliable job training by a subject matter expert. The information contained in the guide structures the training situation and gives the job trainer a precise map of how to conduct instruction. Such documentation allows the organization to utilize multiple subject matter experts as trainers rather than relying on a limited number of individuals with professional instructional skills.

Further examination of the job training guide in Figure 8 reveals that it contains many of the same elements found in a typical instructional plan. The skill description and standards are equivalent to a behavioral objective with notes for preparing a training session. The points cover a series of instructional steps or operations that might be found in a lesson plan. The difference, however, is that this guide is organized and written in a manner easily understood by most people, not just technical professionals. In a comprehensive quality management system, this type of document serves as a bridge between skills inventories and operations documents such as work instructions, manuals, specifications, and job routers.

Documentation that is carefully prepared, presented, and controlled is the key to SOJT. It serves as a series of increasingly detailed skills maps that guide trainer and trainee to their goal of a properly developed skill performed according to predetermined standards. It reduces the need for exotic instructional methodologies and reliance on professional trainers to implement instruction. Since the vast bulk of skills acquisition occurs in the workplace with one trainer and one trainee, it only makes sense to pave the way for job trainers and trainees with clear and effective documentation.

JOB TRAINING GUIDE

CNC and Specialty Machining

Conversational Controls

620 Multiplex - Attend

Skill Description and Standards

Skill Level and Occupation Codes   1   6

Attends the machining center by starting and stopping the machine and loading and unloading parts.

Key Actions: Starts the machine only when the doors are closed and control indicators are green.

Quality Standard: Produces parts according to the specifications outlined in the parts specification setup sheet.

Production Standard: Parts quantities match the production schedule for the shift and machinist.

Underlying Skills: Reads blueprints, control programs, and setup sheets. Uses digital measuring instruments.

Tools and Equipment: Mazak 600 series Multiplex Turning Center.

Information Sources: John Crampton and Susan Kamener

POINTS

1 Orient the machinist to the overall machine, including controller, in-feed and out-feed parts handlers, and turning center components. Emphasize safety requirements, including keeping the doors closed when the machine is in operation.

2 Explain how to load the control program that matches the parts to be produced and point out how to bring the machine up on a "warm start."

3 Demonstrate how to manually step through the control program to insure that a machine crash will not occur.

4 Demonstrate the sequence of indicator lights that must be lit before the cycle starts and how to determine if bar stock is available to the machine's in-feed.

5 Demonstrate how to retrieve finished parts from the machine's out-feed and explain how to verify that the parts conform to specifications.

6 Demonstrate how to perform an emergency stop and then check for machine damage before restarting the operation.

Document Control

Record ID: 241

Recorded By: DB

Record Date: 2/12/94

Entered By: EH

Revised By: MJ

Revision Date: 11/15/94

Print Date: 6/6/95

User Information

Name

Employee Number

FIGURE 8 Sample job training guide.

STRUCTURED ON-THE-JOB TRAINING METHODS

Much has been written on the subject of developing job skills, including material associated with instructional systems design. Systems of analysis, design, development, delivery, and evaluation have been devised to guide trainers through a process designed to produce the best possible instruction. Nevertheless, professional training functions are limited in some companies and virtually unheard of in smaller organizations. The reason is simple: It is often perceived to be less risky and costly to let employees learn job skills through trial and error than to incur the expenses associated with formal instructional services.

Yet, since SOJT occurs almost continuously in every work setting, why not make it as effective and efficient as possible? The answer can be found in instructional techniques developed long ago. Job training saw widespread use during World War II and consisted of a plain and easy four-step method, "show, tell, do, check," where thousands of workers were trained in war production. Variations on these steps have persisted to the present and still produce the same benefits when properly practiced. A common variation consists of the following steps:

(1) Prepare the trainee.
(2) Present the operation.
(3) Observe the trainee.
(4) Provide follow-up.

Coupled with well-organized and up-to-date documentation, this simple four-step method yields excellent results. All that is needed are three key ingredients: (a) a job trainer who knows about and consistently utilizes an SOJT method, (b) a trainee prepared to learn, and (c) sufficient documentation to guide them both towards the intended result—a predefined skill performed at a predetermined standard. When structured and implemented in this manner, SOJT can effectively develop skills even in complex work settings involving computers, automation, and high-risk operations.

CONCLUSION

One alternative to SOJT is to let employees wind their way to competence through trial and error, an option fraught with risks and losses.

Another approach is to enlist professional instructional services which can entail high costs and complex methods. Most companies, however, can afford neither the time nor expense of high-risk experimentation or high-cost overhead services. SOJT is, and has been, the most viable means for developing employee skills. It is safe, simple, and relatively inexpensive. It can produce skills at minimal expense with minimal disruption using existing resources.

Effective SOJT entails a surprisingly straightforward series of steps:

• Ascertain the company's goals and strategic plans.
• Determine how these plans permeate the company and manifest themselves as skills required to fulfill company goals.
• View the opportunities and risks associated with skills gaps as key indicators of where to focus SOJT efforts.
• Assess when and where to develop skills or take other corrective actions in lieu of training.
• Examine how skills are affected by other variables, such as tools and work procedures.
• Structure skills information to match the structure of work to which it is applied.
• Prepare documentation to serve as a series of skill maps.
• Insure job trainers provide consistent and reliable instruction by using a simple SOJT method.

It is obvious that the path to SOJT is long. In fact, getting to the intersection of the trainer, the trainee, and the skill to be developed requires most of the effort. But once there, the ingredients are quite simple: a knowledgeable trainer, a prepared trainee, and good documentation are all that is required. Given this simple combination, it is easy to imagine how powerful a tool SOJT can be for anyone in a work setting.

CHAPTER 8

An Approach to Program Evaluation

DAVID D. L'ANGELLE — *California State University–Long Beach*

THE evaluation of an instructional program is a process, not an event. This suggests that when developing training using the Instructional Systems Development approach (discussed in Chapter 2), course/program evaluation ought to be an integral part of the system. It must be incorporated from the start and must involve measuring both the process and products of training on an ongoing basis. It must also be flexible, so that decision makers can get information relevant to their training program goals. This chapter provides assistance in using the elements of a systematic approach to efficient and effective program evaluation.

RESEARCH ON PROGRAM EVALUATION

America's training effort must effectively contribute to the introduction of new technology, increased productivity, and economic growth. Therefore, professional instructors and trainers must increasingly be concerned with developing effective training courses and programs and substantiating their value. This means a commitment to consistently evaluating the value, worth, and merits of training courses and programs and redesigning those aspects of training that fail to meet the needs of participants and the organization. It also means using a comprehensive evaluation approach that assesses (a) how well the program works when measured against certain criteria, and (b) the quality of the finished product.

Deterline (1977) reported that, in past years, program evaluation was "downplayed," and "its results were of little importance" (p. 14). In addition, many training specialists were engaged in survival evaluation in which they defended themselves or their position in response to pressure from top management. As a result, training specialists often resorted to what Randell (1960) called the use of "joy sheets, in which participants reacted to some nebulous, generalized, and irrelevant criteria that measures nothing" (p. 187).

223

Cook (1980) found that evaluation was not even a major topic area in a study conducted with 2700 members of the American Society for Training and Development (ASTD). Instead of being a basic function of practitioners, evaluation was buried in the general area of training research. This led the ASTD Professional Development Committee to conclude that there was "an absence of a clear function dealing with training evaluation" (p. 4). In a major study on evaluation efforts in industry, a large majority of 285 participating companies evaluated only the reactions of the trainees (did they enjoy the training?) and whether or not they learned anything. Little attention was given to the application of knowledge and skills to the job, or the impact of training on participants and the organization.

This pattern continued, as revealed in a study by Brandenburg (1982) with ASTD training professionals. The researcher found that "no universally accepted model for evaluating training exists, nor are there generally accepted modes of operation or behavior" (p. 14). Brandenburg concluded:

(1) The most commonly used technique of program evaluation is the "reaction" type of feedback. Cognitive and performance-based outcome measures are used less often, with impact measures on the participant and organization practically non-existent.

(2) Most evaluation functions are performed by assigned training personnel who have little or no evaluation expertise. Therefore, "evaluation knowledge and skills" are lacking in most training personnel who are assigned these functions.

(3) Evaluation is viewed by many training professionals as a "one-time event" rather than a continuous activity. As a result, longitudinal data collection techniques are seldom used (p. 14).

Confusion existed among training specialists as to the functions of evaluation and their role in carrying out those functions.

Catalanello and Kirkpatrick (1968) reported that, not only were the function and role in evaluation unclear, but there was a lack of "systematic" methods to assess the effects of training on personnel behavior. Their study, which determined the evaluation techniques used by business, industry, and government, identified the following levels of participation:

(1) *Reaction*—Eighty-five of the firms attempted to measure the participants' reactions to training or how well they liked the program.

(2) *Learning*—Forty-three of the firms measured the amount of learning that took place in the program, or the extent to which the training content was assimilated.

(3) *Behavior*—Twenty-one firms attempted to measure changes in the trainees' on-the-job behavior, that is, how well the skills they learned in the training program were applied to the job.

(4) *Impact*—Sixteen firms tried to determine whether their training created any personnel or organizational change.

The authors concluded that "the state-of-the-art in evaluation is still in its infancy" (p. 258).

Along with an unclear direction, the critical measures of the effectiveness of training were generally neglected. The question, "What measurable improvements in employee performance and organizational productivity can be attributed to training?" was rarely addressed. Dobbs (1980) reported that less than 25% of 3000 ASTD members attempted to measure on-the-job performance changes, in spite of the fact that as few as 1% felt that it could not be measured (p. 14). More recently, Shelton and Alliger (1993) reported on an ASTD study conducted among 300 leading organizations. Only 20% of those surveyed evaluated training in terms of economic effect (level 4). The lack of progression of the state-of-the-art in program evaluation in the 1980s continued to be evident.

Many strategies for evaluation exist; however, they are inconsistently used and infrequently applied. For example, following a 1991 survey conducted by the ASTD's Benchmarking Forum, Kimmerling (1993) reported that only 60% of respondents evaluated training at any of the four levels developed by Kirkpatrick, for every type of training, and only 20% measured effectiveness at all four levels. In addition, the strategies for evaluation ranged from the informal to processes using "multi-colored flow charts for different levels of evaluation" (p. 35).

The literature also reveals that much of the evaluation in education has been psychometric, employing statistical measures. Further, it has been oriented toward finding the "truth" of the matter, appropriate for academic research but demonstrably inappropriate for training program evaluation. Putman (1980) rationalizes that this "truth-seeking" approach concerns itself not with helping evaluate data to determine how it best can be used, but primarily:

> . . . sorting out the one actual version of reality from among the many possible versions. Thus, a researcher takes great pains to eliminate poten-

tial sources of "error" or confounding, by focusing on issues of design, methodology, and analysis. Questions like "OK, what do we do with this information?" or "What actually happened?" seem somewhat ill-mannered or yokelish. (p. 37)

Many training specialists agree with Putman's assessment of "rationalistic research" and understand the need to direct their efforts to more practical evaluation methods which help them choose intelligently among possible courses of action to solve problems. In this type of evaluation, conclusions are drawn and recommendations are made to individuals or groups who have responsibility for making program decisions.

Bakken and Bernstein (1982) laid out the focus for practical evaluation when they suggested the following:

(1) Conduct evaluations based on the needs of the decision makers.

(2) Ensure that the levels of evaluation are consistent with the training objectives.

(3) Use appropriate methods to measure the outcomes.

(4) Correct training problems with evaluation results.

The conclusion to be drawn from these studies is that, with few exceptions, little has changed. Over the past three decades, many authors have correctly concluded that evaluation practices have not adequately proven the effectiveness of training, especially in assessing indicators such as trainee performance, attitudes, morale, and organizational productivity.

There is a glimmer of hope, however. A recent survey (1994 Industry Report, 1994) gave an account of evaluation attempts in employee-sponsored training at the four levels of Kirkpatrick's (1976) evaluation model. Their conclusion, which was based on almost 1200 responses, represented organizations with 100 or more employees:

Respondents' answers surprised us. Conventional wisdom holds that very little evaluation goes on at the two "higher" levels. Yet almost two-thirds of all organizations say they evaluate behavior change—and that they do this for a healthy percentage for all the courses they conduct. More startling yet, nearly half of all organizations say they look for changes in business results attributable to their programs. And they do this not just in an occasional pilot evaluation project, but for 44 percent of their courses. (p. 54)

PRINCIPLES OF PROGRAM EVALUATION

The following statement by Patton (1987) describes program evaluation:

> The practice of evaluation involves the systematic collection of information about the activities, characteristics, and outcome of programs for use by specific people to reduce uncertainties, improve effectiveness, and make decisions with regard to what those programs are doing and affecting. (p. 15)

This description emphasizes the systematic collection of information needed by specific people for decision-making and program improvement.

The development of a practical training program evaluation process begins with the following two principles.

(1) *Evaluation must include a determination of how well a program is developed and operated when measured against certain criteria.* Zais (1976) describes this aspect of evaluation as:

> formative evaluation which provides an assessment of curriculum quality which takes place at a number of intermediate points during the development . . . for the purpose of providing data that can be used to "form" a better finished product. (p. 381)

Evaluating training after implementation is important, but the effectiveness of any training program must also be based on valid program design. Therefore, some evaluation activities must focus on the design and development aspects of a training program. For example, job/task analysis processes are assessed to ensure their accuracy and that the results reflect the job for which students are being trained. In addition, training program documents are reviewed to ensure that the administrative and program testing requirements are consistent with performance-based training concepts. Finally, the training materials are evaluated for technical and instructional adequacy.

Once implemented, this evaluation process permits training activities to be viewed from different perspectives. These evaluations include gathering opinions about the operation of the training program. For example, trainees are asked their opinion about the quality of instruction. The trainees' perspective is important because it reveals whether the program is meeting their personal needs.

In addition, job representatives provide input on whether technical information taught in the program is consistent with job performance requirements. Finally, training administrators and evaluators review the performance of the instructors. Their review helps determine whether the instructional methods used are contributing to the achievement of objectives.

(2) *Evaluation must be concerned with the quality of the finished product.* This aspect of evaluation is referred to by Zais (1976) as summative evaluation. It answers the question, "Does the instructional program actually prepare students for the workplace?" The major considerations of this evaluation are whether the

- skills, knowledge, and attitudes taught in the course or program are necessary to perform the job for which students were trained
- graduates adequately perform the job for which they were trained
- graduates' supervisors are satisfied with their attitudes and performance on the job
- training has had a positive effect on the behavior and productivity of the graduates and the organization
- necessary changes, refinements, and improvements are being fed back into the instructional programs

THE SYSTEMATIC APPROACH TO EVALUATION*

This part of the chapter provides assistance in the use of the systematic approach to evaluation (SAE) shown in Figure 1. By using this approach, trainers can focus on planning evaluation activities as a necessary part of a program development effort rather than treat evaluation as an "afterthought." The process provides useful information about the effectiveness of training and can be used to target as many evaluation goals as necessary, considering time, personnel, and other resource constraints.

The approach has been used with evaluation projects in the nuclear power industry, as well as in apprenticeship and journeyman training, career education, vocational education and training, and instructor training. It is a comprehensive approach in that it focuses on the four levels

*The Systematic Approach to Evaluation (SAE) is copyrighted by David D. L'Angelle, Education and Training Systems.

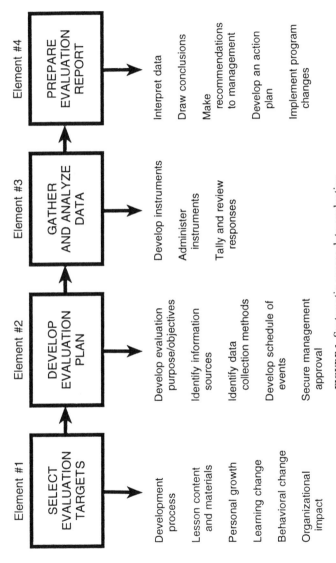

FIGURE 1 Systematic approach to evaluation.

of Kirkpatrick's model, as well as the evaluation of program development. Thus, it is a generic process for evaluating the entire spectrum of evaluation targets.

The evaluation process starts with Element #1—"Select Evaluation Targets." This involves selecting the targets for evaluation, including, but not limited to, the curriculum performance, including the quality of job analysis processes; instructional content and materials; and lesson operation. From there the process moves to Element #2—"Develop Evaluation Plan"—which is the identification of activities, time lines, and personnel involved in the evaluation, as well as a description of the data collection methods. Element #3—"Gather and Analyze Data"—continues with the development and administration of instruments and collection and analysis of data. Finally, Element #4—"Prepare Evaluation Report"—summarizes the data, draws conclusions, and makes recommendations for program improvement.

Element #1—Select Evaluation Targets

The important factor in selecting evaluation targets is to identify some things to measure which both training personnel and management can agree to accomplish. A measurement effort can go awry if the "what to measure" and "how to measure" questions are not addressed carefully from the outset. Therefore, this step consists of identifying the targets for evaluation and focusing them in such a way that the information needed by decision makers in order to improve training programs is obtained.

There are many targets to choose from, as shown in Figure 2. However, in choosing them, the following question must be answered, "What are the needs of the decision makers?" This primary question of the evaluation process should be answered thoroughly and in thoughtful detail because the second, third, and fourth elements refer to and build on the answer.

Meeting the Needs of Decision Makers

The results of an evaluation study are intended to enable decision-making about problems requiring action (Putman, 1980). Therefore, it is important to identify those decision makers who are seeking information about the effectiveness of a training program.

Training specialists have specific needs when it comes to evaluating

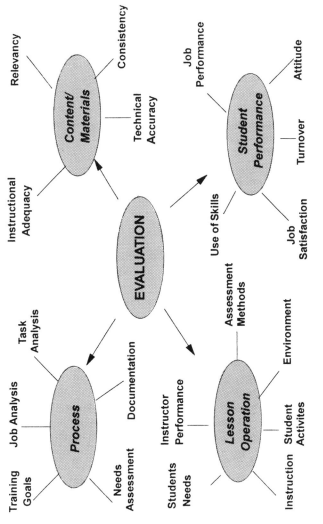

FIGURE 2 Targets for evaluation.

231

training. Typically, they are concerned with training function decisions, such as whether the program taught what it was intended to teach. Certainly, it is important to know if (a) the instructional objectives are relevant to job performance requirements, (b) the instructional methods are effective, (c) participant performance is adequate, (d) skills are transferred to the job, and (e) resources are fully utilized.

However, management decisions are fundamentally different from those made within the training function. The most obvious difference is that, within training, decisions affect only the training function, while management decisions generally affect large portions of an organization. For example, management decision makers are not particularly concerned with course development or the merits of various instructional techniques. Rather, they are concerned with the effects of training on the organization.

It follows then, if the objective is to determine training's impact on sales and profit, do not give "learner reaction to the program" data to management. Putman (1980) made it clear that "once you know by whom your data will be used, find out what kind of data they actually find useful. Then give them that kind of data" (p. 38). Table 1 provides examples of questions asked by management and training specialists for both formative and summative evaluations. As mentioned earlier and shown in Figure 1, the systematic approach for conducting formative and summative evaluation consists of four elements. Different individuals within an organization may be involved in each of these elements; however, training specialists often have overall responsibility for ensuring that each element is carefully planned and carried out.

Evaluation Goals and Outcomes

In their development of the "Systematic Evaluation of Training" (SET) model, Bakken and Bernstein (1982) identified four general goals of training: (a) personal growth, (b) knowledge acquisition, (b) skill acquisition or performance improvement, and (d) organizational development (changes in the "bottom line"). These goals should be written in terms of the contribution made to the overall mission of the organization and matched with training outcomes. The outcomes, which Putman (1980) described as those elements which should be evaluated, were identified in the SET model as learner reaction, knowledge, job performance, and organizational changes (p. 39). For example, if the goal of a

Table 1. Questions asked by management and training specialists for formative and summative evaluation.

Formative Evaluation	Summative Evaluation
Questions Posed by Management	
1. Is the program accomplishing what was intended?	1. What conclusions can be drawn about the program's effectiveness?
2. How can the program be improved?	2. Is the program worth continuing?
Questions Posed by Training Specialists	
1. What are the program goals and objectives?	1. Does the program prepare students for work?
2. Are the program components, e.g., curriculum, instructional materials, and methods effective?	2. Are graduates performing the job for which they were trained?
3. Are the students able to attain the objectives?	3. Are supervisors satisfied with the graduates' job performance?
4. What changes to the program might lead to better attainment of the objectives?	4. Has the training had a positive effect on organizational productivity?
5. What problems are there? How can they be solved?	

Adapted from "A Systematic Approach to Evaluation," by D. Bakken and A. L. Bernstein, 1982, *Training and Development Journal,* p. 45.

course on basic training principles was "personal growth," then it would be a waste of valuable resources trying to assess the impact (outcome) of such a course on organizational sales (Bakken & Bernstein, 1982). However, if the training goal was to "improve performance," such as the development of questioning skills by an instructor, then the effect (outcome) of the training program on the organization's instructional effectiveness ought to be evaluated. Thus, as suggested, it is important to match the outcome that is to be measured to the goal of the training program. Bakken and Bernstein (1982) summarized the importance of selecting evaluation outcomes consistent with training goals, "The key to using this approach to evaluating training is in selecting an outcome that is appropriate to the particular objective of training and to the needs of various decision makers" (p. 45).

Element #2—Develop an Evaluation Plan

There are five steps in the process of developing an evaluation plan: (a) develop an evaluation purpose and objectives, (b) identify information sources, (c) identify data collection methods, (d) develop a schedule of events, and (e) secure management approval.

Step 1. Develop an Evaluation Purpose and Objectives

Bakken and Bernstein (1982) provide clarification on this first step.

One of the primary reasons for evaluating training in the first place is to determine if the goals of the program have been achieved. Unless those goals have been clearly stated at the outset, it may be impossible after the fact to perform a meaningful evaluation. (p. 45)

Wentling (1980) suggested the following statements of purpose: (a) determine what aspects of the total training program need improvement, (b) determine needed curriculum content revisions, (c) identify program graduates' impressions concerning the training they have completed, (d) identify programs needing expansion or removal, (e) determine how well "orientation" courses prepare students for "training" level courses, (f) broaden occupational offerings according to students' needs, and (g) determine the effectiveness of the training in terms of student achievement, program operation, usefulness of skills, and consistency of content (p. 56).

Based on the purpose of evaluation, objectives are created. Evaluation objectives narrow the focus of the evaluation purpose and help operationalize its intent. They reflect what is important to know as a result of the evaluation. A partial sample evaluation plan, containing the evaluation purposes and objectives for a hypothetical Process Control Technician Program, is provided in Table 2. Note that the evaluation objectives are written in the form of questions.

Step 2. Identify Information Sources

Who would be in the best position to answer all of the questions in Table 2? No one person, for sure. As a rule, it is best to gather information from a variety of sources. Getting a cross-section of opinions and ratings gives a reasonably objective picture of program effectiveness. Furthermore, obtaining information from a variety of sources better ensures that all relevant data are gathered. The following sources can typically provide a portion of the information necessary to carry out the evaluation:

Table 2. Sample evaluation plan—process control technician program.

Evaluation Purpose:
To determine the effectiveness of the Process Control Technician Program in terms of the (a) relationship of curriculum content to industry needs, (b) effectiveness of instructional materials, (c) program operation, (d) instructor performance, (e) student achievement, and (f) use of knowledge and skills on the job.

Evaluation Objectives:
Is there evidence that—
1. The program content is consistent with the requirements of the job from the perspective of the Program Advisory Committee?
a. Have job and task analyses been conducted to identify the knowledge and skills to be taught?
b. Are knowledge and skill requirements of the job traceable to the performance objectives and to the technical information to be learned?
2. The instructional materials are effective and help students understand and retain the technical information?
3. The program is operating effectively by meeting the instructional and job needs of participants?
4. Instruction is conducted using proven instructional methods that are designed to help students learn?
5. A criterion-referenced testing program, including written and performance tests, is used to measure student achievement?
6. The skills being taught in the program are being used on the job?

(1) *Administrative personnel*—establish goals, direct activities, evaluate instructor performance, and implement change

(2) *Instructional personnel*—plan and conduct training activities and gather evaluation data

(3) *Students*—perform in training and on the job

(4) *Supervisors*—attest to student performance on the job

(5) *Advisory committees*—evaluate the relevance of the training to the job and assist in establishing training needs

Step 3. Identify Data Collection Methods

Evaluation has been described as an information-gathering and decision-making process. Unfortunately, there are four basic problems that inhibit this process. They are:

(1) *Lack of data*—Many decisions affecting training are based on personal opinions influenced by unsolicited comments or anecdotal information. As a result, training which contributes little to an organization is often continued because the managers thought it was "ok."

(2) *Unreliable data*—Decisions are sometimes made based on inappropriate or irrelevant data. For example, a management course was discontinued because the trainers failed to provide appropriate data to line managers concerning the job improvement aspects of the course. As a result, line managers stopped sending participants to the course because they were not aware of its value. Evaluation data can also be misleading if technical faults bias the data.

(3) *Untimely data*—The most sophisticated evaluation is useless if decision makers are not provided the data in a timely fashion.

(4) *Incomplete data*—Problems are often identified as a result of a course evaluation, but the causes cannot be corrected through training. Adverse management practices, for example, are detrimental to morale and productivity; yet, these practices can be changed only by management. Nevertheless, when decisions are made regarding the training program, data on the real problem is ignored (Brethower & Rummler, 1976, p. 71). These problems can be minimized by carefully identifying information sources and data collection methods consistent with the evaluation objectives. Table 3 shows examples of information sources and appropriate data collection methods for the evaluation objectives which were listed in Table 2.

Step 4. Develop Schedule of Events

The schedule of events identifies the evaluation activities to be conducted along with the responsible person and the target completion date of each activity. Table 4 presents an example of the content and layout for a schedule of events.

Step 5. Secure Management Approval

When completed, the evaluation plan is shared with appropriate decision makers within the training function and at various management

Table 3. Sample evaluation plan—process control technician program.

Program Evaluation Data Collection		
Evaluation Objectives*	Information Sources	Data Collection Methods
Adequacy of training program content (Objective #1)	Program administrator	Document study—Review of the process and results of the job/task analysis efforts
Adequacy of instructional materials (Objective #2)	Instructor	Review of instructional materials using a checklist
Meeting training needs (Objective #3)	Students	Participant reaction questionnaire
Use of instructional methods (Objective #4)	Instructor's supervisor	Instructor observations using an instructor evaluation form
Student achievement of objectives (Objective #5)	Instructors	Review of knowledge and performance test data
Use of skills on the job (Objective #6)	Graduates and their supervisors	Interviews with graduates and their supervisors, using a questionnaire

*Evaluation objectives were stated in Table 2, and objective numbers in this table correspond to the objective numbers in Table 2.

Table 4. Sample schedule of events—process control technician program.

Schedule of Events		
Activities	Person Responsible	Target Date
1. Meet with advisory committee	Evaluation coordinator	15 October 1995
2. Conduct planning meeting with staff	Evaluation coordinator	21 October 1995
3. Develop draft instruments	Assigned staff member	27 October 1995
4. Approve instruments	Evaluation coordinator	15 November 1995
5. Gather data	Assigned staff member	22 November 1995
6. Analyze data	All staff members	01 December 1995
7. Prepare report	Evaluation coordinator	10 December 1995

levels. One of the most important aspects of any training evaluation process is the involvement of management in the plan. Training improvement requires more than just management's approval and endorsement—it requires their commitment and ownership as well.

An important point was made by Cook (1980) regarding the involvement of management in an evaluation effort. He stated:

> It is important to underline the fact that all of this should be worked out by the training staff in close conjunction with line management. Why? Because training cannot expect to receive acceptance and support from the line unless the line sees value in the business objectives toward which training is aimed. (p. 6)

Element #3—Gather and Analyze Data

The primary purpose of a training course or program is to develop skills in an employee, or, in the case of initial training, a potential employee. Therefore, evaluation should be attempted at that level. However, this may not always be possible because the training goal may be at a less critical level, such as an orientation on the benefits of the organization's medical insurance program. If the goal of a particular course or program is personal growth, participants' reactions to training may provide sufficient information. However, as Zenger and Hargis (1982) pointed out, the use of reaction sheets falls short on rigor because "participants have a tendency to report what [they think] a trainer wants to hear" (p. 11). Furthermore, the quality of participants' reaction information varies widely and provides no obvious link to performance goals (Zenger & Hargis, 1982, p. 11).

The following guidelines are useful when attempting to improve "rigor" in reaction sheets:

(1) Ask questions that students are qualified to answer. Identify operational characteristics of a course or program and ask students if they have witnessed those characteristics.

(2) Decide what factors should be addressed, e.g., objectives, instructional and practice time, quality of materials, skills taught, student involvement, quality of instruction, and so forth.

(3) Keep the statements and questions simple.

(4) Ask for comments to support responses.

(5) Select an appropriate rating scale.

(6) Collect feedback at an appropriate time (some weeks after the course or program was completed).

Appendix A is a course evaluation questionnaire that features the above-listed characteristics.

Follow-up Instruments

Typically, behavior change back on the job is measured with follow-up evaluation instruments completed by employees (course or program graduates) and their supervisors. To increase "rigor" in employee follow-up evaluation efforts, the following guidelines should be considered.

(1) Focus on how the training helped the trainee/employee use the knowledge/skills back on the job.

(2) Administer the instrument 30–90 days after training.

Appendix B illustrates an employee evaluation instrument that can be used for a follow-up evaluation.

Supervisors are an excellent source of information regarding both employees' capabilities and training program effectiveness. They are qualified to (a) rate individual job performance, (b) describe common performance problems, and (c) identify anticipated changes in job requirements. Supervisors should be interviewed periodically as to how well training is preparing new employees to perform their jobs and what training is needed for current employees. The following types of questions can be used to collect supervisors' responses:

(1) How well do graduates perform on the job?

(2) For what tasks were they *not* adequately prepared?

(3) How do recently trained graduates compare with those who received earlier training?

(4) Have you observed unexpected results from training?

(5) What additional training is needed to minimize employee errors?

(6) Do you anticipate any changes in job assignments or equipment which will require additional training or changes in current training?

Appendix C is a supervisor follow-up evaluation instrument. It contains eight questions which provide information on whether the course met its purpose.

Impact Survey

Appendix D is an employee survey instrument which can be used to measure the effects of training on employability and maturity skills. With only slight modifications in wording, the instrument can be appropriate for use by employees or their supervisors. When this is done, a comparison can be made of the responses to determine differences in the employees' and supervisors' perceptions of the training success. This information can be used to strengthen, as necessary, training related to these skills.

Evaluation Strategies

Bakken and Bernstein (1982) raise two very appropriate questions in the following quote.

> In many cases, one of the objectives of training is to have impact on the organization. Thus, individuals and organizations are expected to change as a result of some training program. Assessing the impact of training on either individuals or organizations raises two specific questions. The questions: Has a change actually occurred? Are any changes that have occurred actually the result of training? (p. 44)

The first question is often answered by the use of evaluation strategies which emphasize the before-and-after measurement of knowledge, skills, and so forth. This before-and-after comparison is very useful in determining whether changes have occurred. However, it is not as useful as determining whether the changes were a result of the training.

The second question is usually answered by the use of a control group which is not exposed to the training. Changes occurring in only the test group provide a good indication that the training was responsible.

When the use of a control group is not possible, a time-series analysis of before-and-after measurements of the test group is appropriate. These measurements are made at regular intervals and spaced over a period of weeks or months. This strategy is especially useful when dealing with training outcomes such as changes in productivity (Bakken & Bernstein, 1982, p. 48). Kirkpatrick (1976) pointed out that obtaining "proof" of behavior change is complicated, time-consuming, and expensive, but critical if the measurement is to be valid and reliable (p. 11). He made the following suggestions:

(1) Measure behavior before and after training to ensure that the change in performance can be attributed to the training rather than to outside influences or conditions (pre- and post-training measures).

(2) Measure the behavior over a period of time, after waiting long enough to allow the participant to practice the skills on the job, to ensure that the behavior is permanent (successive post-training measures).

(3) Continue the use of a control group under each of these conditions to assure that the training caused the change (pre- versus post-training, using experimental and control groups).

According to Bakken & Bernstein (1982), there are differences between immediate and long-term changes that occur as a result of training:

> Acquisition of skills or knowledge is usually immediate. We can assess any changes at the completion of training. Changes in productivity, turnover, employee attitudes and the bottom line are unlikely to occur immediately. Assessing the impact of training on these outcomes is necessarily a long-term proposition. (p. 49)

Element #4—Prepare Evaluation Report

Element #4 of the SAE process (see Figure 1) deals with the preparation of an evaluation report. This report must provide decision makers with sufficient data on which to make training program refinements and changes. The use of evaluation results is the most important step in the evaluation process. Without proper use of the results, the most extensive data collection process is wasted.

The importance of using evaluation results has traditionally been overlooked. For example, reports of some very sophisticated and well-planned evaluation studies never reach those who may have potential uses for their contents. In other cases, evaluation results are written into a report and distributed; however, no training program improvement action is taken. To attain the primary goal of evaluation, that is, the improvement of training courses and programs, evaluation results must be incorporated into the decision-making and planning process of trainers, supervisors, and managers.

The use of evaluation results can be divided into four interrelated steps:

(1) Interpreting data and drawing conclusions

(2) Making recommendations to management

(3) Preparing the report

(4) Developing an action plan

Interpreting Data and Drawing Conclusions

Interpretation is the act of explaining or telling the meaning of something. The process, when associated with evaluation reports, can be structured around developing an answer to the question, "What do these data mean?" The interpretation of findings from an evaluation represents an important step in the evaluation process. Interpretation can occur at many levels, involving many different individuals and groups. Consider the following example.

A recent evaluation conducted by a technical community college indicated that 60% of their Process Control Technician Program graduates obtained employment upon completion of their program. Over the past five years, the placement results (percentage of graduates placed) were as follows:

1991	96%
1992	95%
1993	80%
1994	90%
1995	60%

Based on the data in the example, consider the following questions:

- Could a trainer legitimately conclude the effectiveness of the instruction and instructional materials?
- Could the program supervisor legitimately conclude the effectiveness of graduate placement?
- Could the advisory committee conclude that the program is meeting the employment needs of the industry?
- Could the college president conclude that the program is meeting state and community employment needs in the most efficient and effective manner?

These questions suggest that the interpretation of data must be directly related to the purpose of the evaluation. That is, if the sole purpose is to

improve program graduate placement, then that data should be interpreted to facilitate placement improvement and nothing else. Since a
conclusion is a statement of judgment, it must be carefully drawn from
a systematic analysis of evaluation information representing the correct
evaluation objectives.

A Case Study

Read the example evaluation objective below; then, review the "tally"
of the evaluation data from supervisors in Table 5 and from employees
in Table 6.

Evaluation Purpose: (1) To determine the effectiveness of the Process
Control Technician Program in terms of (a) how program graduates
rate their training programs, (b) how graduates are prepared to perform in a position requiring entry-level skills, and (c) the effectiveness
of the training equipment; (2) to provide information about placement,
job satisfaction, and turnover; (3) to provide information related to
graduates remaining on the job, satisfaction of supervisors with graduates' performance, and program graduates' satisfaction with their
jobs.

Evaluation Objective #5: Is there evidence that the Process Control
Technician Program is providing the employability and maturity skills
necessary for success on the job?

Data Collection Method—Evaluation Objective #5: Both supervisors and employees (former program participants) completed a survey
instrument with questions related to the success of the employee in
employability and maturity skills, such as human relations, responsibility, coping with conflict and change, and quantity and quality of
work.

Given the tally data in Tables 5 and 6, consider the following questions:

(1) What would be the most appropriate "data display" format?
(2) How should the data be compared, i.e., groups, scale?
(3) What conclusions can be drawn from the data, i.e., agreements, the
    most and least predominant ratings, significant differences in data
    ($\pm 15\%$), appropriateness of instrument?

Compare your ideas for displaying the data with the model data layouts

Table 5. Supervisor responses to training impact survey.

Question #1: Compared to other employees with similar duties, how well does he/she:				
Employability Skills	Better	Same	Not as Well	No Response
1. Follow company rules?	8	10	5	1
2. Accept and follow directions?	9	9	5	1
3. Accept responsibility for his/her actions on the job?	9	10	4	1
4. Work as a member of a team?	9	10	3	2
5. Get along with others?	10	9	4	1
6. Accept supervisor criticism?	5	4	7	0
7. Provide *quality* work according to company standards?	7	7	6	4
8. Provide *quantity* work according to company standards?	6	10	6	4
Grand total	63/34%	69/37%	40/22%	14/8%

Question #2: Compared to other employees with similar duties, how often does he/she:				
Maturity Skills	More Often	Same	Less Often	No Response
9. Come late for work?	3	5	15	1
10. Become angry or frustrated?	3	9	10	2
11. Need disciplinary action?	1	7	15	1
12. Stay absent from work?	1	8	13	2
13. Leave work early?	1	5	17	1
14. Seem bothered by something?	4	5	14	1
Grand total	13/9%	39/27%	84/58%	8/6%

Note: Number of respondents, 24.

Table 6. Employee responses to training impact survey.

Question #1: Compared to other employees with similar duties, how well do you think you are doing on the job in the following areas:

Employability Skills	Better	Same	Not as Well	No Response
1. Follow company rules?	19	17	1	1
2. Accept and follow directions?	21	13	1	3
3. Accept responsibility for my actions on the job?	22	14	0	2
4. Work as a member of a team?	20	15	1	2
5. Get along with others?	24	13	0	1
6. Accept supervisor criticism?	11	11	13	3
7. Provide *quality* work according to company standards?	18	14	4	2
8. Provide *quantity* work according to company standards?	17	17	0	4
Grand total	152/50%	114/38%	20/7%	18/6%

Question #2: Compared to other employees with similar duties, how often do you do the following on the job:

Maturity Skills	More Often	Same	Less Often	No Response
9. Come late for work?	6	5	25	2
10. Become angry or frustrated?	10	5	20	3
11. Need disciplinary action?	4	7	25	2
12. Stay absent from work?	5	5	26	1
13. Leave work early?	6	5	25	2
14. Feel bothered by something?	4	7	25	2
Grand total	35/15%	34/15%	146/64%	12/5%

Note: Number of respondents, 38.

on Figures 3 and 4. Then examine the model conclusions that are presented in Appendix E.

Making Recommendations to Management

In addition to asking "What do these data mean?," trainers, evaluators, and decision makers also need to inquire "What are the implications of these data and what conclusions can be drawn?" Thus, the evaluation effort must also include clear recommendations that are founded on the results of the evaluation activities. Recommendations can be formulated by trainers, supervisors, administrators, and advisory committee members. Better than an individual interpretation, however, is cooperative interpretation by those individuals who have a stake in the evaluation results. The practice of involving training personnel and managers is just as important as it was at the beginning stage. Therefore, the first step of writing recommendations is to assemble a group of individuals who have a say in the interpretation and use of the evaluation data. Remember, the sole purpose of this activity is to create recommendations which will result in program changes. The group should review each of the conclusions that were developed and give their reactions. The following questions can aid in analyzing conclusions:

(1) Is there sufficient evidence to support the conclusions?
(2) Do the conclusions reflect the consensus of the group?
(3) Are the conclusions compatible with the evaluation objective(s)?
(4) Are the statements precise? Are they logical?

Based on the model conclusions for the case study, a set of model recommendations has been prepared. These recommendations, provided in Appendix F, are presented to management in order to correct program deficiencies.

Preparing the Report

The reporting of evaluation outcomes or results is sometimes thought of as a nonessential activity, especially if the evaluator is an administrator or key individual in the decision-making or planning process. However, unless evaluation procedures and findings are documented, the credibility and survivability of an evaluation may suffer. Additionally, an

Summary	Better	Same	Not as well	No Resp.
Sup.% of Responses	33.87%	37.10%	21.51%	7.53%
Emp. % of Responses	50.00%	37.50%	6.58%	5.92%

FIGURE 3 Model data layout for supervisor and employee responses to training program evaluation.

Summary	More often	Same	Less often	No Resp.
Sup.% of Responses	9%	27%	58%	6%
Emp. % of Responses	15%	15%	64%	5%

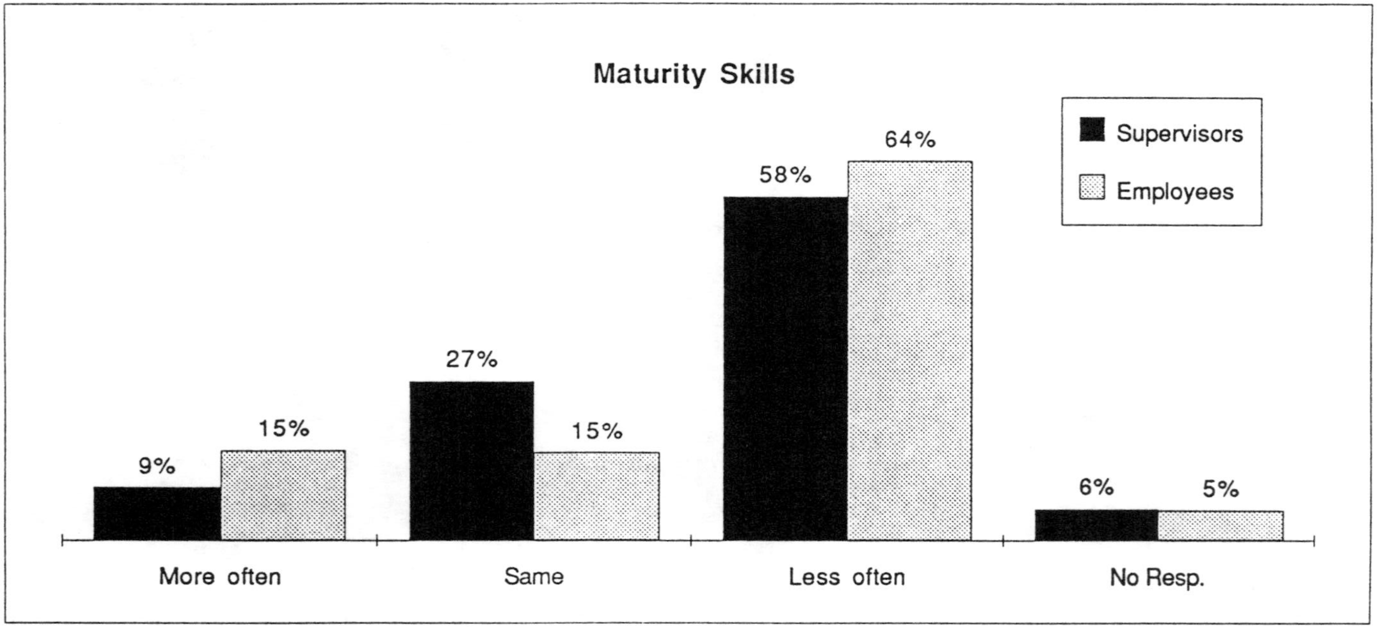

Maturity Skills

Supervisors
Employees

64%

58%

15%

27%

15%

9%

6%

5%

More often

Same

Less often

No Resp.

FIGURE 4 Model data layout for supervisor and employee responses to training program evaluation.

Table 7. Final evaluation report criteria.

	Yes	No	In Part
1. Report states the purpose/objectives of the evaluation project.	____	____	____
2. Report addresses all evaluation objectives.	____	____	____
3. Report describes the activities conducted in the evaluation effort.	____	____	____
4. Data is clearly presented by:			
a. Tables	____	____	____
b. Figures	____	____	____
c. Other graphic means	____	____	____
5. Data collection methods are clearly explained.	____	____	____
6. Findings are based on sufficient data.	____	____	____
7. Conclusions are based on findings.	____	____	____
8. Recommendations are based on findings and conclusions.	____	____	____
9. Material is presented in a factual manner.	____	____	____
10. Writing style is correct, concise, and direct.	____	____	____

evaluation report provides a vehicle through which a variety of individuals may be involved in improving programs and services.

The preparation of an evaluation report should be a straightforward process with a given purpose and scope. In other words, the report should reflect the original evaluation plan. The report should not be an esoteric research report; it should be a tool for communicating the results of evaluation to those individuals or groups who can use them.

Appendix G presents a format as a guide for preparing an evaluation report. The statements in Table 7 serve as a checklist for the preparation of an evaluation report.

Developing an Action Plan

The final element of the SAE process includes considering the training program in terms of refinement and revision. Training may "fail" because of unclear objectives, lack of relevant content, inappropriate instructional methodology, or lack of job emphasis. Organizational

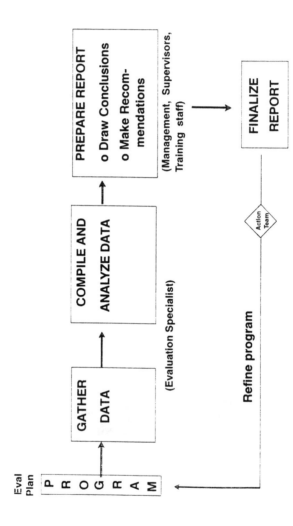

FIGURE 5 Evaluation feedback process.

constraints may prevent the use of the skills on the job. Therefore, it is critical at this point to develop an action plan to correct the discrepancies found through the evaluation.

The importance of the action plan cannot be overemphasized. Training program refinement is achieved only through action. It is not enough to identify a problem and its cause. Training personnel must determine what findings are significant and develop action items that promote the needed changes.

Action plans should specify not only what is to be done, but also who should do it and when it should be done. Someone in the training organization should track and monitor the activities to ensure that (a) they are carried out as planned and (b) changes to the training programs are consistent with the evaluation recommendations.

Lastly, an important thing to keep in mind in devising action plans is that not all identified discrepancies lend themselves to training solutions. There may be a need for more training or better training, of course, but there may also be a need for changes in operating policies and procedures, work design, job responsibilities, on-the-job conditions, or supervisory practices.

The action plans for training staff need to identify those problems which do require training solutions. If the problems are numerous, then they should probably be listed in order of priority:

- Which problems are most critical?
- Which can realistically be dealt with at this time given management or operational conditions?

By systematically seeking feedback, analyzing it logically, and devising realistic and practical solutions, program improvement can indeed be an intrinsic and ongoing part of the training effort. Figure 5 illustrates the course/program evaluation discussed. It presents the various steps and shows that evaluation is a feedback process.

APPENDIX A

Course Evaluation Questionnaire—
Process Control Technician Program

Course title: *Fundamentals of Process Control*   Date: _____

Instructions: Your response to the following statements and questions will be used to improve the course in which you have participated. Please indicate your agreement or disagreement to each statement by making a check mark in the column of your choice. Add comments to support your response in the space provided below each statement.

	Strongly Agree	Agree	Dis-agree	Strongly Disagree
1. The objectives were clearly explained at the start and throughout the course.	_____	_____	_____	_____
Comments: _____				
2. The time allotted for instruction was appropriate.	_____	_____	_____	_____
Comments: _____				
3. The skills taught are important to my job.	_____	_____	_____	_____
Comments: _____				
4. Opportunities were provided to practice the skills taught in the course.	_____	_____	_____	_____
Comments: _____				
5. The instructor encouraged my involvement in the course.	_____	_____	_____	_____
Comments: _____				
6. The instructor used a variety of instructional methods, i.e., lecture, discussion, demonstration, etc.	_____	_____	_____	_____
Comments: _____				
7. The instruction covered all that is necessary for me to perform my job.	_____	_____	_____	_____
Comments: _____				

	Strongly Agree	Agree	Dis-agree	Strongly Disagree
8. Audiovisual media (trans-parencies, etc.) and other training aids helped me to understand the materials.	_____	_____	_____	_____

Comments: _____

9. Rate the quality of instruction by placing a check mark in the appropriate space:

Instructional Area	Excellent	Good	Fair	Poor
a. Process control XT-3000	_____	_____	_____	_____
b. Display features	_____	_____	_____	_____
c. Instruments	_____	_____	_____	_____
d. Materials control display	_____	_____	_____	_____
e. Multi-purpose handling tech.	_____	_____	_____	_____

10. Are there any subject areas that should be added or emphasized?

_____

11. Are there any subject areas that should be deleted?

_____

12. What areas of the training were most helpful?

_____

13. What areas of the training were least helpful?

_____

14. What other comments or suggestions do you have to help improve the program?

_____

_____

APPENDIX B

Employee Evaluation of Process Control Technician Program

Employee's name: _____

Supervisor's name: _____

Training Program: _____ Dates: _____ to _____

Meet with the employee(s) and read/explain the following:

- The objective of this course was to help you learn how to operate the Process Control System. We would like to give you the opportunity to provide feedback to help us improve the training.
- This is not an evaluation of you or your performance, but rather, it is an attempt to find out how you are using the information and skills taught in the course. Your responses will be compiled and judgments made by a neutral party as to the effectiveness of the course.

Have the employee answer the following questions. Make a check mark in the appropriate column. Write any comments the employee may have in the space provided below each question. Be careful not to bias the comment—write the employee's response verbatim.

1. Is the training being used by you as required for correct job performance? _____ Yes _____ No
   Comments: _____

2. Is there a solid connection between this training and the job that you are expected to perform? _____ Yes _____ No
   Comments: _____

3. Did you find the training provided to be based on current and accurate information (as opposed to outdated information)? _____ Yes _____ No
   Comments: _____

4. Are there deficiencies in the training which caused you to be inadequately prepared? _____ Yes _____ No
   Comments: _____

5. Is there a difference between the training that you received and the expectations of your supervisor as to your performance on the job? _____ Yes _____ No
   Comments: _____

6. Are there any performance errors that you have committed since training that require changes in the course? _____ Yes _____ No

Comments: _____

7. Are there changes in knowledge or skills covered in the course that would better prepare you to perform your job? _____ Yes _____ No

Comments: _____

8. Should the Training Department provide you with feedback on any changes that may be made to the course as a result of this evaluation? _____ Yes _____ No

Comments: _____

APPENDIX C

Supervisor Evaluation of Process Control Technician Program

Supervisor's name: _____

Employee's name: _____

Training Program: _____ Dates: _____ to _____

Meet with the supervisor(s) and read/explain the following:

- The purpose of the training in the Process Control Technician Program was to help your employee(s) learn to perform their job more effectively. We would like to give you an opportunity to provide feedback to help us improve the training.
- This is not an evaluation of the employee, but rather, it is an attempt to find out how the graduates are using the information and skills taught in the course. Your responses will be compiled and judgments made by a neutral party as to the effectiveness of the course.

Have the supervisor answer the following questions. Make a check mark in the appropriate column. Write any comments the supervisor may have in the space provided below each question. Be careful not to bias the comment—write the supervisor's response verbatim.

1. Is the training being used by the employee(s) when required for correct job performance? _____ Yes _____ No

   Comments: _____

2. Is there a solid connection between this training and the job the employee(s) is expected to perform? _____ Yes _____ No

   Comments: _____

3. Is the training provided based on current and accurate information (as opposed to outdated information)? _____ Yes _____ No

   Comments: _____

4. Are there deficiencies in the training which caused the employee(s) to be inadequately prepared? _____ Yes _____ No

   Comments: _____

5. Is there a difference between the training that was provided and how you, as a supervisor, expect your employee(s) to perform on the job? _____ Yes _____ No

   Comments: _____

6. Is the employee(s) committing any performance errors which indicate a need for changes in the course? _____ Yes _____ No

   Comments: _____

7. Would you make changes to the training program to better prepare your employee(s) to learn and perform their job? _____ Yes _____ No

   Comments: _____

8. Should the Training Department provide you with feedback on any changes that may be made to the course as a result of this evaluation? _____ Yes _____ No

   Comments: _____

APPENDIX D

Training Impact Survey

Question #1: Compared to other employees with similar duties, how do you think you are doing on the job in the following areas:

Employability Skills	Better	Same	Not as Well
1. Follow company rules?	____	____	____
2. Accept and follow directions?	____	____	____
3. Accept responsibility for my actions on the job?	____	____	____
4. Work as a member of a team?	____	____	____
5. Get along with others?	____	____	____
6. Accept supervisor criticism?	____	____	____
7. Provide *quality* work according to company standards?	____	____	____
8. Provide *quantity* work according to company standards?	____	____	____

Question #2: Compared to other employees with similar duties, how often do you think you do the following on the job:

Maturity Skills	More Often	Same	Less Often
9. Come late for work?	____	____	____
10. Become angry or frustrated?	____	____	____
11. Need disciplinary action?	____	____	____
12. Stay absent from work?	____	____	____
13. Leave work early?	____	____	____
14. Feel bothered by something?	____	____	____

APPENDIX E

Model Conclusions

Question #1—Employability Skills

There is significant disagreement (16%) between supervisors and employees in how well the employees are doing, overall, in "employability skills." The supervisors rated the employees at a lesser rate as compared to other employees. Conversely, the employees rated their own performance at a higher rate than other employees.

- The "better" rating by employees is 50%, compared to the supervisor rating of 34% in the same category. This is the only point of significant disagreement between the supervisors' rating of the employees and the employees' rating of themselves.
- The "not as well" rating by supervisors is 22%, compared to the employee rating of 7% in the same category.
- The ratings by supervisors and employees in the "same" category are comparable, 37% for supervisors, compared to 38% for employees.
- The ratings by supervisors and employees in the "no response" category are also comparable, with 8% for supervisors and 6% for employees.

Question #2—Maturity Skills

There is general agreement between the supervisors and the employees in how well the employees are doing in "maturity skills" except for one area.

- The supervisors and employees are consistent in their ratings on three of the four levels. The one area of disagreement is at the "same" point on the scale. The supervisors rated the employees at 27%, while the employees rated themselves at 15%. Apparently, the employees felt that their maturity was at a higher level than other employees, since they rated themselves slightly higher on the "less often" point of the scale.
- The predominant rating is "less often" for both supervisors (58%) and employees (64%).

In general, employees rated themselves higher in those categories that were favorable to them. There is a natural tendency for employees to engage in the "halo effect" when being asked questions about themselves. It is not unusual for new employees, especially, to view their performance at a higher level of satisfaction than their supervisors view them. Typically, new employees have yet to be exposed to the range of "performance standards" and they measure their success on a day-to-day basis.

APPENDIX F

Model Recommendations

Question #1—Employability Skills and Question #2—Maturity Skills

(1) Strengthen the module "Occupational Survival Skills" in the training program. Help students understand that their behavior is measured against standards of the industry and, therefore, they must perform to those standards.
(2) Make clear the performance standards of the industry as they relate to job performance, behavior, and maturity, and use them as a measure of student performance in training. In this part of the follow-up evaluation, employees rated themselves higher in those categories that were favorable to them. Consequently, performance standards should be made clear throughout the training.

A difficult problem facing young adults today is the transition from school to employment and the resultant "shock" of realizing that they are not performing to standards. Providing increased training is not the total answer; a person frequently finds, even after training, that he/she is unable to hold a job because of unclear job performance standards. Therefore, it is essential that the organization establish, with the assistance of the staff and advisory committee, a set of performance standards that can be used throughout training as a measure for gauging student progress. This is especially critical as it relates to occupational survival skills, since behavior standards are typically not delineated by employers.

As an addition to this process, all staff members could be involved in team sessions in which decisions and recommendations regarding the behavior and maturity of students are made and fed back to the students throughout the training. The major consideration here is that the students be ready for placement with a full range of skills, both technical and employability (behavior and maturity). It is said that a majority of employees lose their jobs not because they lack technical skills, but because of their inability to get along with supervisors and coworkers.

APPENDIX G

Recommended Format for the Evaluation Report

1. *Cover page*—The typical cover page for any report

2. *Table of contents*—Include a table of contents that identifies all section titles, objectives addressed, and attachments

3. *Section I—Summary* (sometimes called an Executive Summary)
   A. Setting
   B. Purpose of the evaluation
   C. Objectives of the evaluation
   D. Summary of the evaluation project
      (1) A short description of how the evaluation was conducted
      (2) A summary of the conclusions drawn from the information collected
      (3) A summary of the recommendations made

4. *Section II—Report body*
   A. Objective 1
      (1) Objective
      (2) Responses, including tables, charts, etc.
      (3) Conclusions for the objective
      (4) Recommendations for the objective
   B. Objective 2
         etc. . . . .

5. *Attachments*
   A. Instruments used in the evaluation effort, i.e. questionnaires
   B. Criterion-referenced tests
   C. Tables, charts, graphs, etc.

REFERENCES

Bakken, D., & Bernstein, A. L. (1982). A systematic approach to evaluation. *Training and Development Journal, 36*(8), 44–51.

Brandenburg, D. C. (1982). What's the current status. *Training and Development Journal, 36*(8), 15–23.

Brethower, K. S., & Rummler, G. A. (1976). Evaluating training. *Improving Human Performance Quarterly, 5*(3–4), 103–120.

Catalanello, R. F., & Kirkpatrick, D. L. (1968). Evaluating training programs—The state of the art. *Training and Development Journal, 24*(4), 252–263.

Cook, M. H. (Ed.). (1980). Page four . . . ASTD and professional development—Two years later. *Training and Development Journal, 34*(3), 4–6.

Deterline, W. A. (1977). Credibility in training: Part V. What do we really want to know? *Training and Development Journal, 31*(4), 14–20.

Dobbs, J. H. (1980). Building training department credibility. *Training and Development Journal, 34*(3), 14–21.

Kimmerling, G. (1993). How training is regarded and practiced in top-ranked U.S. companies. *Training and Development Journal, 47*(9), 29–36.

Kirkpatrick, D. L. (1976). Evaluation of training. In R. L. Craig (Ed.), *Training and development handbook: A guide to human resource development* (2nd ed., pp. 18-1–18-27). New York: McGraw-Hill.

1994 Industry report. (1994), *Training, 31*(10), 29–64.

Patton, M. (1987). *Creative evaluation.* Newbury Park: SAGE Publications.

Putman, A. O. (1980). Pragmatic evaluation. *Training and Development Journal, 34*(10), 36–40.

Randell, L. K. (1960). Evaluation: A training dilemma. *Training Directors Journal.*

Shelton, S., & Alliger, G. (1993). Who's afraid of level 4 evaluation? *Training and Development Journal, 47*(4), 43–46.

Wentling, T. L. (1980). *Evaluating occupational education and training programs.* Urbana, IL: Griffon Press.

Zais, R. S. (1976). *Curriculum: Principles and foundations.* New York: Harper and Row.

Zenger, J. H., & Hargis, K. (1982). Assessing training results: It's time to take the plunge! *Training and Development Journal, 36*(1), 10–16.

Glossary of Terms

THE absence of a standard vocabulary creates misunderstandings. Therefore, it is the aim of this alphabetical glossary to provide definitions of key words and terms used in this book.

Action Verbs   Verbs that convey action (performance) and reflect the type of learning that is to occur. Action verbs express or show behaviors that are observable, measurable, verifiable, reliable, and appropriate.

Apprentice   A qualified person of legal working age who has entered into a written agreement with an employer. Under such an agreement, the employer pays wages and provides an opportunity for the apprentice to learn an apprenticeable occupation.

Apprenticeable Occupation   One which: customarily must be learned by practical, on-the-job training and work experience; is clearly identified and commonly recognized and accepted throughout the industry; involves the development of a skill sufficiently broad to be applicable in like occupations throughout an industry.

Apprenticeship Agreement   A written agreement, registered with an Apprenticeship and Training Council and recorded with the U.S. Department of Labor, providing for a stated number of hours of reasonable continuous employment offering an approved schedule of work experience, supplemented by on-the-job related instruction. This agreement is also known as an apprentice indenture.

Apprenticeship Standards   Document which incorporates procedures for the training of apprentices, terms and conditions of employment, training on the job, and related instruction. The duties and responsibilities, including administrative procedures, of the Joint Apprenticeship Committee (where applicable) are also set forth.

Attitudes   Predispositions or tendencies to react specifically toward objects, stimulations, or values. Usually accompanied by feelings

263

and emotions. Attitudes cannot be directly observed, but must be inferred from overt verbal and nonverbal behavior.

Audiovisual Equipment Equipment used for the recording, production, processing, and exhibition of audiovisual media.

Audiovisual Media Media utilized to facilitate and reinforce learning through one or both of the physical senses of hearing and sight. Examples include audio tapes, overhead transparencies, and video tapes. Require audiovisual equipment for their use.

Behavior A trainee's (visible, audible) action, performance, operation, or product which can be measured by an observer according to specific and discreet criteria.

Behavioral Objective *See* Learning Objective.

Bureau of Apprenticeship and Training (BAT) An agency of the U.S. Department of Labor which stimulates and assists in the development, expansion, and improvement of apprenticeship and training programs. The Bureau's principal functions are to encourage the establishment of sound apprenticeship and training programs as well as to provide technical assistance in establishing such programs.

Coaching An instructional method of one-to-one teaching in which a manager or instructor creates a positive environment for the learner while focusing on the details of learning or understanding a job task. Coaching involves good communication skills (e.g., good eye contact, positive tone of voice, praising), strong encouragement, and skill refinement with the goal of increasing job competency.

Computer An electronic device (usually consisting of a CPU, a monitor, input devices, and output devices) used to store and process information.

Conditions Describes what is presented to the trainee in order to accomplish a specified action; that is, it describes the important aspects of the performance environment. Used in terminal and enabling objectives.

Cooperation Working together to accomplish mutual goals.

Cooperative Learning An instructional method in which small groups of learners work and learn together.

Cost-Effectiveness A comparative evaluation derived from an analysis of alternatives (actions, methods, approaches, equipment, support systems, etc.) in terms of the interrelated influences of cost and effectiveness in accomplishing a learning objective.

Counseling ("Heart-to-Heart" Talk)   A structured discussion aimed at (a) understanding an apparent environmental impediment to learning (e.g., lack of knowledge, personal problem, and difficult relations with other workers) or job-related performance, and (b) developing a strategy to eliminate or reduce the impact of that impediment. This form of counseling is usually used to catch a problem before it becomes serious. In many respects it contains the characteristics of coaching. *See* Coaching.

Course Documentation   Information describing the content of a course (instructional materials, tests, instructor's manual, evaluation plan, trainee's manual) and its developmental history (job analysis, criteria for selecting tasks for training, previous revisions).

Course Objective   A description of the ultimate purpose of a course, including a statement of who is to be trained, what they are to be trained to do, the degree of qualification brought about by the training, and where and under what general conditions the graduate will perform on the job.

Criterion-Referenced Performance Test (CRPT)   A sample work situation in which trainees perform a task which requires them to demonstrate that they have acquired the necessary knowledge and skills. Trainee performance is compared to criteria or attainment standards derived from a task analysis. Also called a Job Performance Measure or Proficiency Test.

Data   Collection of facts or numerical values from which conclusions can be inferred; information.

Data Base   An organized collection of related data about a certain topic or intended for a certain purpose.

Duty   One of the major subdivisions (a large segment) of the work performed by an individual. A job is made up of two or more duties. Duties are groups of closely related tasks.

Electronic Mail (E-Mail)   Text message sent from one computer to another.

Element   The smallest unit into which it is practical to subdivide any work activity without analyzing the separate motions, movements, and mental processes involved. It is a work unit that describes in detail the methods, procedures, and techniques involved in a portion of a task.

Enabling Objective (EO)   Related to a task element, it helps the trainee attain a terminal objective. It includes behavioral action, performance conditions, and attainment standards. Also called a Subordinate Objective, Subobjective, Intermediate Objective, or Enroute Objective.

Entry Behavior The skills, knowledge, and/or attitudes required before beginning instruction; also may refer to the intended trainee's capability prior to new learning.

Entry Skills Specific, measurable behaviors that have been determined through the process of analysis of learning requirements to be basic to subsequent knowledge or skill in the course or program.

Entry Test Contains items based on the objectives that the intended trainee must have attained in order to begin the course or program.

Evaluation The process of interpreting the results of measurement data (e.g., tests, JPMs) for the purpose of making a judgment or decision on the instruction or on the success of a trainee.

Evaluation Plan A method or outline of what set of procedures will be used to gather data and information for the purpose of assessing a course or program.

External Evaluation The collection and analysis of feedback data from outside the training environment to evaluate the graduates' job performance.

Feedback Information on performance is "fed" back to the (a) trainee, in order to improve proficiency; (b) instructional designer, so that the materials and procedures can be improved on the basis of trainee needs; and (c) management system, so it can monitor the internal and external integrity of the instruction and make appropriate revisions. Also refers to the systematic flow of information from one step in the Instructional Systems Development Model to others.

Forecast An assessment of what will happen between a base year and a future date. Calculations are made with a certain degree of confidence in their probability and subject to assumptions concerning future trends.

Formative Evaluation The process of collecting data in order to improve instructional materials and procedures so that they are as effective and efficient as possible. Also called Developmental Testing.

Front-End Analysis Refers to job analysis, selection of tasks for training, and the development of job performance measures.

Go/No-Go Pass-fail; criterion of evaluation whereby a trainee cannot be "partially correct." One is either 100% correct (go) or incorrect (no-go).

Group   Two or more individuals who are interacting with one another, usually in face-to-face communication. A group should be small enough to allow each member to communicate firsthand with all other group members.

Group Dynamics   The scientific study of group behavior to advance the knowledge and understanding of the nature of groups, group development, and the interactions among group members or between groups and larger entities.

Group Maintenance Roles   The activities or functions that group members engage in to help develop cooperation, harmony, and team commitment among group members.

Group Task Roles   The activities or functions that group members engage in to help the group accomplish its tasks or fulfill its mission.

Hard Copy   Information that has been printed on paper.

Hardware   Refers to the physical equipment in a computer system, such as the CPU, monitor, keyboard, printer, etc.

Home Page   The name used to identify a World Wide Web (WWW) site where an organization or individual can store information that can be easily accessed through the Internet. Eventually, it is expected that home pages will be maintained by every university, college, school, department, academic program, and faculty member in every country in the world. Home pages are already being used extensively by business, industry, and government.

Individual Roles   The roles individuals play in a group setting to satisfy their personal needs. These needs do not necessarily relate to the accomplishment of group tasks or contribute to group harmony.

Individualized Instruction   Refers to a management scheme which permits individual characteristics of trainees to be a major determinant of the kind and amount of instruction given. Here, it nearly always implies some form of pacing controlled by the trainee and guided by course or program materials.

Instruction Sheets   Printed instructional materials provided to trainees as an aid in the teaching/learning process. Types of instruction sheets include the (a) information sheet, (b) assignment sheet, and (c) procedure sheet.

Instructional Materials   Tangible trainee-oriented resources, with instructional content. They support the learning process and are an essential component of effective and efficient training courses and programs. Instructional materials can be categorized as (a) printed materials, (b) audiovisual media, and (c) manipulative aids.

Instructional Methods   Methods (strategies) of presentation, practice, and evaluation specifying the ways in which the desired learning outcomes are to be achieved in the instructional setting (e.g., tutorial, lecture/discussion, demonstration, etc.).

Instructional System   An integrated combination of resources (trainees, instructors, materials, equipment, and facilities), techniques, and procedures performing effectively and efficiently the functions required to achieve specified learning objectives.

Instructional Unit   An assembly of lessons which have been integrated, either to complete a usable bit of knowledge or skill, or to aid in scheduling a course or program. The basic components of courses. Same as Unit of Instruction.

Interdependence   Recognition among members of a group that all group members must become actively involved in their work and that goals cannot be reached without the contributions of all members.

Internal Evaluation   The collection and analysis of feedback and management data from within the training environment to assess the effectiveness of instruction in terms of trainee attainment of learning objectives.

Internet   A worldwide, interconnected group of networks. Referred to as the "Information Superhighway" in the popular media.

Interpersonal Skills   Human relations skills that enable individuals to recognize, judge, and balance appropriate behavior; cope with undesirable behavior in others; absorb stress and deal with ambiguity; listen to others; inspire trust and confidence in others; structure social interaction; share responsibility; and easily interact with others in a positive manner.

Job   All the duties and tasks performed by a single job incumbent constitute that individual's job. If identical tasks are performed by several individuals, they all hold the same job. The job is the basic unit used in carrying out the personnel actions of recruitment, selection, training, classification, and assignment.

Job Analysis   The techniques used to obtain a detailed listing of the tasks and elements necessary to perform a clearly defined, specific job. Often involves observations of workers and interviews with those who know the job, in order to describe completely and accurately the work performed and the requirements for successful performance.

Job Description   A detailed description of a job, including qualifications, duties, work environment, tools, equipment, references, and most important, a listing of the tasks to be performed.

Job Incumbent   An individual who performs a job.

Job Performance Aid (JPA)   A procedural guide, worksheet, checklist, decision table, flowchart (algorithm), or other form of reference used to aid in the performance of a task. It reduces the time and effort consumed in memorization by minimizing the amount of information which must be recalled or retained. Also called a Job Aid or Performance Aid.

Job Performance Measure (JPM)   *See* Criterion-Referenced Performance Test.

Joint Apprenticeship Committee (JAC)   A group equally representative of management and labor established to carry out the development and administration of apprenticeship training programs. The Committee may represent labor-management interests at the national, state, or local level.

Journeyman   A worker who has satisfactorily completed an apprenticeship and is classified as a skilled worker in a trade or craft.

Knowledge   Specified information or facts that are not directly observable, required to develop the skills and desired attitudes to effectively accomplish prescribed tasks and jobs.

Learner Characteristics   The traits possessed by trainees that could affect their ability to learn (e.g., age, intelligence, reading level, attitude, aptitude, interests, etc.).

Learning   A change in the behavior of a trainee as a result of experience. The behavior can be physical and overt, or it can be intellectual or attitudinal.

Learning Category   A division of learning behavior. All learning may be classified into one of four learning categories: mental skill, physical skill, information, or attitude.

Learning Hierarchy   Graphically portrays the relationships among learning tasks in which some tasks must be mastered before others can be learned.

Learning Objective   A statement that specifies measurable behavior (performance) that trainees will be required to exhibit after instruction. Properly prepared, it includes the (a) behavioral action (what the trainee does), (b) performance conditions (what the trainee is given), and (c) attainment standards (how well the trainee must perform the behavioral action). Also called a Performance, Behavioral, or Criterion Objective. There are two types of learning objectives: a terminal objective and enabling objective.

Learning Step   The smaller parts into which enabling objectives are broken.

Management Plan   Program for the assignment, monitoring, and assessment of the personnel, materials, and resources dedicated to a specific mission, operation, or function.

Mastery   In terms of learning, refers to meeting all of the specified minimum requirements for a specific performance. Criteria for mastery are defined in the design phase of the Instructional Systems Development (ISD) Model.

Methods   The means, techniques, procedures, etc. of instruction. There are many methods appropriate for use. Included may be such processes as lecture, recitation, practical application, examination, study periods, demonstrations, use of training aids, group discussions, reviews, demonstration-performance, panel discussions, role playing, case studies, programmed instruction, and coach and pupil methods.

Modem   Short for modulator/demodulator—a peripheral device that links a computer to other computers and information services using telephone lines.

Module   A form of specially prepared printed (hard copy) instructional material containing the directions, instructional content, activities, and post-instruction questions which facilitate the attainment of desired learning objectives. Although modules vary in their medium, form, content, length, etc., they offer instructional advantages in terms of self-directed learning and self-pacing. Also called a Training, Learning, or Instructional Package.

Network   Computers linked together to share functions, storage and printing peripherals, and to facilitate communication among users.

On-the-Job Training (OJT)   Workplace-based training designed specifically to train an individual, without the necessity for interrupting assigned duties relative to work assignments. OJT can range in complexity from programs designed for an entry-level trainee to become fully qualified in simple tasks, to programs designed to take an individual who possesses the fundamental principles required to understand the tasks from this level to that of an individual who is fully qualified to perform all the tasks of a position without assistance.

Overlearning   Refers to the continual practice of a learning experience by a trainee who has already correctly performed the task in order to facilitate retention and subsequent proficient performance.

Peer Tutoring   A form of instruction in which trainees at a more advanced level of knowledge or skill provide instruction to other trainees.

Planning   The application of foresight, approaching the future with the aid of systematic analysis, so as to minimize uncertainty and mistakes.

Post-Test   A test administered after the completion of instruction to assess whether a trainee has attained the learning objective(s).

Pre-Test   Administered prior to instruction to determine what the trainee already knows and can do. It can be used to (a) confirm individual trainee qualifications for entering a program, (b) identify remedial training requirements, and (c) identify enabling objectives/instruction the trainee can bypass.

Probationary Period   A period of time served by all apprentices during which the apprenticeship agreement may be cancelled at the request of either party. After completion of the probationary period, the agreement may be cancelled only by the sponsor after adequate cause has been shown and all parties to the agreement have had an opportunity to be heard.

Program Sponsor   An individual employer, a group of employers, or a combination of employer and employee group(s) who have undertaken to establish and operate a formalized apprenticeship program to develop skilled craftsmen in apprenticeable occupations.

Progress Tests   Examinations administered daily or weekly throughout the training course or program to evaluate trainee progress.

Projection   A prediction or estimate of the future based on a past trend, in accordance with assumptions of extrapolation or deviation.

Quality Control   Process of measuring and evaluating in order to maintain course standards through adjustments in instructional materials or procedures.

Related Instruction   Classes in trade-related subjects which apprentices attend each year of their apprenticeship. Usually, 144 hours per year of instruction is considered necessary. To accomplish this, program sponsors request the vocational schools to establish classes of supplemental related instruction for apprentices. They also cooperate with the local vocational school officials in determining the subjects to be taught and the qualifications of the instructors. The program sponsors may further recommend journeymen in the trade who have knowledge and ability to teach related classroom instruction.

Reliability   The consistency with which a test measures the amount of trainee achievement.

Self-Directed Work Teams   A functional group of employees (usually between 8–15) who possess the technical skills and abilities necessary to complete all assigned tasks and who share the responsibility for a particular unit of production. Each team member is encouraged to develop new technical skills in order to increase job flexibility and value to the work team.

Self-Pacing   Mode of instruction whereby trainees work through the instructional materials at their own rate of speed. This procedure enables slower learners to take the time they need while faster learners finish more quickly.

Sequencing   Ordering instruction; proper sequencing allows trainees to make the transition from one skill or body of knowledge to another, and assures that supporting skills and knowledge are acquired before dependent performances are introduced.

Simulation   A technique whereby job-world phenomena are mimicked, in an often low-fidelity situation, in which costs may be reduced, potential dangers eliminated, and time compressed. The simulation may focus on a small subset of the features of the actual job environment.

Skills   Involve physical or manipulative activities. They generally require knowledge for their execution. All skills are actions having special requirements for speed, accuracy, or coordination.

Software   Refers to a wide variety of application programs that are needed for the computer to perform specific tasks, such as word processing.

Standards   Describes the measurable criteria or standards of performance which must be attained. Used in terminal and enabling objectives.

Subject Matter Experts   Persons who are recognized as having professional skill and experience in the performance of some job and who are consulted by a job analyst or an instructional developer in the process of job analysis, instructional materials preparation, etc.

Systems Approach   A generic term referring to the orderly process of analysis, design, development, evaluation, revision, and operation of a collection of interrelated elements. A systems approach is when one element builds upon another.

Target Population The pool of potential trainees for whom instructional materials are prepared and tried out.

Task A distinct measurable work activity that constitutes specific and necessary action by a job incumbent for a meaningful purpose. It is the work unit that deals with the methods, procedures, and techniques by which parts of a job are carried out. Tasks vary in complexity but are made up of at least two elements. Related tasks are grouped together to make up a duty.

Teams A number of diverse individuals organized into a group to accomplish common goals through joint effort and the mutual sharing of information, ideas, opinions, and successes/failures.

Terminal Objective (TO) Represents performance at the task level and is normally derived from the tasks identified in the job analysis. Describes the behavioral action, performance conditions, and attainment standards expected of the trainee when performing a task.

Trade Association A group of firms with similar business or trade interests, joined together for the overall advancement of their industry.

Trade-Offs In any systematic approach to instruction, it is necessary to make compromises between what is desirable and what is possible. Ordinarily, these decisions involve increases or decreases in time, money, facilities, equipment, or personnel. Training aids and simulators represent examples of trade-offs.

Union The duly recognized contractual bargaining agency for a specific company, trade area, or industrial group or groups.

Unit of Instruction *See* Instructional Unit.

Validation The process of developmental testing and revision of instruction until it is effective in realizing its intent.

Validation Process Testing instructional materials on a sample of the target population to insure that the materials are effective.

Validity The degree to which a test measures what it claims to measure.

Vocational and Technical Education and Training (VET) A generic description for a full range of training delivery methods—formal (school-based) and non-formal (workplace-based). Initial and continuing VET is provided in public and private (proprietary) schools, post-secondary colleges, and other institutions, as well as in the workplace and military. It uses practical work experiences and theoretical insights to prepare trainees (students/apprentices) for (a) gainful employment as skilled workers or as technicians or middle-level professionals in recognized vocations, or (b) enrollment in advanced technical education programs.

 VET is concerned with the development of skills, abilities, understandings, attitudes, work habits, and appreciations needed by trainees to enter and progress in employment on a useful and productive basis. It provides a range of skill levels, from basic entry-level skills to technical skills requiring a high degree of specialization and competence. By definition, VET excludes preparation for a baccalaureate degree.

World Wide Web (WWW) A hyper-text-based Internet service used for ease of access to Internet services.

Written Test A test in which individuals demonstrate their capabilities by written techniques. Not usually a performance test and, hence, generally a measure of supporting knowledge rather than skills.

Index

About the Authors

DR. DAVID C. BJORKQUIST is a professor of industrial education in the Department of Vocational and Technical Education at the University of Minnesota. His 38 years of experience have included teaching and administrative roles in industrial arts and technology education, vocational-industrial education, and human resource development.

Dr. Bjorkquist has authored several articles, book chapters, and one book. He has received outstanding manuscript awards from two journals for his writing. He has conducted research projects in technology education, vocational education, and human resource development. His consulting has been with private sector companies and public sector agencies. He is an active member in professional organizations and has held offices in several of them. He chaired the Mississippi Valley Industrial Teacher Education Conference, and the National Association of Industrial and Technical Teacher Educators recognized his contributions to the field with its distinguished service award. He has edited the *Journal of Industrial Teacher Education* and is currently a reviewer for three journals.

DR. PAUL A. BOTT is Chair and Professor of Occupational Studies at California State University–Long Beach, where he has taught for 19 years. He is also the coordinator of the largest vocational teacher preparation program in California. Dr. Bott has taught at the high school level in large inner city schools, in regional occupational programs, and at a private post-secondary institution. In addition, he has served as an industrial training consultant to numerous large corporations, public utilities, and to the military. He is the author of two texts used in vocational and adult teacher preparation programs.

Dr. Bott received his undergraduate education at California State University–Los Angeles, and his master's and doctoral degrees at the University of California–Los Angeles.

DR. CLIFTON P. CAMPBELL is a professor in the Department of Human Resource Development at The University of Tennessee and an international consultant. His career has combined teaching, research, and administration with government service centered in the fields of training and technology transfer.

Dr. Campbell has had leadership roles in international training and technical assistance projects with the Royal Saudi Naval Forces, U.S. Department of Labor, International Labor Organization, The International Center for Advanced Technical and Vocational Training, U.S. Navy, The Kuwait Public Authority for Applied Education and Training, The World Bank, Taiwan (R.O.C.) Ministry of Education, and multinational corporations including ARAMCO, EG & G, and Thiokol. His research focus is on the development, implementation, and evaluation of performance-based education and training.

Dr. Campbell has authored and co-authored numerous books, monographs, journal articles, and other publications in the U.S. and overseas, dealing with human resource development issues. He is active in professional, fraternal, and civic associations and has held offices at the local, state, national, and international levels. Professor Campbell has received awards for his research, writing, and professional service in the field of vocational and technical education and training and for his accomplishments in developing countries.

DR. DENNIS R. HERSCHBACH is an associate professor in the Department of Policy, Planning, and Administration in the College of Education at the University of Maryland. He was formerly Deputy Director of the International Labor Organization's training center at Turin, Italy. He has worked in the field of human resource development for The World Bank, the United Nations Development Program, and the U.S. Agency for International Development.

Dr. Herschbach's publications include work on instructional design, curriculum development, and classroom instruction. Additional research interests include policy and planning issues related to workforce preparation, and education in developing countries. He is a former editor of the *Journal of Industrial Teacher Education* and present editor of the *International Journal of Vocational Education and Training*.

DR. ROGER B. HILL is an assistant professor in the Department of Occupational Studies at the University of Georgia. Dr. Hill holds an undergraduate degree in Industrial Arts Education from North Carolina

State University, a master's degree in Curriculum and Instruction and Educational Administration from Northern Illinois University, and a Ph.D. in Technological and Adult Education from The University of Tennessee.

Dr. Hill's professional experience includes four years as an instructor of technical drawing and wood technology in Raleigh, NC, and 14 years at Hiwassee College (Madisonville, TN), where he was Professor of Technology Education and Coordinator of Academic Computing. He has also worked as a consultant to private industry and as a faculty member for the National Joint Apprenticeship Training Committee's Instructor Training Institute.

A 1990 recipient of the Chancellor's Citation for Extraordinary Professional Promise at The University of Tennessee, Dr. Hill is a member of the Phi Kappa Phi Honor Society, and an active member of American Vocational Association (AVA), Georgia Vocational Association, National Association of Industrial and Technical Teacher Educators (NAITTE), International Technology Education Association (ITEA), and Georgia ITEA. He was a publicity chairman for the 1984 American Industrial Arts Student Association National Conference and has received several awards for leadership and professional service. In 1994, he was a co-recipient of the AVA's Technology Education Division Research Award.

Dr. Hill's research agenda focuses on work ethic, work attitudes, and values which contribute to productive citizenship. His initial work in that area was presented at the 1992 NAITTE Graduate Research Symposium.

DR. DAVID L'ANGELLE is a consultant with Education/Training Systems (San Clemente, CA) and an adjunct professor at California State University–Long Beach. He has 30 years experience in teaching and in education/training program development and evaluation.

Dr. L'Angelle has had a leadership role in training systems development and evaluation with the U.S. Air Force Instructional Systems Design team, university and industry teacher education, career and vocational education, management development, and instructional program evaluation in industry. He has been responsible for the application of the systems approach to training in various education and training efforts.

Dr. L'Angelle has authored numerous monographs, publications, and technical reports dealing with a variety of subject areas, including the development of instructional systems models in teacher education, career and vocational education, and human resource development. He has also published resource guides for vocational education curriculum, sex equity, and post-secondary occupational education and industry cooperation efforts. He is active in numerous professional associations.

BRIAN P. MURPHY is president of the HRD Resource Group, Inc., a company providing human resource development (HRD) services and programs to business and industry. Brian has held positions in the private sector in the areas of human resource planning, training and development, marketing education, and technical training. He also has public education experience in vocational education curriculum development and university-level instruction. Prior to his professional pursuits, Brian worked in the skilled trades as an electronics technician, electrician, and machinist.

Brian earned a B.S. in Industrial Education and an M.Ed. in Career and Technology Education from Bowling Green State University. He has been active professionally in both the training and education fields as an officer in professional societies. Mr. Murphy has published articles in several journals, including the *Journal of Industrial Teacher Education, Performance and Instruction*, and the *Training and Development Journal*.

His areas of expertise include HRD needs assessment and strategy development, job skill development systems and procedures, technical training design and development, media and computer applications in training, coordinating industry/education training efforts, and the development of instruction for job trainers, trainees, and their managers.

DR. GREGORY C. PETTY is an associate professor in the Department of Human Resource Development at The University of Tennessee. He has 21 years of experience in post-secondary vocational-technical education, has taught at the secondary level, and is a veteran of the U.S. Navy. He has worked at all levels of vocational and technical education, from shop/laboratory teaching and professional courses to having served two and one-half years as Acting Head of the Human Resource Development Department.

He has been active in the National Association of Industrial and Technical Teacher Educators for 18 years and currently serves as national secretary. He has consulted with several technical institutes, community colleges, and Fortune 500 companies such as TRW, Martin Marietta, and Battelle Memorial Institute. His specialties include expertise in interactive distance learning, computer multimedia, and identification of employability skills.

Dr. Petty has conducted numerous studies on the occupational work ethic and has developed an instrument (the Occupational Work Ethic Inventory [OWEI]) for measuring the work ethic of individuals. He has published over twenty refereed articles revealing new insight into the affective domain of work. The OWEI has been translated into German, French, Spanish, and Japanese for developing an international data base of the work ethic.